ISBN 978-1-331-23961-1
PIBN 10162888

English
Français
Deutsche
Italiano
Español
Português

www.forgottenbooks.com

Mythology Photography **Fiction**
Fishing Christianity **Art** Cooking
Essays Buddhism Freemasonry
Medicine **Biology** Music **Ancient**
Egypt Evolution Carpentry Physics
Dance Geology **Mathematics** Fitness
Shakespeare **Folklore** Yoga Marketing
Confidence Immortality Biographies
Poetry **Psychology** Witchcraft
Electronics Chemistry History **Law**
Accounting **Philosophy** Anthropology
Alchemy Drama Quantum Mechanics
Atheism Sexual Health **Ancient History**
Entrepreneurship Languages Sport
Paleontology Needlework Islam
Metaphysics Investment Archaeology
Parenting Statistics Criminology
Motivational

PUBLICATIONS

OF THE

UNIVERSITY OF PENNSYLVANIA

HISTORY

THE REVOLUTIONARY MOVEMENT IN PENNSYLVANIA, 1760-1776.
By *Charles H. Lincoln.* Paper, $1.50; Cloth, $2.00.

THE SUFFRAGE FRANCHISE IN THE THIRTEEN ENGLISH COLONIES IN AMERICA.
By *Albert E. McKinley.* $2.50.

CALENDAR OF THE PAPERS OF BENJAMIN FRANKLIN IN THE LIBRARY OF THE UNIVERSITY OF PENNSYLVANIA. $1.50.

SOCIAL CHANGES IN ENGLAND IN THE SIXTEENTH CENTURY AS REFLECTED IN CONTEMPORARY LITERATURE.
By *Edward P. Cheyney.* (*Out of* Print.)

FACTORY LEGISLATION IN PENNSYLVANIA.
By *J. Lynn Barnard.* Cloth, $1.50; Boards, $1.25.

A HISTORY OF AMERICAN WHALE FISHERY.
By *Walter Sheldon Tower.* Cloth, $1.50; Boards, $1.25.

THE ADMINISTRATION OF THE ENGLISH BORDERS DURING THE REIGN OF ELIZABETH.
By *Charles A. Coulomb.* Cloth, $1.50.

A HISTORY OF THE NEW ENGLAND FISHERIES.
By *Raymond McFarland.* Cloth, $2.00.

AMERICAN COMMERCIAL LEGISLATION BEFORE 1789.
By *Albert A. Giesecke.* Cloth, $1.25.

THE RELATIONS OF PENNSYLVANIA WITH THE BRITISH GOVERNMENT, 1696-1765.
By *Winfred Trexler Root.* Cloth, $2.00.

D. APPLETON AND COMPANY, AGENTS, NEW YORK.

STUDIES IN THE HISTORY OF ENGLISH COMMERCE IN THE TUDOR PERIOD

I. The Organization and Early History of the Muscovy Company

By ARMAND J. GERSON, Ph.D.

II. English Trading Expeditions into Asia under the Authority of the Muscovy Company (1557-1581)

By EARNEST V. VAUGHN, Ph.D.

III. English Trade in the Baltic During the Reign of Elizabeth

By NEVA RUTH DEARDORFF, Ph.D.

UNIVERSITY OF PENNSYLVANIA

D. APPLETON AND COMPANY, NEW YORK

1912

J. F. TAPLEY CO.
NEW YORK

GENERAL CONTENTS

INTRODUCTION

Nowhere did the vigor of the English people during the Tudor period show itself more clearly than in the field of commerce. This was especially true in the second half of the sixteenth century. Enterprising merchants, bold navigators and speculating nobles and courtiers united to carry expeditions far into previously unexplored parts of the earth, and to open up lines of trade with regions, well known it is true, but in which Englishmen had seldom been seen as visitors and never before as traders. In accordance with the almost universal practice of the time each of these projects led to the organization of a commercial company and the grant to it by the government of extensive chartered rights.

The group of studies contained in this volume describe this newly organized trade, so far as it was directed toward the north and northeast. The disappearance of most of the records of the early commercial companies, due in all probability largely to the great fire of London in 1666, leaves the story to be pieced together from scattered materials. Such sources as have been printed have been carefully and critically used in the preparation of these papers. This printed material has been supplemented by reference to such manuscript records as still exist in England. Manuscript records existing in the continental countries and still unprinted remain as a possible source of information not yet utilized.

The earliest of the new trading bodies was the Muscovy or Russia Company. Its only predecessors were the Staplers, the Merchants Adventurers, and the Spanish Company. It presented many of the typical characteristics of the period. It was established as the result of a bold effort to reach the much sought trading lands of the far East, and it constantly recurred to this search throughout its early history. It brought England into contact with a new body of people, customs, interests and problems which appealed strongly to the imagination of the curiosity-loving Elizabethan Englishman. The company was given by its charter a complete commercial monopoly, and political rights which were copied but hardly extended in the case of any later chartered body. Its existence gave occasion for most of the diplomatic relations between England and Russia for more than half a century, and the costs of this intercourse were paid for out of its treasury. The difficulties of the Muscovy Company, which constitute the main part of its annals that have come down to us, were the natural difficulties of a company striving to retain a privileged position both in the country of which its members were citizens, and in the country in which its trading interests lay. Its officers were men whose names are well known not only in London civic history but in many other activities of a commercial nature.

The efforts of the Muscovy Company to open up a trade with the far East by this distant route were so early in time, so persistent, so bold in conception, and came so near to attaining success that they seem to justify a special description. This is the subject of the second of the essays in this volume. The successive voyages down the Volga, across the Caspian, and into Persia and the lands where Tartars and Turks were still in conflict, brought Englishmen into contact with still another group of races, whose boundaries they were to approach later from another direction. Notwithstanding its length, this route avoided for Englishmen certain difficulties presented by every other mode of approach to the far East, and for a while it seemed that it might be successfully established. Indeed it has been tried at more than one later period.

But at this time as well as later it proved a failure. The efforts during the sixteenth century have left only too little detailed record, but the main outline of events and the causes of their failure come out with sufficient clearness in the narrative.

English trade to the Baltic during this period, culminating in the organization of the Eastland or Baltic Company and its establishment of a principal settlement in one of the Baltic cities, the subject of the third essay, involves a different set of surrounding circumstances, but one no less typical of the period. The sphere of activity was closer to England, but the struggle with competitors already on the ground and the complications of European politics were all the more intense. The documents connected with this subject are also somewhat more unfamiliar, and a larger part of this study has been made from manuscript materials previously unused. The earliest years only of the company are described in detail and its later history remains to be written. The whole group of questions connected with English trade with the shores of the Baltic, and English relations with the states bordering upon them is a complicated one and involves many political as well as economic factors.

The lines of trade described in this volume represent only one part of the field of Elizabethan commercial enterprise. But if the history of these companies and their congeners in other regions were adequately described and fully understood, we would have gone far toward a comprehension of most of the foreign relations and much of the internal life of England at that period.

EDWARD P. CHEYNEY.

University of Pennsylvania,
    February, 1912.

The Organization and Early History of the Muscovy Company

Thesis presented to the Faculty of the Graduate School of the University of Pennsylvania in partial fulfilment of the requirements for the degree of Doctor of Philosophy, 1910.

By ARMAND J. GERSON, Ph.D.

CONTENTS

THE ORGANIZATION AND EARLY HISTORY OF THE MUSCOVY COMPANY

CHAPTER I

THE ESTABLISHMENT OF RUSSIAN RELATIONS

The idea of a northern route to the Indies made a peculiar appeal to the adventurous and commercial instincts of the Englishmen of the sixteenth century. The reason is easily discernible in the international commercial rivalries of the period. The vessels of Spain and Portugal had rounded the southern extremities of both continents in the race for the jewels and spices of the Orient, and those countries were sharing the profits of that rich trade. It was natural that England should desire her share in the new commercial development. Her geographical position and the preëmption of the southwest and southeast routes by her rivals of southern Europe led her merchant leaders to look toward the north for a new road to the wealth of Asia. That England should have failed to open up a new trade route to India and Cathay is, of course, in the light of modern geographical knowledge, no cause for wonder. That in the attempt she accidentally established a communication and a thriving trade with Russia renders the northern voyages of her traders and explorers of large significance for the historian of European trade and civilization.

Between the northwestern voyages of the Cabots at the close of the fifteenth century and the explorations that led to the discovery of the northern coast of Russia in the middle of the sixteenth there is no record of any serious attempt to try the northern route. That the idea was not entirely lost to view in the interval, however, is clearly indicated by a letter written by one Robert Thorne, a London merchant, in which he urges Henry VIII to organize a voyage of exploration by way of the Arctic regions.[1] The letter contains a very clear statement of the benefits to be derived. Reference is made to the advantages to mariners and explorers of the perpetual daylight of the Polar regions: "Yea what a vantage shal your Graces subjects have also by this light to discover the strange lands, countries, and coasts?"[2] The writer proceeds to point out with rather amusing naïvete that having "past the Pole, it is plaine, they may decline to what part they list,"[2] China and the East Indies if they sail to the east, America and the West Indies if they direct their course to the west.[3]

It remained for the navigators of the next reign, however, actually to put to the test of experience the attractive idea of a northern route. Toward the close of the reign of Edward VI, probably in the year 1552, a number of London merchants took up the project. A contemporary writer explains the motives that led to their action. The falling off of English trade led "certaine grave Citizens of London, and men of great wisedome, and carefull for the good of their Countrey" to take steps looking toward the improvement of this condition.[4] "Seeing that the wealth of the Spaniards and Portingales, by the discoverie and search of newe trades and Countreys was marveilously increased, supposing the same to be a course and meane for them also to obteine the like, they therefore resolved upon a newe and strange Navigation."[5] In search of expert advice, the merchants sought out Sebastian Cabot

---

[1] Hakluyt, *The Principal Navigations Voyages Traffiques, etc. of the English Nation*, vol. II, p. 159.
[2] *Ibid.*, II, 162.
[3] *Ibid.*, II, 163.
[4] *Ibid.*, II, 239.

who was then residing in London.[5] Cabot was at that time a man seventy-five years of age and enjoyed a singular prestige as the result of the remarkable explorations in which his life had been spent, and still more, perhaps, as a result of his remarkable reports of them. His unquestioned services had received substantial recognition from the government in the form of an annual pension of 250 marks.[6] He seems to have been regarded with respect not unmingled with awe by the younger generation of merchants and navigators. Old as he was, he threw himself into the new plan and became the most active spirit in its organization. The result of the conference was a decision to fit out three vessels ''for the search and discoverie of the Northerne part of the world, to open a way and passage to our men to travaile to newe and unknowen kingdomes.''[7]

. Almost immediately the projectors of the venture seem to have recognized the necessity for a definite organization. They accordingly formed a sort of combination and chose Sebastian Cabot to be the governor of the ''company.'' While we have no explicit statement of these early proceedings, indirect evidence is furnished by the document containing the instructions to the officers of the fleet at the time of their departure. That document is headed ''Ordinances, instructions, . . . compiled, made, and delivered by the worshipfull M. Sebastian Cabota Esquier, governour of the mysterie and companie of the Marchants adventurers for the discoverie of Regions, Dominions, Islands and places unknowen . . .''[8] At the close of the instructions we find, '' In witnes whereof I Sebastian Cabota, Governour aforesaid . . .,''[9] clearly indicating his official position.

[5] Hakluyt, II, 240.

[6] Rymer, *Foedera*, Westin, O. XV, 181. H VI. p. III. 170.

[7] Hakluyt, II, 240.

[8] *Ibid.*, 195.   [9] *Ibid.*, II, 205.

In regard to the rest of this early plan of organization we have the further contemporary statement that the merchants made choice "of certain grave and wise persons in maner of a Senate or companie, which should lay their heads together, and give their judgments and provide things requisite and profitable for all occasions."[10] This is the body to which Cabot makes reference in his instructions where he speaks of them as the "Consuls and Assistants in London."[11] The detailed form of organization indicated by this nomenclature is of interest as anticipating the plan prescribed by the Company's charter a few years later.[12] It would seem that the Company from the very first looked forward to a permanent corporate existence.

The funds for the venture were raised by a contribution of 25 pounds from each member of the Company.[13] The fact that 6000 pounds was thus collected is very definite evidence as to the number belonging to the fellowship at the time of its first organization. There were evidently 240 members. This mode of raising the necessary money by equal subscriptions from the whole membership is of significance as indicating a sort of joint stock idea in the Company's very inception.

Three ships were secured and put in condition. They were furnished with arms and ammunition and thoroughly prepared to resist any enemy they might meet at sea.[14] Provisions were purchased and the ships victualed for eighteen months in view of the possibility that the outward trip and the homeward trip might each take six months and that another six months should be allowed for wintering in the unknown lands they hoped to reach.

10 Hakluyt, II, 240.
11 *Ibid.*, II, 201.
12 *Infra*, p. 25 ff.
13 Hakluyt, II, 240.
14 *Ibid.*, II, 241.

Sir Hugh Willoughby under the title of Captain General was given charge of the little fleet and appointed "Admirall with authoritie and commaund over all the rest."[15] He is described by our contemporary narrator as of "goodly personage" and as having "singular skill in the services of warre." Richard Chancellor was appointed to be second in command with the title of Pilot Major.[16] Willoughby's vessel, the *Bona Speranza*, a ship of 120 tons, is spoken of as the "Admiral of the fleete" in couse- quence of carrying the Captain General.[17] The largest of the three ships, however, was the *Edward Bonaventure* of 160 tons, in which Richard Chancellor sailed.[18] The third and smallest of the fleet was the *Confidentia* of 90 tons.[19] Each ship was accompanied by a pinnace and a small boat, and each carried, besides its quota of mariners, pursers, carpenters, cooks, etc., a number of merchants.[20] Every officer, merchant, and servant was put under oath to serve the Company faithfully.[21]

Contemporary writers are silent on the question of the raising of men to man the vessels for the hazardous voy- age to unknown lands. There is clear evidence, however, to show that the practice of impressing sailors was re- sorted to. A warrant among the Admiralty Papers signed by Lord Admiral Clinton and bearing the date of 1553 authorizes Sir Hugh Willoughby to press mariners for his ship about to sail for the north.[22]

Cabot, as we have already mentioned, drew up a list of instructions for the direction of the intended voyage.

[15] Hakluyt, II, 241.
[16] *Ibid.*, II, 242.
[17] *Ibid.*, II, 212.
[18] *Ibid.*, II, 213.
[19] *Ibid.*, II, 214.
[20] *Ibid.*, II, 212-214.
[21] *Ibid.*, II, 215.
[22] Cited by Marsden in *Trans. R. H. S.*, new series, Vol. XVI, p. 80, Cf. Gilbert's request for a similar privilege, *infra*, p. 112.

This interesting document contains thirty-three articles and provides among other things that the rules shall be read aloud on the voyage "once every week . . to the intent that every man may the better remember his othe, conscience, duetie and charge."[23] The instructions are very comprehensive and at the same time practical. The importance of amity and obedience is strongly emphasized and the men reminded of their oath to obey the Captain General and the captains and masters of their ships. A council of twelve, consisting of Willoughby, Chancellor, the masters of the three vessels, their mates, two merchants, "James Dalabere Gentleman" and "Master Richard Stafford Minister,"[24] is given authority to make rules for "the better conduction, and preservation of the fleete, and achieving of the voyage."[25] A careful record of all incidents and observations is to be kept "to remain of record for the Company."[26] No sale of goods is to be made by individual merchants without the consent of those in charge of the voyage,[27] and all wares purchased are to be "wel ordred, packed, and conserved in one masse entirely" and an inventory presented to the Company so that the entire membership may receive the profits of the venture.[28] Besides these important provisions there are a number of detailed rulings such as the requirement of morning and evening religious services,[29] the prohibition of blasphemy,[30] etc. A quaint combination of piety and business sense is evident in the instruction "not to disclose to any nation the state of our reli-

---

23 Hakluyt, II, 196.
24 Ibid., II, 206.
25 Ibid., II, 196.
26 Ibid., II, 197.
27 Ibid., II, 200.
28 Ibid., II, 201.
29 Ibid., II, 199.
30 Ibid., II, 198.

gion, but to passe it over in silence, without any declaration of it, seeming to beare with such laws, and rites, as the place hath, where you shall arrive."[31] The wisdom of the experienced explorer is revealed in the advice, "If you shall be invited into any Lords or Rulers house, to dinner, or other parlance, goe in such order of strength, that you may be stronger than they, and be warie of woods and ambushes, and that your weapons be not out of your possessions,"[32] as well as in the suggestion, "If you shall see them weare Lyons or Beares skinnes, having long bowes, and arrowes, be not afraid of that sight: for such be worne oftentimes more to feare strangers, then for any other cause."[32]

It is evident that the voyage was in many respects a national venture. We have already seen that the Lord Admiral had authorized the impressing of men. Cabot, in the document just cited, says, "you be not ignorant, how many persons, as well the kings majestie, the Lords of his honorable Counsel, this whole companie, . . . be replenished in their hearts with ardent desire to learne and know your estates, conditions, and welfares, and in what likelihood you be in, to obtain this notable enterprise."[33] The most conclusive evidence of the interest of the Government in the new exploration is to be found, however, in a letter written by Edward VI and sent with the fleet. It is directed "To all Kings, Princes, Rulers, Judges, and Governours of the earth and all other having any excellent dignitie on the same, in all places under the universall heaven."[34] The letter makes a general offer of friendship to all princes and suggests the establishing of trade relations. It dwells upon the benefits of universal peace and the efficacy of commercial relations as a

[31] Hakluyt, II, 202.
[32] Ibid., II, 203.
[33] Ibid., II, 204.
[34] Ibid., II, 209.

means to that end. The letter solicits permission for Willoughby and his companions to pass freely through the countries they may reach in their voyage, and promises reciprocal favors to the inhabitants of those lands ''if at any time they shall come to our kingdomes.'' This was the document which was to inaugurate new and important international relations. We are told that copies were also written in Greek ''and divers other languages.'' [35]

The three vessels, provisioned, as we have said, for eighteen months, well manned and armed, loaded with merchandise, carrying the instructions of the Governor of the Company, and the letter of the king, left London May 10, 1553,[36] and proceeded down the Thames. For our knowledge of the events of this voyage we are chiefly indebted to the account of Clement Adams, ''schoolemaster to the Queene's henshmen,'' who received his information at first hand from Chancellor after the return of the latter in 1554.[37] The less literary but more detailed record kept by Sir Hugh Willoughby up to the time of his death has also come down to us [38] and furnishes us with definite statements of detail extremely useful as a verification of Adams' narrative; it is particularly valuable for its record of the fate of the *Speranza* after its separation from the *Edward Bonaventure*. From this contemporary evidence it is not difficult to work out a consecutive account of the outward voyage.

On May 11, the little fleet passed Greenwich, where the

[35] Hakluyt, II, 211.

[36] This is the date recorded in Willoughby's Journal, *Ibid.*, II, 217. The account written by Clement Adams, however, gives the date as May 20, *Ibid.*, II, 244. Willoughby's evidence from its very nature is more to be relied upon for a matter of this sort than that of Adams.

[37] *Ibid.*, II, 239. The date of composition is fixed by the writer's evident ignorance of the fate of Willoughby, word of which reached London in the fall of 1555 (*infra*, p. 12), *Ibid.*, II, 247.

[38] *Ibid.*, II, 212 ff.

court then resided and where King Edward lay in his last illness.[39] In his honor the ships discharged their guns "insomuch that the tops of the hilles sounded therewith" while the mariners shouted "till the skie rang again with the noyse thereof." Crowds collected on the river bank and courtiers waved farewell from the windows and towers of the palace.[40] England was wishing God-speed to her voyagers to "lands unknowen." The fleet continued down the Thames slowly, being obliged to wait on favorable winds and tide.

On May 20 the ships were still in the Thames, having proceeded as far as Gravesend.[41] At last they sailed out to the open sea and turned their course to the north, still, however, keeping close to the English coast. On the 30th of May they "came against Yermouth about three leagues into the sea."[42]

During the first three weeks of June little or no headway was made owing to contrary winds. On the 23rd they put out from the coast and sailed into the North Sea.[42] On the 27th an attempt was made to sail to the northwest "to the ende to fall with Shotland."[43] West winds prevented, however, and the three vessels continued their course to the northeast. Bad weather again delayed their progress. Until July 14 the ships struggled on "traversing and tracing the seas, by reason of sundry and manifolde contrary windes."[43] Then land was sighted to the east, Rost Island, off the coast of Norway. Here the voyagers landed on July 19 and remained for three days.[43]

On July 22 they departed from Rost sailing northeast along the Norwegian coast and continuing in this direc-

[39] *Hakluyt*, II, 245.
[40] *Ibid.*, II, 244.
[41] *Ibid.*, II, 217.
[42] *Ibid.*, II, 218.
[43] *Ibid.*, II, 219.

tion until the 27th when landing was made on another island which Willoughby calls "Lewfoot." [44] On the 30th they set sail once more still keeping land in sight to the east.[45] A boat from one of the islands furnished opportunity to inquire if a pilot might be secured to guide them along the coast to "Finmarke." They were told that if they would land a pilot would next day bring them to "the wardhouse,[46] which is the strongest holde in Finmarke, and most resorted to by report." [45] When they attempted to enter the harbor, however, "there came such flawes of winde and terrible whirlewinds" that the ships were compelled to put out to sea again.[45]

At a council called by Sir Hugh Willoughby an agreement was made that if the ships should at any time be separated by storm "every shippe should indevour his best to goe to Wardhouse, a haven or castell of some name in the kingdome of Norway, and that they that arrived there first in safetie should stay and expect the coming of the rest." [47] On the same day on which this council was held, at about four o'clock in the afternoon, a storm of terrific violence separated the fleet. Willoughby's account says, "And that night by violence of winde and thickenesse of mists, we were not able to keepe together within sight, and then about midnight we lost our pinnesse, which was a discomfort unto us." [48] With dawn the fog cleared, and in the distance the crew of the *Bona Speranza* sighted a ship which on closer view proved to be the *Confidentia;* the *Edward Bonaventure* had disappeared.[48] The two vessels continued in company to the northeast hoping to rejoin Chancellor's ship at Wardhouse as had been agreed upon a few days before. It seems from Wil-

[44] Hakluyt, II, 219.
[45] *Ibid.*, II, 220.
[46] I.e. Vardohuus.
[47] *I*bid., II, 246.
[48] *I*bid., II, 220.

loughby's journal that they now completely lost their way. Soundings were taken and the conclusion reached "that the land lay not as the Globe made mention."[49] They sailed to the northeast, then to the southeast. On August 14 land was sighted in latitude 72° but the water was so shallow that the boat sent out to investigate could not effect a landing;[49] there "was very much ice also, but there was no similitude of habitation." The fact of the case seems to be that they had somehow passed Wardhouse far to their right and they were aimlessly wandering along the desolate coasts of Russian Lapland.

The rest of Willoughby's journal is a concise record of one of those tragic events with which the history of navigation abounds. It continues with almost daily entries up to the end of September. By that time the White Sea had been reached, though the voyagers seem to have had no knowledge whatever of where they were. On the 18th of September they entered into a haven which "runneth into the maine, about two leagues, and is in bredth halfe a league."[50] Here Willoughby and his companions determined to spend the winter. And here they perished to a man. A will later found in the *Speranza* proves that Sir Hugh and most of the company were still alive in January, 1554.[51]

The last entry in Willoughby's journal, written toward the close of September, 1553, is a testimony to the courage of the man and in its very simplicity pictures most vividly the environment in which he met his death. "Thus . . . seeing the yeare farre spent, & also very evill wether, as frost, snow, and haile, as though it had beene the deep of winter, we thought best to winter there. Wherefore we sent out three men Southsouthwest, to

[49] Hakluyt, II, 221.
[50] *Ibid.*, II, 223.
[51] *Ibid.*, II, 224.

search if they could find people, who went three dayes journey, but could finde none: after that, we sent other three Westward four daies journey, which also returned without finding any people. Then sent we three men Southeast three dayes journey, who in like sort returned without finding of people, or any similitude of habitation." [52]

During 1554, after Chancellor had made his memorable visit to the Czar, Ivan the Terrible, the *Speranza* and the *Confidentia* were found by some Russian fishermen with all on board frozen to death. [53] The ships were turned over to Chancellor on his second trip to Russia and word of the tragic fate of the adventurers thus reached England. It seems to have occasioned a great deal of interest there and to have appealed strongly to the imagination of the time. Various embellishments, of more or less artistic merit, seem to have been added to the narrative. Giovanni Michiel, the Venetian Ambassador at the court of England, writing home to the Doge and Senate under date of November 4, 1555, speaks of the return of the second voyage in that year and describes the finding of the *Speranza* and the *Confidentia* "on the Muscovite coast, with the men on board all frozen; and the mariners now returned from the second voyage relate strange things about the mode in which they were frozen, having found some of them seated in the act of writing, pens still in hand and the paper before them; others at tables, platter in hand and spoon in mouth; others opening a locker, and others in various postures, like statues, as if they had been adjusted and placed in those attitudes. They say that some dogs on board the ships displayed the same phenomena. They found the effects and merchandise all

[52] Hakluyt, II, 223.
[53] *Ibid.*, III, 331.

intact in the hands of the natives, and brought them back hither with the vessels.'' [54]

We must now return to consider the progress of the voyage of Richard Chancellor in the *Edward Bonaventure*. In the storm that dispersed the fleet his vessel completely lost sight of the other ships. Left alone he shaped his course toward Wardhouse in accordance with the agreement that had been made. [55] Here he waited a whole week, when, giving up hope of his companions having survived the tempest, he pursued the interrupted voyage, sailing far to the east till " at the length it pleased God to bring them into a certain great Bay, which was of one hundreth miles or thereabout over,'' [56]—the White Sea. Here they entered and made a landing. From the natives it was soon learned that "this Countrey was called Russia, or Muscovie, and that Ivan Vasiliwich ruled and governed farre and wide in those places.'' Chancellor explained that he and his men had been sent by King Edward in search of amity and commerce, "whereby they doubted not, but that great commoditie and profit would grow to the subjects of both kingdoms.'' [57] The "governour of that place'' replied that he did not know what would be the wish of their ruler, but immediately despatched a messenger to the Emperor announcing the arrival of the strangers. [58] A long delay following, Chancellor announced his intention of re-embarking and proceeding further on his journey. [58] At this the Muscovites "fearing the departure in deede of our men who had such wares and commodities as they greatly desired'' offered to conduct Chancellor to the Emperor at once.

Ivan "the Terrible'' was at this time in his city of

---

[54] Cal S. P. (Venetian) 1555-1556, p. 240.
[55] Hakluyt, II, 247.
[56] *Ibid.*, II, 248.
[57] *Ibid.*, II, 249.
[58] *Ibid.*, II, 250.

Moscow, fifteen hundred miles from the spot where the English had landed. The trip had to be made in sledges.[59]   On the way they met the royal messengers with commands from Ivan that all haste should be made in bringing the strangers to his court.[60]   Of the hardships of this long overland trip we know little save that '' after much adoe and great paines taken in this long and wearie journey . . . Master Chanceler came at last to Mosco the chiefe citie of the kingdome, and the seate of the king.'' [60]

1553, the date of Chancellor's voyage, may be said to mark the most brilliant period of the reign of Ivan IV. He had just completed the conquest of Kazan in the southeast and in the following year was to gain possession of Astrakhan, thus extending the limits of his domain from the White Sea to the Caspian.   Only on his western borders might his ultimate success be considered doubtful.   The Teutonic knights in Livonia, the Swedes, Lithuanians, and Poles formed a solid wall between Russia and the civilization of western Europe.   So long as the arts of that civilization were denied to the Czar the subjugation of the powerful neighbors that shut him off from the Baltic would be an impossibility.   Communication by means of his distant Arctic coast suggested brilliant possibilities both of trade and contact with the West. We need go no further than this to explain the cordial reception accorded to Chancellor and his companions at the Russian capital.

Chancellor writing of Russia shortly after his return to England gives us a description of the rude splendor of Ivan's court.[61]   After waiting at Moscow twelve days he was summoned to wait upon the Czar and present the let-

[59] Hakluyt, II, 250.
[60] Ibid., II, 251.
[61] Ibid., II, 224 ff.

ter from Edward VI.[62] An interpreter conducted him
into an outer chamber "where sate one hundred or moe
gentlemen, all in cloth of golde very sumptuous."[62] From
here he was taken to the Council Chamber where he was
presented to the Emperor in the presence of the assembled nobles: "they sate round about the chamber on high,
yet so that he himselfe sate much higher than any of his
nobles in a chaire gilt, and in a long garment of beaten
golde, with an emperial crowne upon his head, and a
staffe of Cristall and golde in his right hand, and his
other hand halfe leaning on his chaire."[63] The Czar
received the letter and bidding Chancellor welcome inquired of the king's health. Chancellor after respond-
ing appropriately presented Ivan with a suitable gift and
departed.[63] Two hours later he dined in state with the
Czar at the golden palace, "but," he writes, "I saw no
cause why it should be so called; for I have seene many
fayrer then it in all poynts."[63] There follows in Chancellor's narration a full description of the banquet.

Ivan formally accepted the suggestion of an alliance
and the establishment of commercial relations between his
country and England. His letter in reply to that of
Edward VI was brought back to England by Chancellor
in 1554.[64] It is addressed to Edward, as to whose death
in the interval both Ivan and Chancellor were of course
in ignorance. The letter grants the request presented by
Chancellor that English subjects may visit Russia and
"frequent free Marts, with all sortes of marchandizes, and
. . . to have wares for their returne."[65] The English king is asked to send a representative with whom
definite arrangements may be concluded for commercial

---

[62] Hakluyt, II, 226.
[63] Ibid., II, 227.
[64] Ibid., II, 271.
[65] Ibid., II, 272.

privileges throughout the Czar's dominions. The letter announces further that the Emperor has given order "that wheresoever your faithful servant Hugh Willoughbie land or touch in our dominions, to be wel entertained, who as yet is not arrived, as your servant Richard can declare."[65]

Of Chancellor's return trip to England we have no detailed account. On his arrival Ivan's letter was presented to Queen Mary. The change of rulers seems to have involved no change of policy so far as commercial relations were concerned. The highest officials in the government were interested in the project. The Company applied for letters of incorporation. These were granted February 6, 1555,[66] from which date the Company's corporate history begins. The charter of 1555 grants to the Company the exclusive right to trade with any of the Czar's dominions, establishes the form of government and organization of the Company, and appoints Sebastian Cabot to be Governor of the Company during the remainder of his life.

On May 1, 1555, the Company adopted articles for the second voyage.[67] This time Russia was the definite destination. Two vessels, the *Edward Bonaventure* and the *Philip and Mary,* were laden with merchandise and sent out under the charge of Richard Chancellor.[68] Two agents, George Killingworth and Richard Gray, were sent with the ships to reside in Russia and take charge of the Company's interests in that country.[69] Detailed instructions were given them as to the limits of their authority and the conduct of the affairs of the Company. On

[66] Hakluyt, II, 316. The closing words of the charter, "Apud Westmonasterium, 6 die Feb. Annis regnorum nostrorum, primo & secundo," fix the date as 1555. February, 1555, falls in the first regnal year of Philip as King of England and in the second regnal year of Queen Mary.

[67] *Ibid.,* II, 281.

[68] *Ibid.,* II, 282.

[69] *Ibid.,* II, 281.

Chancellor's second arrival in Russia Ivan repeated his gracious welcome.[70] In response to a letter from Philip and Mary [71] he granted liberal trading privileges to the merchants,[72] privileges which from the point of view of the Company must be considered as supplementing the charter privileges granted earlier in the year by the English government.

On July 20, 1556, Chancellor departed for England, the *Edward Bonaventure* and the *Philip and Mary* being accompanied on this return voyage by the *Bona Speranza* and the *Confidentia*,[73] which had been found on the coast of Lapland and turned over to the English by the Czar. The *Edward* carried a cargo "in waxe, trane oyle, tallow, furres, felts, yarne and such like, to the summe of 20000. (*sic*) li. sterling."[73] More significant still, it bore the first Russian ambassador to the court of England, Osep Napea,[74] "governor of the town of Vologda." The storms of the Arctic, destined to play so large a part in the history of the Company, soon separated the vessels of the fleet. The *Bona Speranza* and the *Confidentia*, still pursued by their former ill fortune, perished on the coast of Norway.[75] The *Philip and Mary* after long delays finally reached London in April of the next year.[75] The *Edward* with its rich cargo, after four months' buffeting, finally reached the coast of Scotland in November, 1556.[76] Here "by outrageous tempests, and extreme stormes, the said ship . . . was driven upon the rockes on shore, where she brake and split in pieces."[76] Chancellor, attempting to save the life of the ambassador, lost his own life.

[70] Hakluyt, II, 292.

[71] *Ibid.*, II, 278.

[72] *Ibid.*, II, 297 ff.

[73] *Ibid.*, II, 351.

[74] *Ibid.*, II, 350.

[75] "The said Confidentia was seene to perish on a Rocke," *Ibid.*, II, 351. The Bona Speranza was never heard of again.

[76] *Ibid.*, II, 352.

Osep Napea was one of the few persons who survived the disaster. The cargo and the valuable presents sent by Ivan to Philip and Mary were either lost in the sea or seized by the rude natives of that region.[77] In spite of the coöperation of the Scotch government [78] very little of this booty was ever recovered:—"divers small parcels of waxe, and other small trifling things of no value, were by the poorer sort of the Scottes brought to the commissioners, but the Jewels, rich apparell, presents, gold, silver, costly furres, and such like, were conveyed away, concealed and utterly embezelled." [78]

The Company received news of the catastrophe early in December, 1556.[79] They at once secured letters from the Queen to the Scotch government requesting the proper entertainment of the ambassador and the restitution of the goods that had been plundered.[79] They further sent "two Gentlemen of good learning, gravitic and estimation" [80] to bring the Russian ambassador to London. These agents arrived in Scotland on December 23, but the delays attendant on the attempt to secure the stolen and already widely distributed cargo prevented their departure from that country until the following February.[81] On February 18, 1557, they reached Berwick where the ambassador was honorably entertained by the Lord Warden of the East Marches.[82] From Berwick he was conducted toward London,[83] finally arriving in the neigh-

---

[77] Hakluyt, II, 352.

[78] Ibid., II, 353.

[79] Ibid., II, 352.

[80] Ibid., II, 353.

[81] Ibid., 354.

[82] Ibid. Cf. letters of the Privy Council to the Warden, Dec. 1, 1556, and Feb. 24, 1557. A P. C. 1556-1558 pp. 27 and 56.

[83] The ambassador's route from Berwick to London is indicated by the instructions sent by the Privy Council to the sheriffs of Nottingham, Lincoln, Northampton, Cambridge, Huntingdon, Essex and Hertford to conduct the Russian Ambassador safely to the

borhood of that city on February 27. Twelve miles from London Napea was received by "fourscore merchants with chaines of gold and goodly apparell." [84] By these he was conducted to a "marchants house foure miles from London." Next day he was accompanied to the city by one hundred and forty members of the Company.[85] He was formally welcomed by Viscount Montague who had been sent by the Queen to meet him.[85] A procession of three hundred "knights, esquiers, gentlemen and yoemen" accompanied him toward Smithfield Bars, "the first limits of the liberties of the Citie of London." Here he was received by the Lord Mayor "with all the Aldermen in their Skarlet . . . and so riding through the citie of London in the middle, between the Lord Maior and Viscount Montague, a great number of merchants and notable personages riding before, and a large troupe of servants and apprentices following, was conducted through the Citie of London (with great admiration and plausibilitie of the people running plentifully on all sides, and replenishing all streets in such sort as no man without difficultie might passe) into his lodging situate in Fant church [86] streete, where were provided for him two chambers richly hanged and decked . . ." On his entrance into his apartments he was presented with a splendid gift from the Queen.[87]

The formal reception of the ambassador by the court did not take place immediately owing to the absence of Philip in Flanders. Meanwhile the Company attended to his wants. "Daily divers Aldermen and the gravest personages of the said companie did visit him, providing all

next county and see him well attended to "for his reasonable money." A. *P. C.* 1556-1558, pp. 51-52.

[84] Hakluyt, II, 354 . ff. "*A discourse of the . . . receiving . . . of the first Ambassador from . . . Russia.*

[85] *Ibid.,* II, 355.

[86] I.e. Fenchurch Street.

[87] Hakluyt, II, 356.

kind of victuals for his table and his servants, with al
sorts of Officers to attend upon him in good sort and condition, as to such an ambassadour of honour doeth and
ought to appertaine."[88]   In fact during his entire stay
in England the Company assumed the responsibility of
his entertainment.   They invited him "to the Maior, and
divers worshipfull mens houses, feasting and banquetting
him right friendlie, shewing unto him the most notable
and commendable sights of London, as the kings palace
and house, the Churches of Westminster and Powles, the
Tower and Guild hall of London, and such like memorable
spectacles."[89]   Finally, on April 29, shortly before his
departure, the merchants of the Company assembled in
the ambassador's honor at Drapers' Hall and there "ex-
hibited and gave unto ye said Ambassador, a notable sup-
per garnished with musicke, Enterludes and bankets."[89]

Philip arrived in England from Flanders on March 21,
and four days later Napea was formally received by the
English King and Queen at their court at Whitehall in
Westminster.[90]   He presented his letter from Ivan, "made
his oration," and having been graciously dismissed returned by water to his lodging.[90]   The letter does not
seem to have been preserved, but in the light of the reply
sent by Philip and Mary[91] and the contemporary com-
ments of the Venetian ambassador[92] we can infer that a
treaty of alliance had been proposed.

Two days later the Russian ambassador was visited by
the bishop of Ely and Sir William Knight who took the
negotiations in charge.[93]   On April 23 he took formal

[88] Hakluyt, II, 356.
[89] Ibid., II, 358.
[90] Ibid., II, 356.
[91] Tolstoy, Forty Years' Relation between England and Russia, p.
13.
[92] Cal. S. P. (Venetian) 1556-1557, p. 1005.
[93] Hakluyt, II, 357,

leave of their majesties, receiving a written reply to Ivan's proposition. Merchants of both countries were hereafter to enjoy equal privileges of free trade and governmental protection. The Czar's offer of friendship was accepted.[94]

On May 3 the ambassador left London, being accompanied to Gravesend by "divers Aldermen and merchants, who in good gard set him aboord the noble shippe, the *Primrose* Admiral to the Fleete, where leave was taken on both sides and parts, after many imbracements and divers farewels not without expressing of tears."[95]

With the close of this embassy diplomatic relations between England and Russia may be considered to have been firmly established. Thenceforth ambassadors went back and forth between the two countries as special occasion arose. Commercially also the bonds between the two nations may be said to have become firmly established by 1557, the year of Napea's departure. A commercial understanding had been reached and a scheme of mutual benefits established. From that time forward every spring the Company sent out its cargoes to the White Sea, bringing in return the wares of distant Russia.

[94] Hakluyt, II, 357; Tolstoy, p. 13.
[95] Hakluyt, II, 358.

CHAPTER II

Our knowledge of the organization of the Muscovy Company, except for the general provisions contained in its charter, must be based upon indirect evidence in contemporary documents. The official records of the Company, could they be found, would give us a much closer view of the subject than is now possible. That records were kept there can be no doubt. All efforts to locate them, however, have up to the present time proved futile, and it has been surmised with much semblance of probability that the official documents containing the accounts and proceedings of the Company have been destroyed. Certain it is that Muscovy House, the official home of the Company in London and the probable repository of its records, was burned in the Great Fire of 1666. An indenture bearing date of March 30, 1670, makes distinct reference to "that toft peece or parcell of ground whereon that Capitall mesnage formerly called the Muscovie House . . . stood . . . before the late dreadfull fire in London."[1] Whether or not the Great Fire accounts for the present lack of direct source material, the fact remains that for the present at least the student of the history of the Muscovy Company in the sixteenth century has no group of material corresponding in any way to the Court Books of the East India Company or the Acts and Ordinances of the Eastland Company.

Fortunately the Charter of 1555 contains in outline the general plan of organization. We have definite knowledge

[1] Husting Roll, 341 (29).

22

that organization of some sort had been effected at the very beginning of the movement. We have seen that in 1553 the Company had a governor and a governing board definitely referred to as the Consuls and Assistants.[2] It is highly probable that the letters of incorporation, so far as this phase of their content is concerned, merely confirmed the plan of organization under which the Company had been already working for more than two years. The statute of 1566, confirming and enlarging the Company's privileges, specifies no change in this respect. We are probably justified in concluding that the plan of organization outlined in the first chapter represents the form under which the Company existed from its very inception and throughout the period we are considering. An analysis of some of the provisions of the first charter, therefore, and a consideration of the incidental references to be found in contemporary letters and accounts, furnish us with as adequate a comprehension of the Company's organization as, in the absence of the official records, it is possible to secure.

In the first charter the new trading company was organized under the name of "Marchants adventurers of England, for the discovery of lands, territories, Iles, Dominions, and Seigniories unknowen, and not before that late adventure or enterprise by sea or navigation, commouly frequented."[3] This had evidently been the name adopted at the time of the Company's first formation.[4] This cumbrous title the Company bore till the issue of the second charter in 1566. That document mentions the extreme length of this title as one of the reasons for issuing the new charter!—" . . . And for that the name by

---

[2] *Supra*, p. 4.

[3] Hakluyt, II, 305. Not to be confused with the Society of Merchants Adventurers of England. The similarity of official title has led to some confusion in the past.

[4] Cf. the title of Cabot's instructions in 1553. *Ibid.*, II, 195.

which the saide felowship is incorporated by the letters
patents aforesaid, is long, & consisteth of very many
words: Therefore be it enacted, etc."[5]

Accordingly the new charter conferred a new name upon
the Company. "The said felowship, company, society and
corporation made or created by the said letters patents,
shal at al time & times from henceforth be incorporated,
named and called onely by the name of the fellowship of
English merchants, for discovery of new trades."[6] The
lack of contemporary trading companies is clearly seen in
the vague character of this title, specifying as it does nothing as to the nature of the trade or the sphere of the
Company's activities. The "company for the discovery of
new trades" remained its official name throughout the
sixteenth century and beyond.

Usage, however, soon came to apply a more distinctive
appellation. As early as 1555 the Venetian ambassador,
Giovanni Michiel, writing home to the Doge and Senate
refers to "this new Muscovite navigation [company]."[7]
In 1558 Queen Mary writes to Sigismund, King of Poland,
of "the Society of Merchants of London who trade with
Russia."[8] Again in 1566 we find them spoken of as the
"company of Merchant Adventurers into Russia."[9] In
1567 Robert Glover wrote to the "company of Muscovy
merchants."[10] The next year we find them again referred
to merely as the "Muscovy Merchants."[11] A document
dated May 19, 1568, and endorsed by Cecil is headed
"Articles between the Queen and the Muscovy Company."

[5] Hakluyt, III, 86.
[6] Ibid., III, 87.
[7] Cal. S. P. (Venetian) 1555-1556 p. 143.
[8] Hist. MSS. Com. 13th Report, app. part II, p. 10 (Rutland MSS.).
[9] Cal. S. P. (Domestic) 1547-1580 p. 280.
[10] Cal. S. P. (Foreign) 1566-1568, p. 309.
[11] Ibid., p. 462 (2).

This is the form in which we find the name of the Company with extreme frequency thenceforward. This narrowing of the title corresponds with the growth of the trade with Russia and the gradual confining of the merchants' efforts to the exploitation of that country. Particularly in the last quarter of the sixteenth century when trading companies were multiplying did it become necessary to use some distinguishing name. Hence the increasing use of the terms Muscovy Company and Russia Company.

The first charter clearly specifies what officers the Company shall have and gives some intimation of their mode of election. The officials designated consist of a Governor or Governors (either one or two at the option of the Company), four Consuls, and twenty-four Assistants.[12] In general plan this is not unlike the organization of the old company of the Merchant Adventurers, the chief difference being that that body had but one Governor and made no provisions for Consuls.[13] The number of Assistants was the same in both companies, a feature of their organization which was also typical of the later Eastland[14] and East India[15] Companies.

The Governors.—The charter provides in the first place that the Company shall "yeerely name, elect and choose one Governour or two."[16] There is no intimation of any intended superiority of one Governor over the other or any hint that the two officials were to stand in the relation of chief and deputy. In fact, in the later working

[12] Hakluyt, II, 306.

[13] Lingelbach, *The Internal Organization of the Merchant Adventurers of England*, p. 29.

[14] Sellers, *Acts and Ordinances of the Eastland Company*, p. xiii. The portion of the charter cited in Miss Sellers' work omits the provision referring to the number of Assistants.

[15] Charter of the East India Company, in Prothero, *Statutes and Constitutional Documents 1558-1625*, p. 449.

[16] Hakluyt, II, 306.

out of the system there is every indication of an equality in rank: where there are two Governors their names are coupled without any indication of a difference in dignity. We are justified, moreover, in assuming that if any other condition but that of equality had been intended some statement to that effect would be found in the charter. The provision for a dual governorship seems to have been peculiar to the Muscovy Company. No reason for the innovation is suggested, though the analogy to the London shrievalty presents itself, not as an explanation, but as an interesting parallel. The title "Governor" mentioned in the charter seems to have been fairly consistently adhered to. The term "lieutenant" is used, however, in at least one place with evident reference to this official.[17] The expression "Master of the Muscovy House" seems also to have been used with this signification.[18] Whether "cheyff marchand of Muskovea," used by Machyn [19] in speaking of Sir George Barnes on the occasion of his death in 1558, is still another variation of the title is difficult to say in the absence of further information as to the official position held by Barnes in that year. Officially, however, there is very little variation from the regular title.

Sebastian Cabot, the Charter of 1555 provides, "in consideration that . . . he hath bin the chiefest setter forth of this journey or voyage," is to be the first Governor.[20] This position he is to enjoy "during his naturall life, without amoving or dismissing from the same roome." [20] During his life, however, the Company may at their yearly election choose an additional Governor if they so desire.[21] Cabot died in 1557. There is no inti-

17 Hakluyt, II, 375.
18 Cal. S. P. (Colonial) 1513-1616, p. 85.
19 *Machyn's Diary*, p. 166.
20 Hakluyt, II, 305.
21 *Ibid.*, II, 306.

mation in the few contemporary references relating to the history of the Company in the period of less than three years between its incorporation and the death of its first Governor that any one was elected to share Cabot's office. The evidence on this point, however, is in large measure negative. It seems highly improbable in view of the unique position occupied by Sebastian Cabot toward the close of his life that the Company would have chosen any other member to share the governorship with him.

After Cabot's death the dual governorship seems to have been frequently though probably not invariably in use. It has not been possible to compile any complete list of the successive occupants of this position. The following references, however, are among those that seem to indicate the prevalence of a dual governorship. A letter from the Company to its agents written in 1560 mentions the *"Governours."* [22] The instructions to Anthony Jenkinson under date of May 8, 1561, are signed by William Gerrard and Thomas Lodge, *"Governors."* [23] Under date of November 20, 1564, we find a petition of the *"Governors,* Consuls, etc.,"* of the Company to the Privy Council.[24] Other references leave no doubt of the fact of the existence of two Governors in that year.[25] In 1567 we find Sir William Gerrard and Rowland Hawarde jointly filling the office.[26] Again in the following year a letter is addressed to the *"Governors* of the Company of Russia Merchants."* [27] In 1575 the Queen refers to the official heads of the Company, using the expression *"governors of the merchants."* [28] Under date of May 20, 1580,

[22] Hakluyt, II, 410.
[23] *Ibid.,* II, 14.
[24] Cal. S. P. (Colonial) 1513-1616, p. 4.
[25] Cal. S. P. (Domestic) 1547-1580, p. 246 (2).
[26] *Ibid.,* p. 287.
[27] Cal. Clarendon MSS. (Bodl.) Addenda, No. 303.
[28] Cal. S. P. (Foreign) 1575-1577, p. 52.

we find a commission granted by Sir Rowland Hawarde and George Barne, "*Governors* of the Company of English merchants for Discovery of New Trades."[29]   In 1592 Sir George Barne and Sir John Harte are definitely referred to as "*governors* of the Russia and Muscovy Company."[30]

That there were times, however, when the Company exercised its option of electing a single official to act as Governor is indicated by a number of scattered references hardly to be explained on any other supposition. In the following citations the use of the singular number can scarcely be attributed to carelessness on the part of the various writers. Arthur Edwards in a letter of 1566 says: "I have written the prices of wares in my letter to the *governour* both for spices and some drugs which I do know."[31]   The expression "Sir William Gerrard and the Company of merchants trading to Russia" in a document of 1576[32] would hardly have been used if at that time the Company had had two Governors.   Again under date of January 19, 1583, we find a reference to "Mr. Harvie, the *governor,* and others of the Russia company."[33]   Similarly in 1591 reference is made to "Sir Jno. Hart, *governor,* and others of the Company of Merchants trading to Russia."[34]   A letter to Lady Walsingham written in 1583 makes mention of the *Governor* of the Muscovy Company.[35]   It would seem that we are justified in concluding that while we have a number of specific references to prove the existence of two Governors for the Company there are intimations that this was not an invariable practice.

[29] Cal. S. P. (Domestic) 1547-1580, p. 656.
[30] Cal. S. P. (Domestic) 1591-1594, p. 170.
[31] Hakluyt, III, 51.
[32] Cal. S. P. (Domestic) 1547-1580, p. 523.
[33] Cal. S. P. (Domestic) 1581-1590, p. 91.
[34] Cal. S. P. (Domestic) 1591-1594, p. 30.
[35] Cal. S. P. (Domestic) 1581-1590, p. 138.

Unfortunately we have no account of any election of the Company's Governors, so that we have no definite knowledge of the exact form of procedure. It probably did not vary in any important respect from the mode of election employed in other incorporated bodies of the time. On this point the charter provides, "And further-more, we graunt unto the same fellowship . . . that they . . . shall, and may freely and lawfully in places convenient and honest, assemble themselves to-gether, or so many of them as will or can assemble to-gether, as well within our citie of London, or elsewhere, as it shall please them, in such sort and maner, as other worshipfull corporations of our saide citie have used to assemble, and there yeerly name, elect and choose one Governour or two, of themselves, and their liberties, and also . . . the four Consuls and the twenty-four As-sistants." [36] In the event of the death of a Governor during his term of office the Company is to meet and elect a successor "in the place and steade of such as so shall happen to die, to serve out the same yeere." [36] It is in-teresting to notice that seldom if ever were men appointed to this office for a long series of consecutive terms.

The Governors of the Muscovy Company were fre-quently men of considerable standing in the municipal life of their time. Names of Mayors and Aldermen are of frequent occurrence, clearly pointing to the dominance of city influence in the administration of the Company. Those members who held influential positions in the national government seem to have contented themselves for the most part with simple membership. Among the Mayors and Sheriffs who held high office in the Com-pany may be mentioned William Chester, who was Sheriff in 1554 [37] and Mayor in 1560; [38] Thomas Lodge, who was

[36] Hakluyt, II, 306.
[37] Stow, *Survey of London* (edition of 1908), II, 183.
[38] *Ibid.*, II, 184.

Sheriff in 1559 [37] and Mayor in 1562,[40] Rowland Hawarde, who was Sheriff in 1563 [40] and Mayor in 1570 [40] and again in 1590; [39] George Barne, who was Sheriff in 1576 [40] and Mayor in 1586; [39] and John Harte, who was Sheriff in 1578 [39] and Mayor in 1589.[39]

The Consuls and Assistants.—The Charter of 1555 makes provision for twenty-eight other officials to assist the Governor or Governors. Four of these were to be known as Consuls, and the remaining twenty-four as Assistants.[41] They were to be elected by the Company at the same meeting at which the Governors were chosen, and like them were to hold office for one year.[41] This is clearly the meaning of the rather awkwardly worded provision: " . . . also at the election of such said Governour or governours . . . to choose, name and appoint eight and twenty of the most sad, discreete, and honest persons of the saide fellowship, and communalty of Marchant adventurers, . . . and 4. of the most expert and skilfull persons of the same 28. to be named and called Consuls, and 24. of the residue, to be named and called Assistants to the saide Governour or governours, and Consuls for the time being, which shal remain and stand in their authorities for one whole yeere then next following." [41] The difference in function between the two sorts of officials, i.e., Consuls and Assistants, is difficult to ascertain owing to the absence of definite references in documents that have come down to us. The charter provision just cited clearly implies that Consuls occupy a higher rank than Assistants; out of the twenty-eight first chosen "the most expert and skilfull" were selected to be Consuls. We have, however, no explicit reference to the relative amount of authority connected with the two offices.

[39] Stow, *Survey of London*, II, 185.
[40] *Ibid.*, II, 184.
[41] Hakluyt, II, 306.

The Governors, Consuls and Assistants constituted a sort of governing board with extensive powers. When there was one Governor this board consisted of twenty-nine members; when there were two Governors it contained thirty. This group of men were given by the charter full authority to govern the Company,—"to execute and doe full and speedie justice to them, and every of them, in all their causes, differences, variances, controversies, quarrels, and complaints, within any our realms, dominions and jurisdictions onely moved and to be moved, touching their marchandise, traffikes, and occupiers aforesaid, or the good order or rule of them or any of them." [42] A more explicit statement of the authority of this body is found later in the same document. They are empowered to make such statutes for the government of the Company as they shall think proper, and to revoke statutes which in their judgment are unnecessary or hurtful or which may have become obsolete.[43] They are definitely authorized, moreover, to punish by means of fines, forfeitures, and imprisonments any member who may be found "contrarious, rebellious or disobedient" to the officials of the Company or to any statutes that have been passed.[44] They are authorized to "punish every such offendor or offendors, as the quality of the offence requireth, according to their good discretions." [45] That this power was actually used is evidenced by a petition of a certain Thomas Wynington to Sir Francis Walsingham in which he complains that having come from Moscow to London to make complaint of one Northen, a merchant, he had been imprisoned at the instance of the Master (sic) and Governors of the Company of Moscovia.[46]

[42] Hakluyt, II, 308.
[43] Ibid., II, 309.
[44] Ibid., II, 310.
[45] Ibid., II, 311.
[46] Cal. S. P. (Domestic) 1547-1580, p. 695.

In the Governors, Consuls and Assistants, then, the
charter vested full legislative, judicial, and administrative
power. The membership itself had no authority of its own
save that of annually electing its governing board. The
only explicit limitation on the power of this board was
in its relations to the government which gave it being and
to the municipality in whose geographical limits it found
itself, namely the English government and the city of
London. The charter provides that the Company's statutes may not be in disagreement with the "prerogative,
lawes, statutes and customes" of the realm, nor contrary
to any treaty in effect between the English government
and any foreign power.[47] Nor may they conflict with the
authority of the "corporation of the Maior, communalties
and Citizens" of the city of London.[47] In the third place
they may not infringe on the privileges of any other corporation.[47] Finally, to the Governors, Consuls and Assistants was delegated the duty of admitting to membership in the Company "such and as many persons, as to
them shal bee thought good, meete, convenient and necessarie."[48] This provision of the charter, arbitrary as it
seems, is clearly consistent with the other despotic powers
just outlined. No qualifications for admission are mentioned in the charter. The Company is self perpetuating,
but only through the action of its governing board.

Besides the annual meetings at which the election of
officers took place no other regular meetings are provided
for in the charter. The extensive powers delegated to the
officials would suggest that frequent meetings of the whole
membership would have been superfluous. That the annual meetings were not devoted exclusively to the business of election, however, is evidenced by a record of instructions given in 1555 to the Company's first agents by

[47] Hakluyt, II, 311.
[48] Ibid., II, 310.

"the Governor Consuls, Assistants and whole company assembled this day in open court."[49] Similarly in 1580 articles of instruction were delivered to Arthur Pet and Charles Jackman "at the court holden at Muscovy House, 17th May 1580."[50]

Of the times of meeting of the governing board we have no definite knowledge. The charter provides that at meetings of this body fifteen votes shall be necessary to carry any measure.[51] This would constitute a majority if there was one Governor, half of the board if there were two. It is further provided that no measure can be passed unless there be present at the meeting one Governor and two Consuls, or, in the absence of a Governor, three Consuls.[51] This plan in spite of its apparent complexity must have been effective; a majority vote was required to carry a measure and no motion could be carried in the absence of a majority of the higher officials.

The regular place of meeting for the Company was known as Muscovy House. During the earlier years of the Company's existence it was located in Seething Lane. It was here that the Russian emissaries, Twerdico and Pogorella, were entertained during their visit of 1567-1568. A letter from Henry Lane to Hakluyt describes this visit and makes definite reference to the Company's house "then in Seething Lane,"[52] a form of expression which would seem to indicate that at the date of writing the Company's headquarters were no longer located in that street. There seems to be no way of ascertaining the time of removal, though the later situation can be determined with a tolerable degree of precision by a reference in an indenture bearing a much later date. This document fixes the location "in the parish of St. Antholin London in or

[49] Hakluyt, II, 281.
[50] Cal. S. P. (Colonial) 1513-1616, p. 61.
[51] Hakluyt, II, 307.
[52] Ibid., III, 99.

neare a certayne streete since the . . . late dreadfull
fire in London called & knowne by the name of Dukes
street.''[53]

No other regular officers besides those already mentioned
are provided for in the charter. The Company is empowered to employ ''Sergeants'' for the purpose of collecting
fines and enforcing penalties inflicted by the governing
body.[54] These persons, however, were servants in the employ of the Company, not officials in the real sense of the
term. The same may be said of the ''Factors'' to whom
the charter also makes reference.[55] As a matter of fact
the administration of the Company's affairs, particularly

[53] *Husting Roll* 341, 29. "This Indenture made the thirtieth day
of March in the two and twentieth yeare of our soveraigne Lord
Charles the Second by the Grace of God of England, Scotland, ffrance
and Ireland, being defender of the faith. And in the yeare of our
Lord God 1670. Between John Seed sonne and heire of John Seed
late cittizen and haberdasher of London deceased and Elizabeth
his wife on the one parte and William Cooke of Cliffords Inn London
gents of the other part Witnesseth that the said John Seed & Elizabeth his wife for and in consideration of the sume of eleaven hundred
and fifty pounds of lawfull money of England to him the said John
Seed and before the ensealing & delivery of theis presents by the
said William Cooke paid and secured to be paid the receipt and
security whereof the said John Seed & Elizabeth his wife doe sev-
erally and respectively hereby acknowledge have and either of them
hath granted bargained sold aliened enefeoffed released and confirmed and by theis presents doe & either of them doth absolutely
grant bargaine sell alien enfeoffe release and confirme unto the
said William Cooke his heires and assignes for ever in his actuall
possession now being by virtue of an Indenture of Lease beareing
date the day before the date of theis presents from the said John
Seed for one yeare and of the statute for transferring uses into
possession all *that toft peece or parcell of ground whereon that
Capitall mesuage formerly called the Muscovie House with the ap-
purtenaces formerly stood before the late dreadfull fire in London
converted into severall tenements or houses scituate lying and being
in the parish of St. Antholin London in or neare a certayne streete
since the said late dreadfull fire in London called & knowne by the
name of Dukes streete, and also all that toft peece* . . ."

[54] Hakluyt, II, 312.

[55] *Ibid.*, II, 314.

in Russia, necessitated the organization of a whole system
of employees with various functions and powers. These
require some discussion in this place.

As early as 1555 the Company sent Richard Gray and
William Killingworth to take charge of its interests in
Russia. These men were commissioned ''jointly and sev-
erally to be Agents, Factors, and Atturneis general and
speciall, for the whole body of this companie.'' [56] They
were authorized to do all the buying and selling for the
Company in Russia and to supervise the work of all the
lesser employees.[57] They were also to keep careful accounts of the Company's dealings.[58] The privileges
granted to the Company by the Russian government in
1555 specifically grant to its agents the right of governing all Englishmen in Russia: ''Item, we give and graunt
unto the saide Marchants and their successours, that such
person as is, or shalbe commended unto us, our heires or
successors by the Governour, Consuls and assistants of
the said fellowship resient within the citie of London
within the realme of England, to be their chiefe Factor
within this our empire and dominions, may and shal have
ful power and authoritie to governe and rule all Englishmen that have had, or shall have accesse, or repaire in
or to this said Empire and jurisdictions, or any part
thereof.'' [59]

The Company's commercial affairs in England were evidently in the charge of a similar agent. The presence of
the regular officials in London rendered unnecessary the
delegation to this officer of any such plenary powers as
had of necessity to be exercised by their representative
in Russia. In 1575 Michael Lok held the position of
''Agent in London for the Moscovie company.'' [60]

[56] Hakluyt, II, 281.
[57] *Ibid.*, II, 283.
[58] *Ibid.*, II, 284.
[59] *Ibid.*, II, 300.   [60] *Ibid.*, III, 197.

The privileges granted by Ivan in 1555 definitely authorized the Company to "name, choose and assigne brokers, shippers, packers, weighers, measurers, wagoners, and all other meet and necessary laborers for to serve them in their feat of marchandises."[61] In 1557 we find evidences of a fast increasing body of workmen of various sorts in the Company's employ. The raw hemp sent from Russia to England having involved heavy charges of transportation, the Company decided to have it made into rope before importing it. For this purpose they sent to the agents in Russia seven rope-makers. The agents are directed to assign them a "principal overseer . . . and also to furnish them . . . with labourers, workemen and stuffe."[62] At the same time a skinner was sent "to viewe and see such furres as you shall cheape or buy."[63] One Leonard Brian was also appointed to attend to the cutting of certain stores of yew said to have been found in Russia.[64] Two coopers sent at the same time were "to make in a readinesse all such caske as shalbe needful for traine oyle, tallowe, or any thing else."[65] Ten young men " that be bound Prentises to the Companie" were sent to be employed in whatever capacity the agents might think best, "some to keepe accompts, some to buy and sell by your order and commission, and some to send abroad into the notable Cities of the Countrey for understanding and knowledge."[66]

Election to membership, as has been mentioned, seems to have been entirely in the hands of the governing board. Whether confirmation on the part of the Company was necessary we do not know. An oath was administered to

---

[61] Hakluyt, II, 300.
[62] Ibid., II, 381.
[63] Ibid., II, 382.
[64] Ibid., II, 387.
[65] Ibid.
[66] Ibid., II, 383.

all persons on admission to membership.[67] The membership in 1555 included some two hundred names, the list of which in the State Papers presents several points of interest.[68] The grouping is as follows:—There is first a list of twenty-seven names which evidently represent the interest of the Court. These include the Lord Treasurer, the Lord High Admiral, the Lord Chamberlain, the Controller, the Vice-Chamberlain, and the Master of the Horse. In this same group we find the name of Sir William Cecil, a charter member and for half a century a powerful representative of the Company's interests. The next group contains the names of thirteen Aldermen, among them the name of a woman, Mrs. Margarett Kyrtom. Next follows a group designated as "Esquiers"; these are headed by the name of "Sebastian Caboto" and include several names later to be of significance in the Company's affairs. The eleven "Esquiers" are followed by a list of eight "gentlemen." The rest of the document consists of the names of the other members of the Company alphabetically arranged, oddly enough, according to the first letter of their first names. Two more women's names appear in the list. No such complete list of members is available for any other year, so that only through indirect references can we secure any information on the subject of changes in the personnel of the Company. It is of interest to learn that at one time Sir Francis Walsingham was a member,[69] also that Humphrey Gilbert in a letter to the Queen in 1567 laid claim to membership in the Company "for discovery of New Trades."[70]

Any consideration of the organization of the Muscovy Company necessarily involves some discussion of the way

[67] Cal. S. P. (Domestic) 1547-1580, p. 432.
[68] MS. in the State Papers (Domestic) Addenda. Vol. VII, No. 39.
[69] Hakluyt, II, 109.
[70] Cal. S. P. (Colonial) 1513-1616, p. 6.

in which it carried on its trading activities. Was it a
Regulated Company or a Joint Stock? We must be on
our guard, of course, against trying to make Elizabethan
conditions fit modern terms. In the realm of commerce,
as well as in government and religion, the Tudor period
was largely a time of transition. If, therefore, in our
discussion we employ terms that have acquired in modern
times a specific modern. connotation it will be necessary
precisely to define those terms. In our definition we will
follow the lead of the best secondary writers on the subject. By a Regulated Trading Company is meant a group
of persons incorporated by charter, enjoying the monopoly of a certain trade as individuals.[71] None but members
of the company may legally engage in the trade, but these
members do so as individual merchants each with his separate capital. Voluntary and temporary combinations
will, of course, occur with more or less frequency. A
Joint Stock Company, on the other hand, engages in trade
collectively, each member owning a share of the joint stock
and receiving a proportionate share of the profits. Secondary writers, with singular uniformity, have taken the
ground that the Muscovy Company belonged to the class
of Regulated Companies,[72] a position which an examination
of contemporary references does not seem to justify.

While neither of the two charters throws direct light
on the subject under discussion, a significant clause in
the closing section of the Act of 1566 is hardly to be in-
terpreted on any other supposition than that of a Joint
Stock. This section extends the freedom of the Company
to persons of York, Newcastle, Hull and Boston who have
for ten years continually "traded the course of merchandise," on condition that before December 25, 1567, they

[71] E.g., Cunningham, *Growth of English Industry and Commerce*,
II, 215.
[72] It is so classified by Cunningham, II, 239 ff.

"shal contribute, joyne, and put in stocke, to, with, and amongst the said company, such summe and summes of money, as any of the said company, which hath throughly continued and contributed to the said newe trade, from the yeere 1552. hath done, and before the saide 25. of December 1567. shall do *for the furniture of one ordinary, full and intire portion, or share.*" [73]   This certainly is open to the interpretation that a merchant of the towns specified might join the Company by purchasing a share of its stock and paying in addition all assessments which had been levied since the beginning of the trade.[74]

Two years before the granting of this second charter the Company petitioned the Privy Council that interlopers should be restrained from trading with Russia. The petition mentions the great loss with which the trade had been maintained for the previous twelve years. Then follows the statement that the petitioners *"are forced to add 60£ to the former stock, to make every single share 200£,* but finding the trade to the Narve attempted by William Bond, they are so discouraged that they cannot be persuaded to *increase the stock.*" [75]   Obscure as this statement undoubtedly is it still seems to point clearly to some sort of Joint Stock arrangement. Of similar tenor but scarcely less ambiguous is a letter of the Company to their agent Christopher Holme in 1591 in which he is told that the Company "have increased his venture 200£, on account of his having obtained encouragement of the trade." [76]   Still more significant is a notice to the same agent shortly before in which he is directed to prevent private traffic.[77]

[73] Hakluyt, III, 91.

[74] Macpherson states that this clause in favor of the northern towns was due to the fact that they had contributed to the first attempt for a northeast passage, but he cites no authority for the statement.—Macpherson, I, 144.

[75] Cal. S. P. (Colonial) 1513-1616, p. 4.

[76] Cal. S. P. (Domestic) 1591-1594, p. 41.

[77] *Ibid.*, p. 30.

On June 25, 1569, Thomas Bannister and Geoffrey Duckett writing from Russia to the Privy Council on the state of Russian relations and the affairs of the Company mention that one purpose of their mission was "to recover the *Company's stock* out of their factor's hands." [78] Later in their letter they announce that the Emperor "has commanded Thomas Glover to deliver up the *Company's goods* in his hands." [79] Another bit of evidence in the same direction is to be found in a letter of one William Smith written from Russia in 1572 in which after describing certain difficulties he had experienced in the Company's service he says "but there was suche matters layd to my charge, that if I went not the *company's stock* were lyke all to be loste." [80] Evidently the Company was trading as a collective unit, not as separate individuals.

Important in its bearing on the question is a letter to Robert Cecil written November 20, 1595, by Francis Cherry, the Company's agent at that time. Cherry asks Cecil to use his influence in the Company's behalf and reviews its recent vicissitudes. "I thought it much behooful briefly to acquaint you with the present state of our Company; which in times past consisted of many persons to the number of 80, and somewhiles more, who *traded with one entire and common stock* . . . " [81]

The numerous references to the Company buying and selling its wares constitute an important part of the evidence on the point under discussion. The agents in Russia represented the Company there, and attended to matters

[78] Cal. S. P. (Foreign) 1569-1571, p. 90.
[79] *Ibid.*, p. 91.
[80] Wright, *Queen Elizabeth and Her Times*, I, 419. Wright mentions the difficulty of identifying the writer of this interesting letter (p. 418, note). It is probable that this was the same William Smith who was in the Company's employ in 1566, and whom Arthur Edwards mentions as "an honest yong man, and one that doeth good service here."—Hakluyt, III, 48.
[81] Hatfield House MSS. V, 462.

of trade for the Company as a whole. In 1555 Gray and Killingworth were appointed "to be Agents, Factors, and Atturneis generall and speciall, *for the whole body of this companie,* to buy, sel, trucke, change and permute al, and every kind and kindes of wares, marchandizes and goods to the said company appertaining, now laden & shipped in the good ship called the Edward Bonaventure, appointed for Russia, the same to utter and sell to the best commoditie, *profit and advantage of the said corporation,* be it for ready money, wares & marchandises, or truck, presently, or for time, as occasion & benefit of the companie shal require: and all such wares as they or either of them shal buy, trucke, or provide, or cause to be bought for the company to lade them homeward in good order and condition, as by prudent course of marchandises, shall, and ought to appertaine." [82]   The fact that the agents were acting for the Company as a whole is made still more evident by their further authorization "to binde & charge the said company by debt for wares upon credit, as good opportunitie and occasion shall serve, with power to charge and bind the said company, and their successors, for the paiments of such things as shalbe taken up for credite." [83]

The whole tone of these instructions supports our contention for a joint stock basis. For instance it is provided that "no inferiour minister shall take upon him to make any bargaine or sale of any wares, marchandises or goods, but by the Commission and Warrantise of the sayde Agents under their bandes." [84]   Again, the agents are instructed to "learne and observe all kinde of wares, as wel naturals as forein, that be beneficiall for this Realme, *to be sold for the benefit of the company,* and what kinde of our commodities and other things of these West partes bee

[82] Hakluyt, II, 281.
[83] *Ibid.*
[84] *Ibid.*, II, 284.

most vendible in those Realmes with profite, giving a perfeet advise of all such things requisite."[84] Even more significant is the following quotation: "if the Emperour will enter into bargain with you for the whole masse of your stock, and will have the trade of it to utter to his owne subjects, then debating the matter prudently among your selves, set such high prises of your commodities, as you may assure your selves to be gainers in your owne wares, and yet to buy theirs at such base prises, as you may here also make a commoditie and gaine at home, having in your mindes the notable charges that the companie have diffrayed in advancing this voyage: and the great charges that they sustaine dayly in wages, victuals and other things."[85]

The servants of the Company in Russia were required to take a solemn oath to serve the Company faithfully and obey its agents. The oath administered to them ends as follows: "and you shall not directly or indirectly, openly or covertly doe, exercise or use any trade or feate of marchandizes for your owne private account, commodity, gaine or profite, or for the account of or for any other person or persons, without consent or licence of this said fellowship, first obtained in writing. And if you shall know or understand any other person or persons to use, exercise or doe any trade, trafficke or feat of marchandise, to or for his or their own account or accounts, at any time or times hereafter, that then ye shall truely and plainly disclose . . . the same unto this said fellowship, without fraude, colour, covin or delay: So helpe you God, etc."[86] Individual merchants were evidently not to receive any of the benefits of the trade.

All the correspondence of the Company with its agents in Russia seems to point to the same conclusion. Expres-

85 Hakluyt, II, 284.
86 Ibid., II, 290.

sions like the following occur: "the companies goods, and that under their marke," [87]—"You shall receive, . . . God sending them in safety for the use of the Company, these kinds of wares following, all marked with the general marke of the Company," [88] etc. The letter of instructions sent in 1557 to the agents in Russia refers with unusual definiteness to the common trade: "Of furres we desire no great plentie, because they be dead wares. And as for Felts, we will in no wise you send any. . . . We would you bought as much Wexe principally as you may get." [89]

In 1567 Robert Glover, an agent of the Company, wrote home about their affairs in Russia. He mentions that certain English merchants were selling "better cheap English commodities than the company" and closes his letter with the statement that he will "seal up the *goods of the company* till such time as he has answer." [90] The next year when Bannister and Duckett were sent to Russia by the Company to investigate certain charges that had been made we find them writing to Cecil that they "find the estate of the Company to stand very evil, as well touching their accounts as also with the Prince." [91]

That the Company not only traded in Russia on a Joint Stock basis, but sold its wares in England on the same plan is indicated by the fact that the English government purchased cordage from the Company, not from its individual members. Under date of May 19, 1568, we have a definite record of articles between the Queen and the Muscovy Company in which the Company contracts for the delivery of "cables, hawsers, cordage and other tacke at Deptford dockyard to the value of 4000£ 8s 10d." [92] All

[87] Hakluyt, II, 319.

[88] Ibid., II, 380.

[89] Ibid., II, 381.

[90] Cal. S. P. (Foreign) 1566-1568, p. 309.

[91] Ibid., p. 518.   [92] Ibid., p. 462.

the references to the relations of the Company to the government tend to substantiate this idea. The government was frequently indebted to the Company for goods delivered. In 1582 Walsingham wrote to Burghley that the Muscovy Company request payment of the money due to them for wax taken these two years past for the use of her Majesty's household.[93]

After all, perhaps the chief argument to prove that the Muscovy Company's business must have been managed on a Joint Stock basis is to be found in the physical fact of the actual distance of Russia and the numerous difficulties of communication. These would almost inevitably have rendered impossible any extensive trading by individual English merchants. The other alternative, that the trade was managed through a succession of temporary combinations of members of the Company, while in itself a possible supposition, conflicts with most of the references just cited. The numerous indications of the whole membership trading as a single group contained in the directions to the agents and in the references to the government's dealings with the Company would seem absolutely to preclude this possibility.

With one more argument we shall bring this portion of our discussion to a close. A Joint Stock basis is the most plausible, if not the only, explanation of the presence of a group of noblemen among the members. These would hardly have engaged in individual trade. That they actually derived a profit from their membership in the Company is evidenced by a letter written to Lord Burghley in 1568 by Humphrey Lok and John Fenton. They write to complain of the Company's oppressive and unjust actions but add significantly that they "are sorry that Cecil is one of the voyage, for where in three or four years he gains one hundred pounds he sells for the same one thou-

[93] Cal. S. P. (Domestic) 1581-1590, p. 75.

and pounds worth of honour." [94]   In those days as in our own time the connection of government officials with wealthy corporations was evidently looked at askance.

[94] Cal. S. P. (Foreign) 1566-1568, p. 463.

CHAPTER III

We have already had occasion to notice the close connection between the English government and the Muscovy Company. This connection is so important as to warrant separate and definite consideration. Our discussion of the topic will fall under four main heads. In the first place we shall need to examine the nature and extent of the privileges, both governmental and commercial, granted to the Company by the crown and by Parliament. In the second place the question of the exportation of contraband to Russia will need some consideration inasmuch as this question necessarily involves the relation of the Government to the only authorized carriers of merchandise from England to the dominions of the Czar. A third phase of our discussion will treat of the Company's part in the diplomatic relations between the two nations. Finally we shall devote some attention to the commercial dealings of the English government with the Muscovy Company.

1. *The Government's Grant of Privileges to the Company.*

The letters of incorporation of 1555 guaranteed that the Company should have perpetual succession. This furnishes a decided contrast to some of the later Companies whose charters set definite time limits to the privileges they conferred. The same clause of the Muscovy Company's char-

46

ter authorizes the use of a common seal and provides that
the Company shall be forever capable in law to purchase,
possess, grant and let lands and other possessions to the
annual value of one hundred marks.[1]   The corporation is
further given the right "in the law to implead, and be
impleaded, to answere, and to be answered, to defende,
and to be defended" in all courts in cases touching the
Company's affairs, "in as ample manner and forme, as
any other corporation of this our Realme may doe."[2]

The right of self regulation conferred by the charter and
by it vested in the Governors, Consuls and Assistants has
been referred to in another connection.[3]   The only limitation on this power is that no regulations of the Company
may conflict with the royal prerogative, statute or common
law, or with the privileges of the corporation of London
or of any other corporation established by royal grant.[4]
Otherwise the control of the Company over the affairs of
its members is supreme.   This right of self-regulation is
supplemented, moreover, by the guarantee of government
assistance in the carrying out of its decisions.   The sergeants appointed by the Company to collect fines, forfeitures, etc., are authorized by the charter to seize the
property and person of offending members "in every place
and places not franchised."[5]   If the offender should be
in any "place franchised or priviledged where the said
officer or officers may not lawfully intromit or intermid-
dle" (e.g., in cities, boroughs or "townes incorporate") the
regular officials of those places shall seize and turn over to
the Company the offender's goods and person, formal request having been made by the Governors, Consuls and
Assistants "under the common seale."[5]   Mayors, sheriffs,

[1] Hakluyt, II, 308.
[2] Ibid., II, 309.
[3] Supra, pp. 31, 32.
[4] Hakluyt, II, 311.
[5] Ibid., II, 312.

bailiffs or other officials who assist the Company in the manner specified "shall not be impeached, molested, vexed or sued in any our court or courts, for executing or putting in execution of any of the said precept or precepts." [6]

The Company is authorized to send its vessels on voyages of discovery under the English flag.[6] Further they may take possession, in the name of the English government, of any "lands of infidelity," i.e., non-Christian regions, which they may discover.[7] Formal possession is to be taken by planting on those places "our banners, standards, flags, and Ensignes." [7] The natural narrowing of the Company's interest to the Russian trade, and the unsuccessful outcome of their attempts at further exploration to the northeast and southeast account for the relatively slight historical importance of this grant of the right to subjugate distant nations, a right of much greater significance in the history of some of the later trading companies.

The Company's trading privileges were fully as extensive as its grant of jurisdiction. The Charter of 1555 granted to the Company the right to trade with any lands they might come upon in their voyages, not hitherto frequented by English merchants, "in whatsoever part of the world they be situated." [8] This general privilege is not, however, in the nature of a monopoly. It merely extends to the Muscovy Company the right to enjoy any new trades that it may discover.

Exclusive trading privileges, on the other hand, were granted by this charter so far as the trade with Russia was concerned. All Englishmen except the Company and its employees were forbidden under penalty to engage in trade with that country save by express license granted

[6] Hakluyt, II, 313.
[7] Ibid., II, 314.
[8] Ibid., II, 313.

by the "Governour, Consuls, and Assistants of the said fėlowship and communalty."[9] In fact the wording of the provision would seem to imply that not only English merchants, but Englishmen of any degree, were prohibited from visiting for any purpose whatever, except by special permission, the lands of whose trade the Company enjoyed the monopoly. At least this restriction would seem to arise from a strict interpretation of the statement that these lands "shall not be visited, frequented, nor hanted by any our subjects, other then of the sayd company and felowship."[9]

Another extensive grant of commercial privilege was contained in the sweeping provision of the charter which delegated to the Company the exclusive right to trade with any lands not previous to that time frequented by English merchants and "lying Northwards, Northeastwards, or Northwestwards."[9] In regard to these lands the same prohibition was to apply to trade by other Englishmen as in the case with Russia. Of the three grants, i.e., the right to trade with all parts of the world with which the Company might establish relations, the exclusive right to trade with Russia, and the exclusive right to trade with any other northern country not before that time engaged in commerce with England, the monopoly of Russian trade seems to have appeared of most practical value to the Company and to have determined in the main the field of its activities.

The alternate successes and failures of Ivan IV in his wars with his neighbors led to a frequent shift of Russian boundaries. In 1554 the conquest of Astrakhan had given Russia a port on the Caspian. It was this outlet toward the south that suggested to the Company the series of efforts to establish an overland trade to Cathay and to Persia which occupied its attention, more or less intermit-

[9] Hakluyt, II, 315.

tently, for more than twenty years. In 1558 Anthony Jenkinson secured from the Czar permission to open a trade with the far south-east. The next year he returned to Moscow from his first Persian voyage,[10] having demonstrated the practicability of the overland route to that country.

Another change in the geographical limits of the Company's trading interests occurred in 1558 when Narva fell into Ivan's hands, thus giving Russia an outpost on the Baltic. The question whether the privileges of the Company extended to a port which had not been part of the Czar's dominions at the time the charter was granted was a difficult one. English merchants who were not members of the Company claimed the right of trading with Narva. The Company's very existence was threatened.

The Act of 1566 settled definitely and finally the question of the Company's exclusive right to the trade with Narva, and the further question of the Company's monopoly of the overland trade with Persia. As to the latter, the act specifically adds "the countries of Armenia major or minor, Media, Hyrcania, Persia," and the Caspian sea to the list of places not to be visited by any Englishmen except with the Company's consent.[11] This was a specific enlargement of the original grant, which could not in any way be construed to include a monopoly of a trade with southwestern Asia.

It is held by most writers on the subject that to the Act of 1566 the Company also owed its exclusive right to the trade with Narva.[12] The great trouble caused by merchants not of the Company trading with Narva before

[10] Jenkinson's account of this interesting trip is in Hakluyt, II, p. 449 ff.

[11] Hakluyt, III, 88.

[12] Wheeler, *Treatise of Commerce*, p. 55. Wheeler is followed by Cunningham, II, 239, and by modern writers generally. Cf. Stählin, "Françis Walsingham und seine Zeit," I, 196.

the grant of the second charter and the specific mention of Narva in that charter indicate, it is contended, that the Charter of 1555 did not of its own force extend the rights of the Company to the Baltic port when that region became Russian territory. The facts of the case, however, point to a different conclusion and merit brief consideration in this place.

The grant to the Company of the exclusive right to trade with any lands to the north, northwest or northeast with which they should establish relations must clearly have included Narva, for up to 1560 English merchants had not engaged in trade with that port.[13] Beginning in that year individual Englishmen trading independently with Russia by way of its town on the Baltic struck a blow at the Company's dearest privilege. In November, 1564, the Company made formal complaint to the Privy Council asking that "William Bond and his partners be restrained from trading with the Narve."[14] This petition was not a request for an extension of the Company's privilege, but an appeal for the enforcement of its monopoly.

Wheeler in his "Treatise of Commerce," 1601, takes the ground that the Act of 1566 by its mention of Narva specifically enlarged the scope of the Company's exclusive privilege. He cites Narva prior to the date of the second charter as an instance of the evils of unregulated trade competition. "In the yere 1565," he says, "a number of stragling merchants resorting thither out of this Realme, the trade was utterly spoiled, . . . which being made knowne to her Maiestie, and her Highnes right Honourable privie Counsell, order was taken at the next Parlia-

---

[13] Hakluyt, III, 335.—"And at this time (1560) was the first traffic to the Narve in Livonia . . . this trade to the Narve was hitherto concealed from us by the Danskers and Lubeckers."

[14] Cal. S. P. (Colonial) 1513-1616, p. 4.

ment, that the Towne of Narue should be comprized within the Charter of the Muscovie Company, to prevent the like pedlarlike kinde of dealing ever after."[15] Secondary writers from that time forward seem to have taken the ground that the including of Narva in the second charter implied an additional grant of privilege. Careful reading of the first charter, however, leads to the conclusion that the provision referring to Narva in the Act of 1566 must be construed as a mere emphasis of a privilege concerning which there had been some controversy and considerable difficulty of enforcement. As we shall see, even this reiteration failed to secure to the Company the enjoyment of its exclusive right in the Baltic.

An interesting and conclusive bit of evidence on the point under consideration is to be found in the case of an interloper sued in the Court of Admiralty under date of 1572. The defendant had traded with Narva without the consent of the Company. The verdict of the court was against him. The fact of significance, however, is that the court cited the first Charter of 1555 as the basis of its decision.[16]

The matter of interlopers was one of the most serious difficulties of the Company and one which must have frequently brought it into direct relation with the English government. Both charters definitely prohibit Englishmen not of the Company from engaging in trade with Russia.[17] The penalty for this offense is forfeiture of ship and cargo, "the one halfe of the same forfeiture to be to the use of us, our beires, and successors, and the other halfe to

[15] Wheeler, *Treatise of Commerce*, p. 55.

[16] *Select Cases in the Court of Admiralty*, p. 149. In this decision the company is referred to by the name given it in its first charter. The document contains a recital of the letters patent from Philip and Mary granting monopoly of trade to Russia with prohibition of interlopers upon pain of forfeiture of ship and cargo.

[17] Hakluyt, II, 315; III, 88.

be to the use of the sayd fellowship and cummunaltie.''[18] Suit may be brought against offenders either by the crown or by the Company ''in any court of Record, or in any other Court or courtes within this Realme, or els where, by Action of debt, action of detinue, bill, plaint, information, or otherwise: in which suite no essoine, protection, wager of lawe, or injunction shall be allowed, for, or on the behalfe of the partie or parties defendant.''[19] The Charter of 1566 makes special provision that persons not of the Company who had unlawfully engaged in the trade to the Company's lands shall not be impeached for past offenses, and such persons are given until June 29, 1568, to bring their goods and ships back to England.[20] That the government actually carried out the provisions against interlopers is indicated by the typical admiralty case cited above.

An interesting restriction of the Charter of 1566 provides that only English vessels, ''sailed for the most part with English mariners,'' shall be used by the Company in the exportation of its goods and in the carrying of merchandise ''from their saide new trade'' into England or into Flanders.[21] The penalty prescribed for each infringement of this ruling is a fine of 200£, one-half to go to the crown and the rest to be used for the repair of harbors of any port town that ''will sue for the same in any Court of Record.''[21] That this provision was carefully observed is evidenced by a memorial of the Company under date of May, 1576, in which they explain that ''having great store of wares lying at the Narve in great danger, they were forced to hire three Lübeckers' vessels to transport the same, and request license to bring the same into the

[18] Hakluyt, II, 315; III, 88.
[19] Ibid., III, 88.
[20] Ibid., III, 89.
[21] Ibid., III, 90.

realm." [22] Another prohibitive restriction in the same charter forbids the exportation of any "clothes or karsies" before the same shall be "all dressed and for the most part died within this Realm, upon paine of forfeiture for every such cloth and karsie . . . five pounds," half to go to the crown and the rest to the "Master and Clothworkers in the Citie of London." [23]

Finally, the second charter provides that if at any time the Company shall "willingly withdraw, and discontinue wholy by the space of three yeers in time of peace" their trade with Russia, it shall be lawful during that interval [24] for all English subjects to engage in trade with that country, only, however, by way of Narva and only in English ships.[25]

2. *The Exportation of Contraband.*

One of the chief motives that led Russia to establish relations with England was her need for the implements of western civilization in her struggle with the powers on the Baltic. To secure an alliance with a member of the European family of nations, she was willing to go to great lengths in the direction of granting extensive commercial privileges. After the accession of Elizabeth in 1558 the isolation of England was in many respects analogous to that of Russia, and would at first glance seem to suggest that the English government would feel the need of firm friendships fully as much as the distant Czar. It must be remembered, on the other hand, that offensive and defen-

[22] Cal. S. P. (Domestic) 1547-1580, p. 523.
[23] Hakluyt, III, 90.
[24] This clause is not very clear. The words of the charter are, "during the time of any such discontinuance and withdrawing."
[25] Hakluyt, III, 91.

sive alliances were entirely at variance with Elizabethan policy. England, moreover, would have little to gain and much to lose in making Russia's quarrels her own. At the same time her commercial interests forbade any break in the newly established Russian relations and brought about a willingness to perform unofficial acts of friendship wherever they could be indulged in without serious risk. This sufficiently explains the exportation of munitions of war to Russia. The Muscovy Company were the authorized carriers of whatever English merchandise reached the White Sea and Narva.

At the time of Osep Napea's embassy to England (1557) the Venetian ambassador in a letter to the Doge and Senate said, ''There is now here an ambassador from the Muscovites who demands a loan of ammunition and artillery, his lord being at war, and subsequently another ambassador arrived from the King of Sweeden to prevent the grant of this demand . . . ; but their majesties here have not yet formed any decision.''[26] The English reply to Ivan's requests, whatever they may have been, was entirely favorable. Napea carried back a letter from Philip and Mary promising advantages to Russian merchants if they should come to England.[27] While the letter makes no specific reference to the sending of munitions it does contain a significant statement that all Ivan's requests have been granted (''Omnia libenter concessimus que ad vestram expectationem et peticionem pertinebant.'')[28] It specifically promises, moreover, that English artificers will be at liberty to go to Russia (''Placet etiam nobis vt mercatores et artifices regni nostri si qui volent in vestre ditionis urbes et loca proficiscantur bona cum venia et fauore.'')[29]

[26] Cal. S. P. (Venetian) 1556-1557, p. 1005.
[27] Tolstoy, p. 13. *Minut to the Emperor of Russia from queene Mary concerning the priuileges of the marchants.*
[28] Tolstoy, p. 13.
[29] *Ibid.*, p. 14.

Suspicion that England was sending assistance to "the Muscovite" soon found expression in the various countries interested. In 1558 Thomas Alcock traveling through Poland on the Company's service was seized as a spy. Mary wrote to King Sigismund in July demanding his release.[30] In a letter to Richard Gray and Henry Lane, at that time agents for the Company in Russia, he gives an account of the questions that were put to him in the course of his examination. "Then he demanded of mee," writes Alcock, "what wares wee brought into Russia, and what wee carried from thence. I declared the same unto them. Then they burdened mee, that wee brought thither thousandes of ordinance, as also of harneis, swordes, with other munitions of warre, artificers, copper, with many other things." [31]

After the accession of Elizabeth the suspicion incurred by Mary of secretly aiding Ivan in his struggle against his neighbors continued to fall with undiminished force upon the English government. On August 17, 1559, the Emperor Ferdinand addressed a letter to the Queen in which he speaks of the danger to Christendom if Ivan should get possession of Livonia. "If he shall conquer the Livonians he will not be content, but will turn his arms against the Queen and other Christian Princes; but if the Livonians, who act as a sort of bulwark, are helped to repulse him . . . there will be no danger of such a calamity." [32] Elizabeth is invited to join in the league against Russia.

Two years later the German emperor made the Livonian disorders the subject of another letter to the English Queen. This time she is not asked to join any anti-Russian alliance, an evident recognition of the futility of that

30 Hist. MSS. Com. 13th Report, app. part II, p. 10 (Portland MSS.).

31 Hakluyt, II, 399.

32 Cal. S. P. (Foreign) 1558-1559, p. 484.

request. The letter makes specific reference, however, to the subject of contraband: "The Muscovites are greatly encouraged by obtaining from abroad such war-like stores as they lack, viz., guns, shot, powder, nitre, sulphur, lead, iron and the like, provisions, especially salt and herrings, various goods, as silks and cloth; they have also obtained artizans and men skilled in war-like matters. He . . . begs her to see that none of her subjects go into Muscovy, and most especially that none transport stores to that country." [33]

At about the same time a similar complaint was made by the Senate of Hamburg [34] and by the Senate of Cologne. [35] In a letter to Elizabeth from the former city under date of April 14, 1561, the statement is made that certain large quantities of armor and cannon shipped from their port are said to be intended for the Russians in their war against the Livonians, which is in contravention of the Imperial decree. The vessel has been stayed until they can hear from Elizabeth that these arms are for her own use.

That the idea that England was assisting Ivan with supplies had gained credence in the lands about the Baltic and North Seas is further evidenced by a letter written to Cecil from Antwerp, July 11, 1561, by his secretary, W. Herlle. The writer says, " . . . The rumour of the Queen having transported armour into Russia is very brym (sic) here; and it is told to all the Princes of Germany that the losing of Livonia is through the furniture of ammunition which the English sent to the Russians." [36]

To these various charges Elizabeth responded by a prompt denial. In answer to the Emperor's demand that she prohibit intercourse with Russia she promised to prevent the export of war material or supplies, but added that

[33] Cal. S. P. (Foreign) 1561-1562, p. 126.
[34] Ibid., p. 59.
[35] Ibid., p. 90.
[36] Ibid., p. 174.

she must allow her merchants to trade in skins.[37]   To the
Senate of Hamburg she sent the assurance ''on her royal
word'' that ''all the arms and munitions shipped in her
name from Hamburg are intended solely for the defence
of her realm.''[38]   She further expressed the desire that
the author of the rumor that they were intended for the
Muscovites might be sought out and punished, and that
the import of her letter might be widely made known.[38]

In fact Elizabeth seems to have felt very strongly that
public repudiation of the charge of sanctioning the sending of contraband to Russia should be made promptly and
emphatically.   On June 28, 1561, she wrote to Cecil in
reference to the injurious reports that armor was being
conveyed from England to Muscovy and asked that strict
orders be given that no sort of armor or artillery be
transported out of the realm.[39]   Accordingly, on July 8,
a royal proclamation was issued prohibiting the transportation of armor into Russia, ''or to any other place in war
with any nation in Christendom,'' and boldly asserting
that the rumor that the Queen had caused arms to be
made in Germany and transported into Russia was ''false,
vain, and malicious.''[40]

Denial and proclamation notwithstanding, the complaints continued.   Formal protest was made by the Danish ambassador in 1565,[41] and reply made that ''as not past
two or three vessels go yearly to Muscovy, it will be easy
to give order that no armor or victual be put into them
but such as shall be necessary for their navigation.''[42]
In 1568 the King of Poland wrote to Elizabeth that he
had ''interdicted all commerce with his enemy of Mus-

[37] Cal. Clarendon MSS. (Bodl.) Addenda, No. 92.
[38] Cal. S. P. (Foreign) 1561-1562, p. 102.
[39] Cal. S. P. (Domestic) 1547-1580, p. 178.
[40] Cal. S. P. (Foreign) 1561-1562, p. 171.
[41] Cal. S. P. (Foreign) 1564-1565, p. 279.
[42] Ibid.

covy, and placed vessels to seize all ships doing so, which he has commanded to be impounded together with their cargoes.''[43]

That assistance was actually given to Ivan by the sending of supplies from England is indicated by Anthony Jenkinson's account of his embassy to Russia in 1572. In reminding the Czar of his obligations to England he said, ''And since the first time of their traffiking in thy Majesties dominions, which is now nineteene yeres, the said merchants have bene, and are alwayes ready and willing truely to serve thy highnesse of all things meete for thy Treasurie, in time of peace and of warre in despite of all thy enemies . . . and have brought, and do bring from time to time such commoditie to thee, Lord, as her Majestie doeth not suffer to be transported foorth of her Realme to no other Prince of the world.''[44] Later references are even more explicit and leave no doubt whatever as to the fact. Giles Fletcher, ambassador to Russia in 1588, specifically refers to the fact, that the Queen and the Company had for many years served the emperor ''with necessarie commodities for his wears.''[45]

In regard to the sending of English workmen to Russia the evidence is also conclusive. We have already seen that Queen Mary in 1557 had explicitly granted Ivan's request for English artificers. Ten years later the Czar demanded that ''the Q-s ma-tie would lycence maisters to come unto him which can make shippes, and sayle them.''[46] That Englishmen were ready to take advantage of opportunities in Russia is shown by a letter written

[43] Cal. S. P. (Foreign) 1566-1568, p. 424.

[44] Hakluyt, III, 177.

[45] Fletcher's account of his embassy in *Russia at the Close of the Sixteenth Century*. Appendix IV, pp. 347-348.

[46] Tolstoy, p. 38. *Antho. Jenkinson's message done to the Q. Ma-tie from the Emperor of Moscouia.*

from Russia in 1572. The writer,[47] after complaining of the difficulties and dangers incurred in the service of the Company, says, "I could have had fifty robulls a year, and meat and drink, to have served the Emperor."[48] He goes on to explain that "There is as good as a sixteen Englishe maryners at the Narve, which dothe serve, and hathe good entertaynment: he that is worst hathe thirty robulls a year, and fifteen d. a daye besides, to find him meat and drink, and a house they have every man at the Emperor's charges."[48] In the case of men as in that of munitions there can be little doubt of the friendly coöperation of the English government as well as of the Company.

3.   *The Company's Part in Diplomatic Relations.*

It is very difficult to make a sharp distinction between the Muscovy Company's activities in its attempts to maintain and enlarge its commercial privileges in Russia, and the diplomatic activities of the English government which frequently had the same object. The interests of the Government and of the Company, so far as Russian relations were concerned, were identical: both desired the protection and extension of English mercantile rights. It was natural, therefore, that the Company's agents should for the most part have been entrusted with the management of diplomatic relations with the Czar, and that special ambassadors from the English court should have been sent seldom and only on the occasion of some serious danger to the Company's commercial privileges.

From the Russian point of view, however, there was no such identity of mercantile and political interests. From

---

[47] I.e., William Smith. Cf. *supra*, p. 39, note.
[48] Wright, *Queen Elizabeth and Her Times*, II, p. 420.

the first Ivan desired a firm league of amity with England. As we have seen he had great need of English arms and munitions and of English workmen. Later he made offers of marriage with a kinswoman of Elizabeth's. These were obviously matters that involved a direct relation to the English government. Special embassies were consequently sent to England from time to time to treat directly with the English sovereign and her ministers. Osep Napea, of whose visit in 1557 we have already had occasion to speak, was the first of these. Other embassies were sent by the Czar in 1569, 1582, and again in 1600.

The Company's part in the diplomatic activities of the two countries can best be considered under three heads:— (1) the Company's agents as ambassadors, (2) the Company's relation to special ambassadors sent to Russia, and (3) the Company's relation to the ambassadors sent by the Czar to England.

To the extent that the agents of the Muscovy Company treated with the Russian government as official representatives of the English sovereign we may be justified in considering them as diplomatic agents. Chancellor may be said to have been acting in this capacity when in 1553 he presented to the Czar the letter of Edward VI "to all Kings, Princes, Rulers, etc.," and when he brought Ivan's reply back to England the following year. The same may be said of his mission in 1555 when with Killingworth and Gray he bore the official letters of Philip and Mary to the Czar.[49]

In 1557 Anthony Jenkinson, who had taken service with the Company for four years at an annual salary of 40£,[50] was captain of the vessel that carried Napea back to Russia.[51] In 1561 Jenkinson once more left England for Rus-

[49] Hakluyt, II, 278 ff.
[50] Ibid., II, 390.
[51] Ibid., II, 413.

sia and Persia, this time carrying not only instructions
from the Company [52] but also letters from Queen Elizabeth to the Czar [53] and to the "great Sophy of Persia." [54]
That on this occasion the English government considered
him its official representative is clearly indicated by the
wording of the letter to Ivan in which Elizabeth, asking
for the same consideration that had been accorded to
Jenkinson on his previous visit, says, "And we doubt not
but that at our request, you will againe graciously shew
unto the same Anthony, now admitted into our service,
the like favor as heretofore Your Majesty of your meere
motion did exhibite unto him, being then a private person." [55]   The same double function is evident in Jenkinson's mission of 1566 when he represented both the Company and the Queen.   This time detailed instructions were
framed by the Company and, at their request,[56] officially
given to Jenkinson by the Queen.   The commercial phase
of his activities is shown by the extensive privileges he
secured for the Company at this time.[57]   The diplomatic
side is shown by the fact that the Czar intrusted him with
secret proposals of alliance to be presented to Elizabeth
on his return.[58]

Jenkinson's subsequent and last visit to Russia in
1571-2 is even more specifically diplomatic in character.

[52] Hakluyt, III, 9 ff.
[53] Ibid., III, 1 ff.
[54] Ibid., III, 6 ff.
[55] Ibid., III, 5.
[56] Tolstoy, p. 24. "The Societe of the marchaunts adventurers
trading in Russia doe desier most humbly that Anthony Jenkynson
may have in commission from the quenes ma-tie to the emperor of
Russia to the tenor ensewing."   At the close of the document is ap-
pended in Jenkinson's handwriting, "the true copy of the artykles,
comytted unto me by the quenes ma-tye to be declared in her
gracs name to th' emperour off Russia.—By me Anthony Jenkynson." Ibid., p. 26.
[57] Infra, p. 76.
[58] Tolstoy, pp. 38-39.

The Company's interests at that time were in serious danger. Ivan had for the second time within a period of three years withdrawn their privileges and had gone so far as to seize their wares. Whether Jenkinson's mission on this occasion should be considered purely as a special diplomatic embassy from the English government, or as a Company affair in which a Company agent incidentally took charge of an international misunderstanding is difficult to say. There is no doubt that Jenkinson stood in a twofold relation. The Company's part in the event is evidenced by their request for "lettres . . . from her ma-tie to the Muscouit for Jenkinson."[59] On the other hand, however, he treated not only of commercial affairs but, as the Queen's representative, discussed the matter of an offensive and defensive alliance. His mission was successful. The Company's privileges were restored, and restoration of its confiscated goods promised.[60] The last words of the autobiographical statement written by Jenkinson soon after illustrate once more the ambiguous nature of his functions as diplomatic agent and Company employee: "And thus being weary and growing old, I am content to take my rest in mine owne house, chiefly comforting my selfe, in that my service hath bene honourably accepted and rewarded of her majestie and the rest by whom I have bene imploied."[61]

On special occasions, as we have said, special ambassadors were sent by Elizabeth to the Russian court. Ivan's objection to merchants' affairs being given precedence over affairs of state, the injection into the international relations of matters essentially diplomatic, and, finally, the special request from the Czar that embassies be sent, probably explain the missions of Sir Thomas Randolph in

[59] Tolstoy, p. 117. *The Requeste of the Marchants Adventurers for Russia.*
[60] *Infra*, p. 83.
[61] Hakluyt, III, 196.

1569, of Sir Jerome Bowes in 1583, and of Giles Fletcher in 1588. The Company's part in the conducting of these embassies furnishes us with a problem of peculiar difficulty. In the nature of things commercial relations constituted the central motive of all the English diplomatic dealings with the Czar. Though Randolph, Bowes and Fletcher in all probability had no official connection with the Company, the Company unquestionably had a real and direct interest in their respective missions.

The first ambassador extraordinary was Thomas Randolph, one of Elizabeth's courtiers and a tried diplomat. He was accompanied by two agents of the Company, Geoffrey Duckett and Thomas Bannister, and carried a letter from Elizabeth to the Czar.[62] This embassy took place between Jenkinson's two visits of 1567 and 1571. Ivan, angered at Elizabeth's failure to reply to the propositions he had made to Jenkinson, had withdrawn the Company's privileges.[63] Randolph managed to secure a restoration of trading rights.[64] The Company seems to have been as influential in the management of this embassy as if the ambassador had been one of its own agents. The concluding section of Randolph's instructions reads, "whereas the societie of the merchants haue made choice of ij trusty wyse merchants of their companye, Tho: Bannister and Geofries Ducket, to whom also we haue for their more credit giuen commission with your help to treate with the same emperour, about the maters of their traffike. Because the said societye hath best knowledge how to aduance that treaty, we must wholly referr you to suche instructions as the said socyetie hathe in that behalfe deuised."[65]

[62] Tolstoy, p. 49 ff. *Hir Ma-ties lettre to the Empe*ror *of Muscouia, by Mr. Thomas Randolphe.*

[63] *Ibid.,* p. 46.

[64] *Infra,* p. 79 ff.

[65] Tolstoy, p. 46.

Sir Jerome Bowes was sent to Russia in 1583 in response to a request made by the Czar. The Company's influence in the selection of envoys is exemplified in the contemporary account of Bowes' appointment. The first choice had fallen upon Sir William Russell, third son of the Earl of Bedford.[66] Russell, however, was unwilling to take the hazardous journey. We are told that "then the company of merchants intreated for Sir Jerome Bowes."[66] Bowes was accordingly appointed, his commission bearing date of June, 1583.[67] He left England June 22, bearing a letter from Elizabeth to the Czar.[68] Not only was the Company influential in his selection, but it bore the expense of his embassy. Our contemporary narrator says "he was waell sett forth most at their charge."[69] The large part played by the Company in the management of this embassy is further evidenced by a clause in Bowes' instructions directing him to follow the Company's wishes in the handling of "causes of our merchants."[70]

Giles Fletcher, who was sent as ambassador to Russia in 1588, four years after the death of Ivan, secured a partial confirmation of privileges from Czar Feodor.[71] There is no indication that his relations to the government and the Company were essentially different from those of Randolph and Bowes. In general, we are probably justified in concluding that the Company took an important but indirect part in the selection of special ambassadors. They also shared in the framing of their instructions and bore the expenses of their missions.[72]

[66] *Travels of Sir Jerome Horsey*, p. 196.
[67] Hakluyt, III, 308 ff.
[68] *Ibid.*, III, 312 ff.
[69] Horsey, p. 196.
[70] Tolstoy, p. 205. *Copie of instructions giuen to Sir Jerome Bowes.*
[71] *Infra*, p. 90 ff.
[72] Hakluyt, VIII, 135. Carlile's Discourse—"The charges of all

To turn now to the other party in the diplomatic intercourse, we find in the first place that the Russian government frequently sent official messages to the English
Queen by means of the Company's servants. Chancellor
in 1553 carried the first official communication from the
Czar to his own country.[73] Jenkinson in 1567 was entrusted by Ivan with confidential messages to the Queen,
most serious in their import and in their consequences.[74]
Later in the century Jerome Horsey and Francis Cherry
while in the pay of the Company acted as diplomatic
agents for Elizabeth and Ivan's successors. This diplomatic function merely supplements the employment, already mentioned, of these men by the English government
for the same purpose.

The relation of the Company to the special embassies
sent to England by the Czar presents a separate problem.
Osep Napea, to whose embassy in 1557 we have previously
made reference, was, as we have seen, lodged and entertained at the expense of the Company.[75] At the banquet
given by the Company in his honor shortly before he left
England "a cup of wine being drunke to him in the name
and lieu of the whole companie, it was signified to him that
the whole company with most liberal and friendly hearts,
did frankly give to him and his all maner of costs and
charges in victuals riding from Scotland to London during
his abode there, and untill setting of saile aboord the ship,
requesting him to accept the same in good part as a testimony and witnes of their good hearts, zeale and tender-
nesse towards him and his countrey."[76]

The visit of Stephen Twerdico and Theodore Pogorella,

Ambassadours between that Prince and her Majesty, are always borne
by the merchants stocke." Also cf. *infra*, p. 88.
[73] Hakluyt, II, 271.
[74] *Supra*, p. 63.
[75] *Supra*, p. 20.
[76] Hakluyt, II, 358.

who came from Russia to England in 1567, need not detain
us long in this place, as they were clearly not ambassadors,
Camden's implication to the contrary notwithstanding.[77]
They were Russian merchants bearing a letter from the
Czar in which permission was asked that they might dispose of the Czar's wares which they carried and secure for
him "Saphires, Rubies and apparelling, such as in our
tresorie we haue neede of."[78]   Freedom from custom and
safe conduct were requested "that noe man may hurte or
moleste them, sufferinge them in your shipps by godes
helpe to come safe to us agayne."[79]   Some years later
Ivan complained that his request had not been granted
and made that grievance the pretext for confiscating the
goods of English merchants in Russia.[80]

Andreas Gregorowich Saviena, who accompanied Thomas
Randolph to England in 1569, must be considered the next
Russian ambassador after Osep Napea. Ivan's propositions to Elizabeth had been entrusted to Jenkinson by the
Czar in 1567. He had proposed a firm alliance which
would put each nation under obligation to engage in war
with the enemies of the other, and had suggested a secret
agreement by which each monarch in the event of being
obliged to leave his own kingdom might find refuge in that
of his ally.[81] No reply had been made by Elizabeth to
this proposition, the letter brought by Randolph to the
Czar referring only to trade affairs.[82] Randolph's instructions, moreover, definitely directed him to avoid committing England to a treaty of alliance:—"And in such good
generall sorte we wold haue you satisfie him without giuing
occasion to enter into any speciall treaties or capitulacon

[77] Camden, *History of Elizabeth*, p. 103.
[78] Tolstoy, p. 34.
[79] *Ibid.*, p. 35.
[80] *Ibid.*, p. 157.
[81] *Ibid.*, pp. 38-39.
[82] *Ibid.*, p. 49 ff.

of any suche legue as is called offensiue and defensiue betwixt vs Whereof though the sayd Anthony Jenkinson
made mention to vs, yet we wold have you pass those matters with silence.'' [83]   These directions Randolph followed
to the letter if we can judge by Ivan's complaint to Jenkinson three years later:—''but all his talk with us was
about Merchants affaires, and nothing touching ours
. . . and thereupon wee sent our Ambassadour into
England with him to ende the same.'' [84]

Saviena arrived in England in 1569. After long negotiations the Queen agreed to the offensive and defensive
alliance but with a condition she must have known Ivan
would not accept: if either party to the alliance ''shalbe
iniuried by any other Prince, uppon significacon made
thereof by the party iniuried and the justice of his cause
made manifest'' the other party shall call upon the offender to ''returne to honnorable condicons of peace according to the lawes of Almighty God''; if this warning
is not heeded then the allies shall unite their forces against
the enemy.[85]   In a secret letter Elizabeth grants the request for refuge in case of need, although she does not
follow his suggestion so far as to ask a similar favor of
the Czar.[86]

We have little knowledge of the relation between the
Company and Saviena during the time of his sojourn at
the English court. The Company's interest in and influence upon the subject of the embassy, however, are indicated by a message from Sir William Gerrard to Anthony
Jenkinson during the ambassador's visit, containing ''ser-
ten instrokysons . . . to move the Ryght honnorabell
S-r W-m Syssyll.'' [87]   The document gives advice on the

83 Tolstoy, p. 45.
84 Ibid., pp. 174, 175.
85 Ibid., p. 75.
86 Ibid., p. 97.
87 Ibid., pp. 82, 83.

granting of trading privileges, the sending of another ambassador to Russia, and the calling home of Englishmen who are staying in Russia against the Company's will. The seventh item requests "that the sayd ambassador maybe ffvlly ansred at thys next metyng so as he may take hys leve ffor that the shypes atend only upon hym and the yere ys ffare spent."

The embassy of Pissemsky in 1582 dealt again with the subject of an alliance. He was to conclude the negotiations of a treaty and to propose a marriage for the Czar with Lady Mary Hastings, daughter of the Earl of Huntingdon. Elizabeth was to be asked to send a special ambassador to the Czar to treat with him about it. Pissemsky had an interview with the lady; "fell prostrate to her feett, rise, ranne backe from her, his face still towards her, she and the rest admiringe at his manner. Said by an interpritor yt did suffice him to behold the angell he hoped should be his masters espouse."[88] He departed with Bowes in 1583. Of the relation of the Company to his embassy and to that of Gregory Mikouleve in 1600[89] we have little definite information, but there is no reason to suppose that there was any large change in the Company's interest or influence.

The expense attached to the entertainment of Russian ambassadors in England was borne by the Company. The scant references we find of this phase of our topic clearly point in this direction.[90] Corroboration is furnished by two references at the time of an embassy a generation later. The Privy Council on November 18, 1628, wrote to the Lord Mayor requiring him to confer with the governor of the Muscovy Company "and provide a convenient house

[88] Horsey, p. 196.

[89] Cal. S. P. (Domestic) 1598-1601, pp. 477, 478, 543.

[90] Hakluyt, VIII, 135. Carlile's Discourse.—"The charges of all Ambassadours betweene that Prince and her Majesty, are always borne by the merchants stocke."

for the Ambassador's lodging, and to give orders for such attendance on his arrival as was usual . . ."[91] A letter written the next month describing the reception of the ambassador says, "To-morrow being Sunday he will be received in audience by His Majesty with the usual pomp. He has not brought any presents, such as sables and other rich furs of that country, consequently the merchants here who pay all his expenses may send him home without presents or with some of little value . . ."[92]

On the whole the Company's connection with the diplomatic relations between England and Russia seems to have been very close. Even when its own servants were not employed on diplomatic missions the Company seems, sometimes at least, to have been a factor in the selection and instructions of ambassadors. The burden of bearing the expense, in any event, fell to its share.

4. *The Government's Commercial Dealings with the Company.*

The trade in cordage was one of the most profitable activities of the Muscovy Company. If we can take the word of a member of the Company there was "not the like cordage in Europe to be had." Less liable to bias was the judgment of William Burrough, "Treasurer of the ships," who in 1582 writing of the Russian cordage characterizes it as "the best brought into this country."[93] It is not surprising that the English government in that period of the extension of her naval activities should have proved one of the Company's best customers.

[91] Remembrancia, VI, 188.
[92] Hist. MSS. Com. 11th Report, app. part I, p. 177 (Salvetti Correspondence).
[93] Cal. S. P. (Domestic) 1581-1590, p. 74.

In 1568 the Queen contracted with the Company "for the delivery of cables, hawsers, cordage, and other tackle into Deptford dockyard to the value of 4000£ 8s. 10d."[94] In March, 1588, the year of the Armada, Hawkins in a letter to Burleigh mentions that "great cables to the value of 3000£ had been ordered in Muscovia."[95] The following year he makes mention of the fact that he has written for thirty cables "to be brought by the ships of the Muscovy Company."[96] Other references in 1591[97] and 1593[98] indicate a continuance of the sale of cordage to the government in those years.

The last decade of the century witnessed a remarkable increase in the amount of the sale of this commodity to the English government. In 1595 it amounted to almost 6000£.[99] In 1596 the government's purchase amounted to 9254£ 8s.[100] In 1597 it reached the sum of 13,922£ 15s. 2d,[101] and in December of that year the government ordered "10,000£ worth of cordage against the next year."[102]

For the cordage furnished by the Company, as for the wax it supplied for the use of Her Majesty's Household, money was not always paid as promptly as might have been desired. Complaints by the Company on this score were frequent. In 1582 Walsingham wrote to Burghley that the Company was demanding payment of the money due them for wax "taken these two years past" for the Queen's use.[103] Hawkins and Burrough writing to

[94] Cal. S. P. (Foreign) 1566-1568, p. 462.
[95] Cal. S. P. (Domestic) 1581-1590, p. 467.
[96] Ibid., p. 615.
[97] Cal. S. P. (Domestic) 1591-1594, p. 154.
[98] Ibid., pp. 397, 408.
[99] Hatfield House MSS. V, 399.
[100] Ibid., VI, p. 511.
[101] Ibid., VII, 484.
[102] Ibid., VII, 505.
[103] Cal. S. P. (Domestic) 1581-1590, p. 75.

Burghley in 1593 refer to the "debt due to the Muscovy Company for cordage, and debts to sundry other merchants for hemp long since delivered." [104]   In 1595 Francis Cherry wrote to Burghley, "The late sum we received in part for our cordage taken for her Majesty's navy will scarcely serve to provide such other cordage as is given us in charge to furnish the next year; and the money behind for that already delivered is with the rest to be returned, else shall we not be able to set out our shipping, maintain our trade, and satisfy our creditors." [105]   A year later the account had not been settled.   A petition sent by the Company to the Queen in December of that year points out that three months before the Admiralty had made choice of cordage to the value of over 9000£ and asked for the payment of this "as well as of the 658£ 11s. 8d. unpaid for cordage delivered last year." [106]   At the close of 1597 the Company was still endeavoring to secure payment; more cordage had been ordered by the government, "which we cannot do," complains Cherry in a letter to Robert Cecil, "without our money, now twenty-two months owing." [107]

[104] Cal. S. P. (Domestic) 1591-1594, p. 324.
[105] Hatfield House MSS. V, pp. 462-463.
[106] Ibid., VI, 511.
[107] Ibid., VII, 505.

CHAPTER IV

The history of the relations of the Muscovy Company and the Russian government consists for the most part of a discussion of the various privileges granted at different times to the Company, and the successive modifications, withdrawals or extensions of these privileges by the Czar. It must be borne in mind that the English grants embodied in the two charters of the Company would have been practically valueless without some corresponding concessions by the Russian government. The English crown by letters patent and Parliament by statutory enactment could after all do no more than prohibit the Russian trade to Englishmen who were not members of the Company. Whether the English were to be permitted to trade in Russia at all and on what terms, and the whole problem of their relation to the merchants of other European nations trading in the Czar's dominions were questions which could be settled by Russia alone. It is the purpose of the present chapter to trace the history of the privileges which the Russian government granted to the Muscovy Company in the period under consideration.

Ivan's reply to the letter of Edward VI, although sent a year before the incorporation of the Company, embodied a definite promise of freedom of trade to English merchants. The Czar says in so many words, "And if you send one of your majesties counsel to treate with us whereby your countrey marchants may with all kinds of wares, and where they will make their market in our dominions, they shall have their free marte with all free liberties to my whole dominions with all kinds of wares to come and goe at their pleasure, without any let, damage or impediment, according to this our letter, our word and our seale which we have commaunded to be under sealed."[1] The following year Chancellor returned to Russia with a letter from Philip and Mary in which assurance was given Ivan that England was willing to reciprocate:—" Which your benevolences so to bee extended, wee bee minded to requite towards any your subjects Marchants, that shal frequent this our realm at your contemplation therefore to be made."[2]

"Chiefly upon the contemplation of the gratious letters, directed from the right high, right excellent, and right mighty Queene Mary, by the grace of God Queene of England, France, etc.," in favor of the newly incorporated Company the Czar issued the first formal grant of privileges in the very year of the Company's incorporation. The grant bears the date of 1555 and includes eleven articles relating to affairs of trade and administration.[3]

The trading privileges of 1555 extended to the merchants of the Company and their agents and servants the right to visit any part of the Emperor's dominions with their ships and merchandise, and buy and sell all sorts of wares without the payment of toll or tax of any kind.[4] A special clause authorized the Company to employ "brokers, shippers, packers, weighers, measurers, wagoners, and all other meet and necessary laborers for to serve them in their feat of merchandises."[5] These employees they may put under oath "to serve them truly," punish or dismiss

1 Hakluyt, II, 272.
2 Ibid., II, 280.
3 Ibid., III, 297 ff.
4 Ibid., III, 299.
5 Ibid., III, 300.

for poor service, and replace "without disturbance . . . from us, our successors, or any justices, officers, ministers or subjects whatever."[6]

The grant further specified definite and extensive rights of jurisdiction which the Company was to enjoy. The Company's factor was given "full power to rule and govern all Englishmen that have had or shall have access to these dominions."[6] This grant of jurisdiction was evidently intended to apply equally to those who had no connection with the Company and to the Company's own members or employees. The article goes on to specify that this grant includes the right to make rules and ordinances and to punish offenders by fines and imprisonments.[7] Russian officials were to aid in enforcing obedience to the factor and, on his request, were to put at his disposal "prisons and instruments for punishment."[7] We find in these governmental provisions the parallel and complement of the rights of jurisdiction granted by the English government in its first charter to the Company.

Besides these grants of trading privilege and rights of government the document contains a number of specific promises of protection by the Russian government. In difficulties arising between Englishmen and Russian subjects speedy justice is promised.[8] Merchants' goods are not to be seized for offenses committed by their servants.[9] No Englishman is to be arrested for debt if he can furnish surety, nor before the factor is asked whether he will be surety for the debtor.[9] Condign punishment is to be administered to any person who kills or wounds an English merchant.[9] The Czar will do what he can to secure reparation in cases of piracy against English ships.[9] The dictation and foresight of the Company itself is quite evi-

[6] Hakluyt, II, 300.
[7] *Ibid.*, II, 301.
[8] *Ibid.*, II, 300.
[9] *Ibid.*, II, 302.

dent in this list of privileges intended to cover all possible vicissitudes or calamities.

The grant of 1555, then, contained three groups of privileges: the right to trade in any part of Russia and to employ persons necessary for the carrying on of this trade; the right to govern all Englishmen in Russia whether of the Company or not, and the assistance of Russian officials in the enforcement of this right; a group of special grants of privilege and protection. It is worthy of note that there is no grant of any monopoly. This first trading privilege did not specifically exclude from a share in the Company's privileges the merchants of other countries.

In 1558 the capture of Narva, by giving to Russia a port on the Baltic, opened to the Company a new route to the Czar's dominions. We have in another place considered the effect of this acquisition on the Company's charter rights and have reached the conclusion that the charter of 1555 of its own force extended to any lands that the Czar might acquire subsequent to the date of that grant and lying north of London.[10] Similarly on the Russian side any extension of the Czar's territory involved an extension of the sphere of the Company's activity under Russian protection. Nevertheless Narva constituted a source of trouble to the Company, the attempts of Englishmen not of the Company to establish a trade there leading to vigorous complaints to the Privy Council. The second charter in 1566, as we have seen, attempted to settle the difficulty by specific mention of Narva in the grant.[11]

One of the purposes of Jenkinson's mission to Russia in 1566 was to secure for the Company the exclusive right to the White Sea trade, "And that no other straungers may be admytted or lycencyd to land or trade that

10 *Supra*, p. 49.
11 *Supra*, p. 50.

waye." [12] Jenkinson was successful, securing from the Czar a second set of privileges for the Company under date of September 22, 1567. The most important additional privilege over the grant of 1555 was this definite closing of the northern coasts to all vessels except those of the Company. This was the first grant by Russia of a definite monopoly. "We for our sisters sake Elizabeth have granted, that none besides sir William Garrard and his company, out of what kingdome so ever it be, England or other, shall not come in trade of merchandise nor otherwise to Colmogro, nor to the river Ob, nor within Wardhouse,[13] . . . nor to any mouth of the river Dwina, nor to any part of the North countrey of our coast." [14] The penalty for infringement of this restriction is confiscation and forfeiture of "the people and goods, ship or ships" to the Czar.[14]

The grant contains a restatement of the Company's right to trade free of custom in all parts of the Czar's dominions.[15] As in the case of the second charter here also we find specific mention of Narva, evidently with the purpose of leaving no doubt of its inclusion in the grant. The right of the Company to pass to the lands beyond the Caspian by way of Astrakhan is also definitely granted.[16] Except for the "north parts," however, there is no grant of any monopoly or exclusive privilege.

In return for this extension of privilege it is required in the grant of 1567 that all goods "needful or necessary" brought by the Company to Russia shall, before being placed on sale, be examined and selection made of such

[12] Tolstoy, p. 25. *Anthony Jenkinsons Instructions sent by the merchants adventurers into Russia to the Emperor there.*

[13] The English Charter of 1566 had explicitly opened Wardhouse to all Englishmen. Hakluyt, III, 89. Colmogro is the modern Kholmogory.

[14] Hakluyt, III, 97.

[15] *I*bid., III, 93-94.

[16] *I*bid., III, 94.

as "shalbe needfull for our treasury," the rest being delivered back to the Company to sell and barter at their
pleasure. The Company is " to sell none of the fine wares
before they be seene by our, chancellers, except sorting
clothes, and other wares not meet for our treasury."
Another interesting phase of the Company's relation to
the Russian government is seen in the provision that the
Company's agents shall, at the request of the Russian
Chancellor, take with them "treasure out of our treasury"
and " sell and barter it for wares meet for our treasury,
and bring it to our treasury." They are forbidden,
however, to handle "other mens wares to barter or sell
with them." In other words the Russian government
was to have first choice of the Company's goods for its
own use and reserved the right to employ the Company as
its own commercial agent.

Other provisions of the privilege grant the Company the
right to retain its house in Moscow without payment, and
to set up houses at their own charges at Vologda and Kholmogory "or in any other place where they can chuse for
themselves any good harbour." [17] At their Moscow house
they are licensed to keep "one Russe porter or two," at
their other houses "two or three," who shall not, however, buy or sell for the Company.[17] This provision is in
line with the further restriction that the Company may
not employ Russians "to buy or sell for them their
wares." [18] Lawsuits that may arise between the merchants and Russian subjects are to be judged by royal
officials without the charge of any fee; [19] "and when they
cannot be judged by law, they then shalbe tried by lots,
and whose lot is first taken out, he shall have the right." [20]

[17] Hakluyt, III, 96.
[18] Ibid., III, 95.
[19] Ibid., III, 97.
[20] Ibid., III, 96-97.

The grant of 1567, notwithstanding several new restrictions not included in the previous grant, constituted on the whole an extension of the Company's trading privileges. Unfortunately the settlement was of short duration. Jenkinson's failure to return to Russia with a reply from Elizabeth to Ivan's secret message concerning an alliance between the two countries, together with the disloyal activities of the Company's agents at Narva, was responsible for a decided change in the Czar's attitude toward the Company. Christopher Bennet, Thomas Glover and certain other servants of the Company shortly after the conclusion of Jenkinson's successful mission seem to have entered into a plot to defraud the Company of the goods in their charge and secure special privileges from the Emperor for themselves.[21] They persuaded him that the Company was responsible for Jenkinson's failure to return to Russia, in that they had brought him "in displeasure with the Queen only because he went about to further the Emperor's matters."[22] The plot was successful, the conspirators receiving a special privilege from the Czar.[23] They adopted a "mark of Company" in imitation of that of the Muscovy Company and proceeded to trade with the Company's goods on their own account.[24] This was the situation, when, in 1568, Randolph was sent to Russia as special ambassador accompanied by two agents who had been deputed by the Company to recover its goods out of its factors' hands and to act with Randolph to secure the annullment of the privilege granted to Bennet and Glover.[25] The success of Randolph's mission [26] and his return to England in 1569 accompanied by an

[21] Cal. S. P. (Foreign) 1569-1571, p. 90.
[22] Cal. S. P. (Foreign) 1566-1568, p. 519.
[23] Tolstoy, p. 74.
[24] Cal. S. P. (Foreign) 1566-1568, p. 519.
[25] Cal. S. P. (Foreign) 1569-1571, p. 90.
[26] Hakluyt, III, 118.

ambassador from Ivan, Andreas Saviena, has already been mentioned. The important point in the present connection is the grant of privileges secured for the Company by Randolph before his departure from Russia.

The privileges thus granted in 1569 were made up of thirty-four separate articles. The provisions of the grant secured by Jenkinson in 1567 are practically repeated but with important extensions. The monopoly of the trade to the northern coast is confirmed.[27] This time, moreover, forfeitures that result from the capture of interlopers instead of going to the Czar alone are to be shared by the Czar and the Company, a provision similar to that in the Company's charter. A more important extension of privilege, however, is to be found in the grant to the Company of the exclusive enjoyment of the overland route to Persia. The Persian trade like that of the northern coasts is granted to the Company as a monopoly right.[27]

The privileges of 1569 once more grant the right to trade freely without payment of custom in all parts of Russia.[28] Without definite knowledge of the privileges enjoyed by other nations in Russia at this time it is impossible to say to what extent this right was monopolistic. Camden's statement that "the Merchants of other Nations might not go a mile beyond the City of Moscow"[29] would make this grant almost the equivalent of a monopoly. In regard to Narva, however, a special provision declares that all strangers are permitted to trade "to our towne of Narve, Ivanogorod, & other our towns of Liefland, as they have done beforetime."[30] It would seem that only to Englishmen who were not members of the Company was the trade with Narva closed.[31]

[27] Hakluyt, III, 117.

[28] Ibid., III, 109, 110.

[29] Camden, p. 124. The statement is hardly consistent with the activities of Venetian and Dutch merchants of which we have evidence shortly after this time.

[30] Hakluyt, III, 118.   [31] Ibid., III, 117.

The provisions that the Russian government is to have
the right to select for its own use those of the Company's
wares that it needs before they may be placed on sale, and
that the Company is to act in the capacity of agent for
the Czar are repeated in the grant of 1569. In fact the
provision goes so far this time as to state that "when we
shall sende any adventure into England then our Chaun-
cellour to give them a yeeres warning, that their ships
may be provided thereafter, that by taking in of our wares,
they leave not their owne behind them."[32] The Company
was also required to "take our adventure yeerely when
they goe into Persia."[33]

The houses of the Company were transferred by this
same document to the jurisdiction of the Oprichnina,[34]
i.e., the direct control of the Czar's personal government.
The inclusion of the Company's affairs in this depart-
ment freed its members from various forms of local control and interference; it is definitely ordered that "none
of our Captaines, or authorized people, or officers in any
other our townes, give judgement upon the said English
Merchants for any thing."[35]

Among the new privileges included in the grant of 1569
are the right to have money coined at Moscow, Novgorod
and Plesko (Pskoff), "without custome, allowing for
coales, and other necessaries with the workemanship";[36]
the right to search for iron mines at Wichida (Vychegda),
setting up houses for the working of the metal and enjoying the use of the woods "five or sixe miles compasse
about the sayd houses, to the making of the sayd iron";[37]
the grant of ground in Vologda to build a house;[37] and

[32] Hakluyt, III, 110.
[33] Ibid., III, 111.
[34] Ibid., III, 113.
[35] Ibid., III, 114.
[36] Ibid., III, 116.
[37] Ibid., III, 113.

a definite statement of the right of the English in Russia to keep their own law and faith.[38] Section 33 provides for the revocation of the privileges which the Czar had granted to Bennet, Glover and their companions.[38]

The grant of 1569 represents an advance over that of 1567 fully as great as the advance of the latter over the grant of 1555. The monopoly of the White Sea trade had been confirmed and to it had been added the monopoly of the overland trade with Persia. The Company's affairs were placed under the immediate jurisdiction of the Czar. The dangerous competition caused by Englishmen trading to Narva on their own account was prohibited. Glover, the chief cause of the recent trouble, was handed over to Randolph and brought back to England by him to answer for his actions before the Company.[39]

Unfortunately the settlement of 1569 was almost as short-lived as that of 1567. This time the difficulties that arose were even more serious. Saviena's failure to secure the absolute committal of Elizabeth to all Ivan's propositions and his return to Russia without Jenkinson seem to have angered the Czar beyond measure. He withdrew the merchants' privileges and seized their wares. Jenkinson writing to Burghley in 1571 from Kholmogory says, "The late ambassador (Saviena) at his return slanderously reported to his lord that he was evil entertained and used in England, which, with the spiteful practices of such abjects and runagates of the English nation as are here, has caused him not only to take away their privileges from the company, but also forbidden them traffic throughout his dominions, and what he has taken from them he has given the companies of other nations." [40] Thirteen ships of the Company which had expected to sail from Narva

[38] Hakluyt, III, 118.
[39] Cal. S. P. (Foreign) 1569-1571, p. 91.
[40] Ibid., p. 504.

in 1570 laden with Russian wares could only find goods enough to load half of them; in a letter to the Emperor the Company's agents complain, "And the cause is, we have this winter (by your majesties order) bene kept from trafiquing to the companies great losse."[41]

In 1571 Anthony Jenkinson was sent to Russia once more to straighten out these difficulties and secure the restoration of the privileges granted to Randolph. There was a long delay before he was admitted to the Czar's presence. In the course of the interview that finally took place, a full account of which was sent by Jenkinson to the Company, the Czar's anger seems to have been entirely allayed. He refused, however, to give Jenkinson an immediate answer to his requests. Later the ambassador presented his demands in the form of sixteen articles to which separate replies were made by the Russian government. To article 3, which contained a petition to the Emperor to take the Company into his favor again "and to restore them to their former privileges and liberties, for free traffike in, and through, and out of al his Majesties dominions, in as ample manner as aforetime,"[42] the Emperor gave answer "that his great goodnes and favour againe unto the merchants shall be restored, and the same to be knowen by his gratious letters of privilege now againe granted."[43] Article 4 asked for reparation for the Company's losses and injuries during the time of the Czar's displeasure;[44] in reply the merchants were recommended to make formal complaint to the Secretary and were assured that they would receive prompt justice.[45] Article 6,[46] requesting payment to the Company

41 Hakluyt, III, 169.
42 Ibid., III, 180.
43 Ibid., III, 189.
44 Ibid., III, 180.
45 Ibid., III, 189.
46 Ibid., III, 181.

for goods taken into the royal treasury, was answered with the statement that the accounts would be looked into and some settlement made: "such as is due, & found meete to be paid, shall be paid forthwith." [47]   Article 7 complains that the return of Ducket and Bannister from beyond the Caspian had been prevented by the hostile attitude of the officials of Astrakhan; [48] the Czar promised to send commands at once to have these agents with their Company and goods out of Persia safely conducted up the Volga out of danger of enemies.[49]   Article 11 cited the loss suffered by the Company through the burning of Moscow and requested the Czar "to give the said company so much as shal seeme good unto his Majestie towards their said losses"; [50] to which answer was given that restitution would not be made, "for that it was Gods doing, and not the Emperours." [51]

On the whole, while Jenkinson succeeded in securing a renewal of the Company's privileges, the tone of the replies to many of his requests indicate a decided lessening of friendliness on the part of the Russian government. This is further borne out by the fact that Jenkinson was compelled to set sail from Russia without having received a copy of the granted privileges.[52]   He carried a letter to Elizabeth in which Ivan says, "And for your sake we have granted to your merchants and ordered them in all our realms to trade free and have given order to let them pass out of our dominions into any other dominions according to their wish without any lett or hinderance.   And we have ordered for your sake to give them a charter of privileges such as is convenient." [53]

---

47 Hakluyt, III, 190.
48 *Ibid.*, III, 181.
49 *Ibid.*, III, 190.
50 *Ibid.*, III, 183.
51 *Ibid.*, III, 190.
52 *Ibid.*, III, 194.
53 Tolstoy, p. 147. *Czar John to Q. Elizabeth.*

From 1572 until his death in 1576 Daniel Sylvester was the chief go-between for the two governments, frequently carrying diplomatic messages bearing upon the Company's privileges. In 1574 Ivan brought up once more the question of the offensive and defensive alliance. A long letter under date of August 20 contains the significant sentence, "And if you wish for more amity and friendship from us, ponder upon that subject and do that business, by which you may increase our amity towards you."[54]

Some two years later the Czar complained bitterly to Sylvester of the Queen's haughtiness and scrupulous answers; he also on this occasion gave expression to his old grievance that "affayres of merchaunts ar preferred and made of more emportance than the affayres of ours."[55] This was followed by a definite threat: " And how ample our goodnes hathe bene and ys towards them ys aparaunte by the many-foulde lybertyes whearwith we have graced them . . . Of all the which with the rest of all their lybertyes they ar to be restrayned yf we fynde not further lyberalyte then this from our systar. And will traunporte the same trade vnto the Veneatianes and Garmaynes . . . ; wherein wee will yett staye vntill we shall here from our sister towchinge her determynation therin: either a liberall graunte or flatt denyall."[55] Elizabeth's reply, carried by Sylvester, was destined never to reach the Czar. At Kholmogory the bearer was struck by lightning, "whereat the Emperour was much amassed when he heard of it, saieng 'Gods will be donn!' "[56]

The instructions given to Bowes at the time of his embassy in 1583 clearly indicate that the Company's privileges at that period were again in serious danger. Pis-

[54] Tolstoy, p. 158. *Czar John to Q. Elizabeth.*
[55] *Ibid.*, p. 184. *A note of speche with th' emperour of Rowsia vsed vnto me Daniuell Siluester in his towne of Muscouia the 29 of January 1576.*
[56] Horsey, p. 184.

semsky had intimated to Elizabeth that the closing of the northern coasts to all merchants except those of the English Company constituted a rather large grant. When we remember that Narva was definitely lost to Russia in 1581, thus closing once more after a period of twenty-three years the Baltic road to Russia, the exclusion of all nations but England from the White Sea was indeed a policy of questionable wisdom on the part of the Russian government. The only argument advanced in Bowes' instructions for the continuance of this privilege is that "we request nothing therein but that he hath allready graunted to the said company, in respect of the great charges ther (sic) haue bene at in finding out that trade."[57] English privileges moreover were being seriously threatened by the presence in Russia of large numbers of Dutch merchants "who had intruded themselves to trade into those countries"[58] and who had by questionable means won several powerful nobles to their cause. Bowes in his account of his mission brings charges against these Dutch traders who "besides dayly gifts that they bestowed upon them all, they took so much money of theirs at interest at five and twenty upon the hundred, as they payd to some one of them five thousand marks yeerely for the use of his money, and the English merchants at that time had not one friend in Court."[59]

In spite of the difficult prospect Bowes succeeded in securing from Ivan a full ratification of the old exclusive grant. Payment of debts due to the merchants was promised, as well as the restoration of certain sums which had

[57] Tolstoy, p. 203. *Copie of instructions giuen to Sir Jerome Bowes.*

[58] In May, 1582, complaint was made in a memorial to the Queen that custom had been collected in Russia in violation of the Company's privilege and that "a Dutche merchant, against the priuiledges graunted to her subiects, is permitted to vse trade to their great hindrance in the parts priuiledged." Tolstoy, p. 194.

[59] Hakluyt, III, 317.

been exacted in violation of their privilege.[60] The negotiations thus auspiciously begun, however, were destined to come to nothing. In the words of the ambassador, "All these were granted, . . . the olde privilege ratified, newly written, signed and sealed, and was to be delivered to the ambassadour at his next comming to Court, before when the Emperor fell sicke of a surfet, and so died."[60]

The death of Ivan the Terrible is an event of great significance in the history of the Muscovy Company. In spite of a brief and temporary withdrawal of privileges and frequent threats to take from the Company its exclusive trading rights the first thirty years of the Company's history, i.e., from the first voyage to Ivan's death, show a fairly consistent policy of friendship and protection on the part of the Russian government. The right to trade all over Russia without payment of duties had been granted in 1555; the monopoly of the trade with the northern coasts had been granted in 1567; the monopoly of the overland trade with Persia had been granted in 1569. The mission of Bowes shows that in the very last year of Ivan's life he still adhered to the policy of friendship for England and exclusive privilege for the English Company.

Ivan's death dealt the prosperity of the Company a blow from which it never fully recovered. The blow fell, moreover, at the period when the interest of English adventurers was turning definitely toward the west. In the very year of the Czar's death appeared Hakluyt's "Discourse on Western Planting." In this work the poor condition of Russian trade is advanced as an argument for the discovery of new fields for commercial enterprise in America. Hakluyt summarizes the Russian situation as follows: "Our trade into Muscovye . . . stoode them in fourscore thousande poundes before they broughte it to any goodd passe. And nowe after longe hope of gayne, the

[60] Hakluyt, III, 325.

Hollanders, as also the men of Diepe, are entred into their trade by the Emperours permission; yea, whereas at the firste our men paid no custome, of late yeres, contrarie to their firste priviledge, they have bene urged to pay yt. Also the chardges of bringinge the Emperours embassador hither, and mayneteyninge him here, and the settinge furthe of her Majesties embassador thither with presentes to the Emperour, lyenge all upon the poore marchantes neckes, is no easie burden unto their shoulders. . . . And nowe the Emperour of Russia beinge late deade, yt is greatly feared that the voyadge wilbe utterly overthrowen, or els become not worthe the contynuance."[61]

The immediate result of the death of Ivan was the complete cessation of the negotiations which Sir Jerome Bowes had almost brought to such a satisfactory termination. It seems that Bowes had made many enemies among the dignitaries of Ivan's court. Now their turn had come. The ambassador was imprisoned in his own house for a period of nine weeks "and was so straightly guarded and badly used by those that attended him, as he dayly suspected some further mischiefe to have followed."[62]   At last he was brought to the council chamber and there notified by the Chancellor "that this Emperour would not treat of further amity with the Queene his mistresse."[62]   Boris, whose influence was not yet strong enough to allow him to declare himself openly, gave the ambassador to understand that he was friendly to the English and would later do what he could to remove these differences.[63]   Bowes was sent to St. Nicholas and there set sail for England after having

[61] Hakluyt's *"Discourse on Western Planting,"* in Collections of the Maine Historical Society, second series, Vol. II, p. 16. Cf. Carlile's statement of the same tenor in Hakluyt, VIII, pp. 134 ff.

[62] Hakluyt, III, 326. Ivan was succeeded by his son Feodor, a weak-minded prince, during whose reign (1584-1598) actual power was in the hands of his brother-in-law, Boris Godounof. In 1598 Boris succeeded to the throne.

[63] *Ibid.*, III, 327.

issued an unsuccessful call upon all the English merchants
to accompany him.[64]   The agent at Kholmogory wrote to the
Company, "Wolde he had never come here   . . .   The
Lorde sende vs all his grace." [65]

During the next few years the most prominent figure in
the affairs of the Company was Jerome Horsey. He has
left us an account of the embassy of Bowes in which he
takes credit to himself for the ambassador's escape with his
life.[66]   In September, 1585, Horsey carried a letter from
Czar Feodor to Elizabeth.[67]   This letter indicates that the
Company had lost the favor of the Russian government.
The chief complaints were that they had sold goods at retail in violation of their privileges and had also handled
"other straungers comodities vnder color of their owne."
Renewal of the old privilege was absolutely refused. The
only special rights they were to enjoy were the payment of
half custom and possession of their own houses.[68]

Horsey's influence is clearly indicated by his success in
securing a new grant of privilege for the Company within
a year of the Czar's written refusal and in spite of the
strong opposition of the Chancellor. For this grant of
1586 he was chiefly indebted to the friendship of Boris
Godounof. Horsey's own account, however, grossly exag-
gerates the importance of the new grant. His absurd boast
that he obtained for the Company "those privileges which
in twentie yeeres before would not be granted" [69] is absolutely disproved by a careful reading of the grant itself,
which was not nearly so generous as those previously granted
by Ivan IV. The only important concession was the restoration of the right to trade all over the Czar's dominions

64 Hakluyt, III, 328.
65 Tolstoy, p. 228.
66 Horsey, p. 205.
67 Ibid., p. 210.
68 This letter is given in full in Tolstoy, pp. 261-269.
69 Hakluyt, III, 346.

without the payment of duties.[70]   The Company is prohibited from engaging in retail trade, from handling "any
other mens goods but their owne,"[71] from sending their
servants to England overland without the Emperor's
knowledge,[72] and from employing Russian agents to sell
their goods.[73]   The jurisdiction of the Treasurer of State
and the Secretary of Embassies is to extend to all cases between the Company and Russian subjects.[74]   No monopoly
right is mentioned, either of the White Sea trade or of the
overland route to Persia.[75]

In spite of Horsey's success in securing the new privilege the Company had reason to suspect his honesty in the
handling of its affairs.   The embassy of Giles Fletcher in
1588 was partly for the purpose of treating with the new
Emperor about the matter of a new alliance, partly "for
the reëstablishing and reducing into order the decaied trade
of our Englishmen there."[76]   Fletcher on his arrival in
Russia found the Company in disfavor and their privilege
of trade "of no account."[77]   Moreover a league between
Russia, Spain and the Pope was in contemplation, a circum-
stance which together with a false report of the success of

[70] Hakluyt, III, 348-349.
[71] Ibid., III, 349.
[72] Ibid., III, 352.
[73] Ibid., III, 349.
[74] Ibid., III, 353.
[75] In spite of the apparent definiteness of the privilege secured
by Horsey and the inclusion of the grant in Hakluyt there is some
reason to doubt its authenticity.   The Company in presenting complaints against Horsey a few years later said among other things,
"And whereas he, by vertue of her Majesties letters, obteyned and
brought over with him, two years since, a graunt of privilidge for the
Companie, free of all custome, which privilige is called in againe,
and, as yt is said by her Majesties late ambassador (Fletcher), was
constantlie affirmed by Andrea Shalcan *to be either never graunted
by the Emperour, or unorderlie gotten out under seale* . . ."—
Russia at the Close of the Sixteenth Century, appendix III, p. 333.
[76] Hakluyt, III, 353.
[77] *Russia at the Close of the Sixteenth Century*, appendix IV, p.
349.   Fletcher's account of his embassy.

the Spanish Armada rendered the task of the English ambassador doubly difficult.   However, Fletcher soon received news of the English victory through letters from Drake which the ambassador ''cawsed to bee translated into the Russ toongue togeather with your Highnes oration made to the armie in Essex,'' whereupon ''all this conceipt of a Spanish league vanished away.'' [78]

Fletcher succeeded in overcoming the initial difficulties and managed to secure from the Emperor a new grant. A claim on the Company to the amount of 23,503 marks was reduced to 7,800 marks.[79]   The customs exacted the year before amounting to 1840 marks were remitted.[79] The Company is not to be held responsible for the actions of persons save those whose names have been registered by the agent in the office of the Treasury.[80]   Hereafter the Company is not to be under the office of the Chancellor (consistently their enemy) ''but pertein to the office of the Treasurie, so that they may appeal to the Lord Boris Godonove if they thinck they have wrong.'' [81]   On the important question of the payment of customs all that Fletcher could secure was that ''half-coustoom is claimed hearafter.'' [81]   Finally, the monopoly of the route to Persia is regranted,[81]—rather an empty privilege in view of the total discontinuance of the overland trade with that country.

In the letters that passed between Boris Godounof and Lord Burghley during the next few years the Russian min-

[78] *Russia at the Close of the Sixteenth Century*, pp. 346-347.
[79] *Ibid.*, p. 349.
[80] *Ibid.*, p. 350.
[81] *Russia at the Close of the Sixteenth Century*, appendix IV, p. 350.   The privilege is printed in full in Hakluyt, III, pp. 353-356. On the question of duties this document is silent.   Just when entire freedom from customs was restored it is difficult to say, but a letter from Feodor to Elizabeth in 1591 says, ''. . . we have been gratyous to your marchaunts and geoven theyme libertie to trade into our kingdome withoute payinge any custome.''—*Russia at the Close of the Sixteenth Century*, introd. p. cxvii.

ister gives repeated expression of his good will to the English merchants. A new grant of privilege dated 7104 (i.e., 1596) contains the significant statement that it was granted by "our princely Majestie at the request of our brother in lawe Boris Feodorowich Godenova our servant."[82]   This lengthy document does not differ in any important feature from the previous grant to Fletcher except that freedom from all payment of customs is this time specifically included,[83] and that cases between English merchants are to be heard and determined by the Chancellor.[84] The vigorous and exclusive manner in which officials are called upon to follow to the letter the requirements of the grant would seem to indicate that previous grants had not been strictly enforced.   The document closes with the striking sentence, "And whosoever shall withstand & not regard these our gracious letters shalbe in our high displeasure, and shal incurre the losse of his life."[85]

Two years after this grant Czar Feodor died (1598) and his brother-in-law Boris Godounof, " Protector of the English," succeeded to the throne.   This involved no change of policy toward the English merchants, as Boris had practically been in control of affairs during most of the reign of his predecessor.   In 1600 the embassy of Gregory Mikouleve to Elizabeth brought the century to a close with a confirmation of the friendship established between the two nations in 1554.   Despite repeated assurances of friendship, however, there is no indication of any renewal of the Company's monopoly of the White Sea trade after the death of Ivan the Terrible.

82 Hakluyt, III, 439.
83 Ibid., III, 440.
84 Ibid., III, 444.
85 Ibid., III, 445.

CHAPTER V

A. *The Nature and Extent of the Company's Trade.*

The first agents sent by the Company to reside in Russia were directed to "diligently learne and observe all kinde of wares, as wel naturals as forrein, that be beneficiall for this Realme, to be sold for the benefit of the company, and what kinde of our commodities and other things of these West partes bee most vendible in those Realms with profite, giving a perfect advise of all such things requisite."[1] In other words a systematic investigation of what sort of import and export trade might with most advantage be entered upon was undertaken by the Company in the very year of its incorporation. On September 11, 1555, the agents arrived at Vologda.[2] Two months later Killingworth sent to the Company a detailed account of his experiences and observations.[3] It was of course impossible in such a short time to have reached any final conclusions as to the most advantageous sorts of commerce to develop. Killingworth takes the ground that the Company's efforts should be directed toward securing general privileges; experiment is the only means of ascertaining what trades will pay. "And thus may we continue three or foure yeeres, and in this space we shall know the countrey and the marchants, and which way to save our selves best, and where to plant our houses, and where to seeke for wares."[4] The subsequent correspondence between the Company and its agents furnishes a model of business-like co-operation.

[1] Hakluyt, II, 284.
[2] *Ibid.*, II, 291.
[3] *Ibid.*, II, 291 ff.
[4] *Ibid.*, II, 296.

Of the articles imported by the Muscovy Company the most important was without question cordage. To avoid the heavy charges involved in the transportation of the raw hemp the Company as early as 1557 arranged for the establishment of the rope industry in Russia. Seven ropemakers were sent out in that year and the agents instructed to arrange a place for them at Kholmogory or Vologda,[5] to assign an overseer "to see the deliverie of the stuffe unwrought, as also to take charge of the stuffe wrought, & to foresee that neither the yarne be burnt in tarring, nor the hempe rotted in the watering."[6] Provision was to be made for the training of other workmen in this industry to carry it on when the English workmen should return home. The letter sums up the importance of the trade in cordage in the clause, "for we esteeme it a principal commoditie, and that the Counsel of England doth well allowe."[6]

"Traine oyle," i.e., sperm oil, was also from the first an important import. In fact oil, tallow, wax, flax and cordage constituted by far the greatest part of the goods carried in the Company's ships from Russia to England. In 1557 the agents were definitely directed to see that the "chiefest lading . . . be principally in wexe, flaxe. tallow and traine oyle," the letter continuing "for wee doe purpose to ground our selves chiefly upon these commodities, as wexe, cables and ropes, traine oyle, flaxe and some linen yarne.[7] In 1560 the Company wrote, "The wares that we would have you provide against the coming of the shippes are, Waxe, Tallowe, trayne Oyles, Flaxe, Cables and Ropes, and Furres, such as we have written to you for in our last letters by the shippes."[8] That in the last dec-

---

[5] The agents finally decided upon Kholmogory. Hakluyt, II, 393.
[6] Hakluyt, II, 381.
[7] Ibid., II, 382.
[8] Ibid., II, 403.

ade of the century these were still the chief articles brought
to England by the Company is indicated by a letter written in 1595 by Francis Cherry, an agent of the Company,
in which he says, "There is yearly brought into the realm,
and that without any contradiction of any prince or potentate, tallow, wax, flax, train oils, buff hides, cow hides, cordage and hemp, and this present last year was there returned 9000£ worth of cordage."[9]

One would expect the trade in furs to have furnished one
of the Company's most lucrative sources of profit. The
discouraging attitude of the government, however, prevented the free development of this branch of the Company's trade. In 1557 a "Skinner" was sent "to viewe
and see such furres as you shall cheape or buye."[10] The
Company warned the agents, however, that it desired "no
great plentie,"[11] exception being made only in the case
of "marterns" and "minnivers," "otherwise called Letis
and Mynkes."[10] The direction adds, "As for Sables and
other rich Furres, they bee not every mans money: therefore you may send the fewer, using partly the discretion of
the skinner in that behalfe."[10] A few years later (1560)
the agents received word to curtail still further the exportation of furs from Russia: "for now there is a Proclamation made that no furres shall be worne here, but such as
the like is growing here within this our Realme."[12] Another letter of the same year says, "As for Allard the
skinner, if you thinke good, he may come home in these
shippes."[13] A tone of regretful reminiscence is discernible in Camden's reference to "rich Furrs of Sables, Lu-
serns, and others, which at that time and in former Ages

[9] Hatfield House MSS. V, 462-3.
[10] Hakluyt, II, 382.
[11] Ibid., II, 381.
[12] Ibid., II, 403.
[13] Ibid., II, 409.

were in great request amongst the English, both for their Ornament and Wholesomness.'' [14]

The heavy charges which we have already mentioned as the cause of the discontinuance of the importation of raw hemp from Russia had a similar effect in the case of masts, tar and feathers,—''they would not beare the charges . . . considering our deere fraight.'' [15] This was not true of the less bulky and more valuable silks and spices which came to be included in the Company's cargoes after the establishment by Anthony Jenkinson of the overland route to Persia, a temporary phase of the Company's trading activity which was not destined to fulfill the promise of its early years.

As cordage was the Muscovy Company's chief article of import so English cloth constituted the chief staple of its export trade. Russia presented a new market for this greatest of English commodities. The Company's correspondence which has come down to us is much less explicit and detailed on the question of exportations from England than on that of importations from Russia. It is possible that there was less need for elaborate directions on that side of the question, since the problem of what English wares could be best disposed of in Russia presented fewer difficulties than the question of what Russian products would be most profitable to import. Suffice it to say that the chief part of the outgoing cargoes was made up of cloths of various sorts and colors. There was also some pewter exported,[16] and, as we have mentioned in another connection, probably large quantities of munitions of war.[17]

In the absence of the Company's records the question of the extent of its trade and the amount of its profits pre-

[14] Camden, p. 102.
[15] Hakluyt, II, 382.
[16] *Ibid.*, II, 380.
[17] *Supra*, p. 59.

sents numerous and serious difficulties. All that we shall attempt in this place is to cite a few scattered references from various sources which may be considered as suggestive though not in any sense conclusive.

The number of ships sent out annually by the Company may be said to furnish a fair index of the condition of its trade. In 1555 two vessels, the *Edward Bonaventure* and the *Philip and Mary*, were sent out.[18] We have evidence to show that in 1556 [19] and 1557 [20] fleets of four vessels were sent out by the Company to the White Sea. That cargoes were also sent out in 1558 and 1559 is clearly indicated by the fact that the venture of 1560 is referred to as the Company's seventh voyage; [21] in that year the fleet consisted of three vessels. By 1565 there had been no increase in the number of ships engaged in the Russian trade if we can judge by the official statement to the Danish ambassador that "not past two or three vessels go yearly to Muscovie." [22] In 1570, however, a fleet of thirteen vessels was

---

[18] Hakluyt, II, 281, 286.

[19] In Nov., 1555, the *Edward Bonaventure* and the *Philip and Mary* returned to England bringing with them the *Bona Speranza* and the *Confidentia* (Cal. S. P. Venetian, 1555-1556, p. 240). In May, 1556, the *Searchthrift* was sent out from London on a voyage of exploration to the Northeast under the command of Stephen Burrough. Burrough tells us that the *Searchthrift* set out in company with the *Edward Bonaventure* (Hakluyt, II, 323). The *Philip and Mary*, the *Bona Speranza* and the *Confidentia* must also have gone to Russia at this time as in the fall of the same year these three vessels left Russia with the *Edward Bonaventure*, the *Philip and Mary* alone surviving this return voyage (Hakluyt, II, 351). In 1556, therefore, the Company sent four vessels to Russia exclusive of the *Searchthrift*.

[20] In 1557 Jenkinson was sent with the *Primrose*, the *John Evangelist*, the *Anne* and the *Trinity*. This was the fleet that carried Napea back to Russia (Hakluyt, II, 375).

[21] Hakluyt, II, 401. In numbering the voyages the trip of Willoughby and Chancellor in 1553 is counted as the first, that of 1555 as the second, and thereafter annually.

[22] Cal. S. P. (Foreign) 1564-1565, p. 279.

sent by the Company to Narva.[23]   The northern route to
St. Nicholas was by no means given up; in fact in 1582 a
fleet of eleven ships was sent out by the Company to the
White Sea.[24]   This increase, however, was not destined to
be permanent.   The loss of Narva to Russia, followed a
few years later by the death of Ivan the Terrible and the
loss to the Company of its exclusive privileges in Russia,
probably explain the poor state of the trade which marked
the close of the century.   Whatever the cause, in 1591 only
five ships were sent out.[25]   Nor is there any indication of
a revival of the Company's prosperity.

The wealth of the Company is even more difficult to estimate than the extent of its trade.   Horsey says that in
1581 the Company's stock in Russia was worth at least
one   hundred   thousand   marks   sterling   (66,666⅔£).[26]
The burning of the Company's warehouse in Moscow was
said to have involved the loss of ten thousand rubles
(6000£).[27]   Government contracts to the amount of 3000£
and 4000£ do not seem to have been unusual.[28]   In 1597
the government's debts to the Company amounted to almost
14,000£.[29]   Fragmentary   and   isolated   items   of   debit,
credit, expense or loss, however, give little indication of
the actual condition of the Company's affairs.   Its im-
poverished state shortly after the close of our period is indicated by the fact that in the next century the poverty of
the Muscovy Company had passed into a proverb.   In the
records of the East India Company for 1639 we find this
significant expression, "For if the debt be not lessened it

[23] Hakluyt, III, 167.

[24] *Ibid.*, III, 303.

[25] Cal. S. P. (Domestic) 1591-1594, p. 30.

[26] Horsey, p. 184.

[27] Hakluyt, III, 183.   The computation here made is on the basis
of 12 s. to a ruble.   Cf. Hakluyt, II, 391.

[28] Cal. S. P. (Foreign) 1566-1568, p. 462; Cal. S. P. (Domestic)
1581-1590, p. 467.

[29] Hatfield House MSS. VII, p. 484.

will consume the [East India] Company and bring them a 'Muscovia reckoning' ''![30]

B. *The Company's Exploring Activities.*

It will be remembered that one of the original purposes of this Company had been the discovery of a passage to the Indies.[31]   While the accidental establishment of a means of communication with the northern coasts of Russia unquestionably centered the thought and activity of the Company on the development of trade relations with that country the original idea was by no means given up.   That neither the government nor the Company regarded the work of the latter as having been completed with the establishment of the Russian trade is clearly indicated by the charter of 1555, which besides granting a monopoly of this trade specifically conferred on the Company the exclusive enjoyment of any other trades it might establish to the north, northeast or northwest.[32]   This provision, evidently looking toward the continuance of the Company's original plans of exploration, was repeated in the charter of 1566.[33]

As early as 1556 we have record of a serious attempt being made by the Company to continue the interrupted search for a northeast passage.   Stephen Burrough, "master of the Pinnesse called the *Searchthrift*," was the hero of this adventure, of which he has left us a full account. Burrough had been master of the *Edward Bonaventure* on its first outward voyage under Chancellor in 1553.[34]

The *Searchthrift* departed from London on Thursday, April 23, 1556.[35]   The following Monday Sebastian Cabot came aboard at Gravesend and wished the voyagers Godspeed.[35]   In company with the *Edward Bonaventure* the

[30] Court Minutes of the East India Company, 1635-1639, p. 306.
[31] *Supra*, p. 2 ff.
[32] Hakluyt, II, 316.
[33] *Ibid.*, III, 85.
[34] *Ibid.*, II, 213.
[35] *Ibid.*, II, 322.

Searchthrift sailed across the North Sea.[36]   On May 23 the
North Cape (so named by Burrough on the first voyage)
was passed.[37]   Soon afterward the *Searchthrift* separated
from the *Bonaventure* which proceeded on its way to the
White Sea: "at eight of the clocke, we heard a piece of
ordinance, which was out of the *Edward,* which bade us
farewell, and then we shot off another piece, and bade her
farewell: wee could not one see the other, because of the
thicke miste."[38]

The *Searchthrift* pursued its way alone along the northern coast of Russian Lapland.   A few days after the
separation from the *Edward* it put into the safe harbor
afforded by the mouth of the Kola River.[38]   It was not
until June 22 that the cessation of northerly winds permitted them to put out to sea again.[39]   During this delay
the explorers noticed a large number of small Russian boats
coming down the river on their way to Pechora to fish
for morse and salmon.   "And amongst the rest, there was
one of them whose name was Gabriel," who showed much
friendship toward the Englishmen, and informed them
that with a fair wind they might reach the river Pechora
in seven or eight days.[40]   He promised to act as pilot and
give warning of shoals; "as hee did indeede," adds Burrough.

The English vessel now pursued its voyage in company
with the Russian boats.   They stayed close to the shore,
saved from the shoals by the advice of their friendly guide.
Near the entrance of the White Sea much time was lost by
the recurrence of stormy weather.   By July 8, however,
they had sailed past the entrance of the White Sea and had
sighted the headland "which is called Caninoz" (Cape

[36] Hakluyt, II, 323.
[37] *Ibid.,* II, 325.
[38] *Ibid.,* II, 326.
[39] *Ibid.,* II, 331.
[40] *Ibid.,* II, 328.

Kanin).[41] From this point Burrough found himself in regions hitherto unsailed by any Englishman. On the 14th the island called "Dolgoieve" (Kolguev) was sighted.[42] The next day the *Searchthrift* sailed over the bar of Pechora,[42] Burrough being the first Englishman to visit the mouth of that river. On the 20th they recrossed the bar and resumed their hazardous journey toward the northeast.

The next day, July 21st, the English ship was almost destroyed by icebergs. "We thought that we had seen land . . . " writes Burrough, "which afterwards proved to be a monstrous heape of ice. Within little more than halfe an houre after we first saw this ice, we were inclosed within it before we were aware of it, which was a fearfull sight to see: for, for the space of sixe houres, it was as much as we could doe to keepe our shippe aloofe from one heape of ice, and beare roomer from another. . . . The next day we were again troubled by the ice."[43] For this time, however, the danger was escaped and on July 25, "S. James his day," the exploring party came upon several islands.[44] Near one they cast anchor and made a landing, naming it "S. James his Island" in honor of the day.[44] According to Burrough's statement of the latitude (70° 42′) this must have been one of the small islands off the coast of Nova Zembla.

On July 31 the *Searchthrift* came to anchor "among the Islands of Vaigats"[45] (Waigatz), probably in the strait which separates Nova Zembla from Waigatz. During the month of August little or no progress was made. Burrough has left us, however, an interesting record of his observations in these regions, particularly of the relics of

[41] Hakluyt, II, 333.
[42] *Ibid.*, II, 334.
[43] *Ibid.*, II, 335.
[44] *Ibid.*, II, 336.
[45] *Ibid.*, II, 337.

the absent natives, the Samoeds. He saw a large number
of their idols, "in number above 300, the worst and the
most unartificiall worke that ever I saw: the eyes and
mouthes of sundrie of them were bloodie, they had the
shape of men, women and children, very grosly wrought
. . . some of their idols were an olde sticke with two or
three notches, made with a knife in it . .. and before certaine of their idols blocks were made as high as
their mouthes, being all bloody, I thought that to be the
table whereon they offered their sacrifice."[46] A Russian
who was with the party told Burrough that these Samoeds
did not live in houses but "onely tents made of Deers
skins, which they underproppe with stakes and poles," also
that "their knowledge is very base, for they know no letter."[47] This Russian, whose name was Loshak, offered to
accompany the English party toward the river Obi.[47]

On August 5, however, the approach of "a terrible heape
of ice" induced the voyagers "with all speed possible to
depart from thence."[47] They changed their course to the
west and for the following week were pursued by frightful storms along the northern and western coasts of Waigatz. "The ice came in so abundantly about us," writes
Burrough on August 7, ". . . that it was a fearefull
sight to behold: the storme continued with snow, rain, and
hayle plenty."[48] On August 12 they came to anchor off
the southwest corner of the island.

On Saturday, August 22, the bad weather abated. The
perils they had so barely escaped and despair of discover-
ing "any more to the Eastward this yeere" led Burrough
to give up the attempt for that time. He mentions three
causes for this decision: the continual northerly winds,
"which have moe power after a man is past to the East-

46 Hakluyt, II, 338.
47 Ibid., II, 339.
48 Ibid., II, 340.

wards of Caninoze (Cape Kanin) then in any place that I
doe know in these Northerly regions;'' the abundance of
ice,—''I adventured already somewhat too farre in it, but
I thanke God for my safe deliverance from it;'' and the
darkening of the nights with the approach of winter.[49]
''And therefore,'' says Burrough, ''I resolved to take the
first best wind that God should send, and plie towards
the Bay of S. Nicholas.'' [49] On the 24th they were off the
coast of Kolguev once more.[50] By the 29th Cape Kanin
had been reached.[50] Two days later the *Searchthrift*
doubled that cape and entered the White Sea.[51] On September 11 the party landed at Kholmogory.[51] The voyage
was finished.

Burrough expected to make another attempt the following summer. Other business, however, prevented.[51]
We may say of his voyage that while it is of interest as indicating the intention of the Muscovy Company to pursue
its exploring activities even after the establishment of its
Russian trading rights it was not of much actual benefit
either to the Company or to the English nation. It did,
however, clearly indicate the tremendous difficulties connected with any attempt to discover a northeast passage.

Between 1556 and 1568 there is no definite record of any
systematic attempt on the part of the Company to explore
the seas east of Cape Kanin. This is probably to be explained, in part at least, by the attempts made during that
period to reach Cathay by an overland route. We have
already seen that in 1558 Anthony Jenkinson set out from
Moscow on that enterprise. He crossed the Caspian and
penetrated Asia as far as Bokhara. Cathay, of course, he
failed to reach, but he did establish for the Company a
trade with Persia. The monopoly of this trade remained

[49] Hakluyt, II, 342.
[50] *Ibid.*, II, 343.
[51] *Ibid.*, II, 341.

for many years one of the Company's most cherished privileges. It was realized, however, that the original problem, the discovery of a new route to China and India, was still unsolved.

Of the exploration planned in 1568 no positive record has come down to us. All that we know is that at that time a voyage of exploration to the northeast was definitely arranged for and its leaders appointed. We have copies of their instructions. The subsequent silence of the records may possibly indicate the suspension of the plan at the last moment. A disastrous outcome suggests itself as the other possible solution.

It will be remembered that in 1568 Thomas Randolph was Elizabeth's ambassador to Ivan IV and that he had been accompanied to Russia by two special agents of the Company, Thomas Bannister and Goeffrey Duckett.[52] On August 12, the agents in a letter to Cecil concerning the Company's affairs in Russia state their intention of appointing "Bassington (sic) with two mariners and interpreters" to explore toward the northeast.[53] Evidently mindful of Burrough's account of the Russian boats he had met on his voyage the agents decided to send the explorers out this time in a Russian vessel "which will be done at a small cost and . . . to more purpose than if two barks should be sent out." [53] The voyagers are " to pass from Pechoray . . . with the first open water in the spring along the coast eastward for the trial of the northeast passage." [53]

The commission had been drawn up by Randolph and the agents on August 1st.[54] It appoints James Bassendine,

---

[52] *Supra*, p. 64.

[53] Cal. S. P. (Foreign) 1566-1568, p. 518.

[54] Hakluyt's date of 1588 (Hakluyt, III, 119) is manifestly an error. The period of Randolph's embassy fixes the date as 1568. The position of the document in Hakluyt among other documents of the same period would seem to indicate that "1588" was a slip.

James Woodcocke and Richard Browne "joyntly together, and aiders, the one of them to the other, in a voyage of discovery to be made (by the grace of God) by them, for searching of the sea, and border of the coast, from the river Pechora, to the Eastwards."[55] Bassendine and his companions were instructed to sail directly to the mouth of the Pechora, "where is an island called Dolgoieve."[55] Thence they were to sail to the eastward, keeping close to the coast until they should reach the river Obi.[56] They were not to enter that river, however, but to sail past its mouth, keeping ever in sight of land until the approach of winter should compel them to return, "which travell may well be 300 or 400 leagues to the Eastwards of the Ob, if the Sea doe reach so farre as our hope is it doth."[56] Careful observations of latitude and coast configurations were to be made and soundings taken at frequent intervals.[57] A full record was to be kept "of all such things as shall fall out worth the knowledge, not forgetting to write it, and note it, that it may be shewed and read at your returne."[58]

The directions contained in the articles of commission evidence an absolute ignorance of the vast stretch of Siberian coast that would have to be passed before the dream of a northeast passage should become a reality. The hope is expressed "that the said border of land and sea doth in short space after you passe the Ob, incline East, and so to the Southwards."[59] The difficulty they anticipated was not the three thousand miles of Arctic coast but was based on the curious fear that this coast might be found "to incline and trend to the Northwards, and so joyne with Nova Zembla, making the sea from Vaigats to the Eastwards but a bay"![59]

[55] Hakluyt, III, 119.
[56] Ibid., III, 120.
[57] Ibid., III, 122-123.
[58] Ibid., III, 123.   [59] Ibid., III, 121.

Instructions given by the Company on the occasion of their next attempt are entirely silent on the subject of Bassendine and his companions. This would seem to indicate that the plan of 1568, even in the event of its having been undertaken, had led to no useful result. 1580 is the date of the next venture of which we have any definite knowledge. This time the most elaborate preparations were made not merely for an investigation of the coast east of the Obi but for the actual discovery of Cathay by way of the northeast. Arthur Pet and Charles Jackman were placed in charge of the voyage, their commission being dated May 20, 1580.[60] Their vessels, the *George* and the *William*, then lying in the Thames, were provisioned for two and a half years.[61] Interest in the voyage was widespread. Besides the elaborate directions contained in the commission, William Burrough wrote the leaders of the enterprise a letter full of detailed advice.[62] "Master Dee," probably John Dee, the mathematician and astrologer, also wrote them "certaine briefe advises."[63] Richard Hakluyt himself has left us a record of "notes in writing, besides more privie by mouth," that he gave to Pet and Jackman, "not altogether unfit for some other enterprises of discovery, hereafter to be taken in hand."[64] Finally Gerard Mercator, the geographer, writing to Hakluyt shortly after the departure of the explorers, expressed his regret that he had not had an opportunity to add his word to the advice with which the leaders of the voyage had been besieged: "I wish Arthur Pet had bene informed before his departure of some speciall points. The voyage to Cathaio by the East, is doutlesse very easie and short,"[65] etc.

[60] Hakluyt, III, 251.
[61] *Ibid.*, III, 256.
[62] *Ibid.*, III, 259 ff.
[63] *Ibid.*, III, 262 ff.
[64] *Ibid.*, III, 264 ff.
[65] *Ibid.*, III, 278.

Mercator's letter ends with the striking sentence, "At Arthur his returne I pray you learne of him the things I have requested, and whether any where in his voiage, he found the sea fresh, or not very salt: for I suppose the Sea betweene Nova Zembla and Tabin to be fresh." [66]

The commission clearly brings out that the prime purpose of the venture is to establish trading relations with the empire of Cathay. Pet and Jackman carried letters from Elizabeth to the Emperor and were instructed to try to procure from him in return definite trading privileges.[67] The Company was clearly attempting to realize the object implied in its official title, "the Company for the Discovery of New Trades." Nicholas Chancellor, a merchant, was sent with the expedition, evidently to superintend the commercial activities of the venture.[68] Pet was given the title of Admiral and Jackman that of Vice-Admiral.[68]

On the subject of the route to be followed the commission is very definite. The ships were to set out from London as soon after May 22 as the weather would permit and proceed to the North Cape.[69] Thence they were to pass to the east. In this part of their voyage the explorers were to try to ascertain whether Nova Zembla was identical or contiguous with certain lands to the north mentioned by Willoughby in his journal.[69] Passing Waigatz they were to sail past the mouth of the Obi.

The directions as to their subsequent route reveal the same ignorance of conditions as we found in the directions to Bassendine in 1568. Three contingencies are specifically provided for. The first course outlined provides that the coast east of the Obi is to be followed until Cathay is reached, "whether it incline Southerly or Northerly (as at

[66] Hakluyt, III, 281.
[67] *Ibid.*, III, 255.
[68] *Ibid.*, III, 253.
[69] *Ibid.*, III, 254.

times it may do both)." [70] If on the approach of winter
they have not reached their destination they shall wait until the spring "in some convenient harborow and place." [71]
Here, if the inhabitants seem to warrant it, commercial relations may be established, one of the Queen's letters being
delivered to the prince and trading privileges if possible
procured. Whether in this attempt they are successful or
not, the following spring they shall proceed on their way
to Cathay,—"for that is the Countrey that we chiefly desire to discover." [71]

The second contingency mentioned in the commission
refers to the possibility "that the land of Asia, from beyond the river Ob, extende it selfe Northwards to 80. degrees, or neerer the poole . . . that small or no hope
may be looked for, to saile that way to Cathay." [71] In
that case the coast is to be followed, nevertheless, during
the summer. The following winter, however, shall then
be spent on the banks of the Obi, exploring that river the
next summer if it should prove wide and deep enough to
permit. "Happely you may come to the citie Siberia, or
to some other towne or place habited upon or neere the
border of it, and thereby have liking to winter out the
second winter." [72]

The third direction makes provision for the explorers'
course in case the Obi should be found to be too shallow to
admit of the exploration referred to. In that case, after
wintering in that river, the explorers shall turn back
through "Boroughs streights" (Kara Strait). Thence
they shall sail westward, keeping in sight of the coast of
Nova Zembla until they reach "Willoughbies land." [73]
The instruction adds, "and from Willoughbies land you
shall proceed Westwards alongst the tract of it (though it

[70] Hakluyt, III, 254.
[71] Ibid., III, 256.
[72] Ibid., III, 257.
[73] Ibid.

incline Northerly) even so farre as you may or can travell, having regard that in convenient time you may returne home hither to London for wintering." [74]

In comparison with these ambitious plans the actual trip must be regarded as an absolute failure. The *George* and the *William* departed from Harwich at the end of May, 1580.[75] On June 6 the vessels were separated but met once more at Wardhouse.[76] From here they put to sea on July 1.[76] Next day, however, the *William* was seen to be in need of repair and made her way to Kegor, Arthur Pet continuing his voyage with the *George* with the idea of rejoining the *William* at Waigatz.[77]

Pet continuing his eastward course sighted land to the north on July 5.[77] Wind and ice prevented him from getting close to it. For the next two weeks the progress of his vessel was very slow. Much time was wasted in the attempt to pass the island of Waigatz, but at last the *George* sailed through the strait which separates that island from the mainland and passed out into the Kara Sea. On the 24th the *William* was sighted, but "there was a great land of ice betweene her and us, so that we could not come one to the other." [78] Next day, however, the two vessels did come together. The *William* was again out of repair but with the *George's* assistance was put in condition to continue the voyage.[78]

The story of the struggle of the explorers to make their way through the Kara Sea is largely a repetition of the difficulties encountered by Burrough twenty-four years before. Icebergs impeded their progress and threatened their very existence. "Windes we have had at will," writes the contemporary narrator, "but ice and fogge too much against

[74] Hakluyt, III, 258.
[75] *Ibid.*, III, 282.
[76] *Ibid.*, III, 283.
[77] *Ibid.*, III, 284.
[78] *Ibid.*, III, 290.

our willes, if it had pleased the Lord God otherwise.'' [79]
On July 28, Pet and Jackman held a conference and decided to put back to Waigatz, "and there to conferre further.'' [80] The return to Waigatz took nineteen days and constituted one of the most hazardous episodes of the whole voyage. The account is full of items like the following: "At 3. in the afternoon (July 28) we did warpe from one piece of ice to another to get from them if it were possible: here were pieces of ice so great, that we could not see beyond them out of the toppe;'' [80] . . .
"We did our best untill ten of the clocke (July 31), and then perceiving that we did no good, and being inclosed with ice, wee made our ships fast to a piece of ice: All this day the *William* lay still, and did as much good as we that did labour all the forenoone;'' [81] . . . "This day (August 3) we lay still inclosed with yce, the weather beeing darke with fogge: thus abiding the Lords leasure, we continued with patience;'' [82] . . . "The eleventh day (August 11) we were much troubled with yce, and by great force we made our way through it, which we thought a thing impossible: but extremity doth cause men to doe much, and in the weakenesse off man Gods strength most appeareth.'' [83] On August 16 they at last reached the southeast coast of Waigatz.[84]

There is no record of further conference between the leaders. Their experience had probably proved to them that the task they had undertaken was impossible, at any rate for vessels the size of theirs.[85] They did not resume

[79] Hakluyt, III, 290.
[80] *Ibid.*, III, 291.
[81] *Ibid.*, III, 292.
[82] *Ibid.*, III, 293.
[83] *Ibid.*, III, 295.
[84] *Ibid.*, III, 296.
[85] The *George* was a vessel of 40 tons, and the *William* of 20 tons. In the former were nine men and a boy; in the latter five men and a boy. Hakluyt, III, 252.

the abandoned northeast course. Instead the two ships sailed west through Waigatz Strait, went aground on Kolguev on August 20 [86] but managed to get off, and proceeded on their return voyage. Arthur Pet arrived at Ratcliffe December 26.[87] Jackman with the *William* had parted from the *George* on August 22,[88] wintered at a port in Norway, "And from thence departed againe in Februarie following, and went in company of a ship of the King of Denmarke toward Island: and since that time he was never heard of." [89]

The contrast furnished by the elaborate preparations for the Pet-Jackman expedition and its absolute failure to accomplish anything might lead us to expect a cessation of this form of activity. While we have no full account or definite statement of any other northeast voyages sent out by the Company during the remainder of the century there is reason to believe that the idea was not abandoned. A document bearing date of 1584 contains a letter from certain Russian traders to Anthony Marsh, the Company's factor at that time, on the subject of the route to the Obi. Whether the plan advocated in the letter of reaching that river by sailing up the Pechora and across by way of the Ouson (Ussa?) was ever tried we do not know. One sentence in this document, however, indicates that at some time before 1584 Englishmen had reached the Obi. "Heretofore," writes Marsh's correspondent, "your people haue bin at the said riuer of Obs mouth with a ship, and there was made shipwracke, and your people were slaine by the Samoeds." [90] Even if this statement does refer to an unrecorded expedition of the Company its disastrous conclusion forbids us to consider it in the light of an actual

[86] Hakluyt, III, 297.
[87] *Ibid.*, III, 303.
[88] *Ibid.*, III, 298.
[89] *Ibid.*, III, 303.
[90] *Purchas His Pilgrimes* (edit. by MacLehose) XIV, pp. 292-293.

discovery. In 1589 the Company was still seeking a route to the Obi "and a passage by the northeast of St. Nicholas into Asia." [91]

No discussion of the explorations of the Muscovy Company in the sixteenth century could be considered complete without at least passing reference to the Company's connection with the attempts of the Elizabethan seamen to find a passage by the northwest. The Company's part in those ventures, which bore so close a relation to the exploitation and colonization of the western continent, has not in the past received due recognition. With a brief consideration of this phase of the Company's activities we will bring this portion of our discussion to a close.

The Charters of 1555 and 1566, it will be remembered, granted to the Muscovy Company the monopoly of any new trade routes that it might discover to the northwest as well as to the northeast. While its activities were largely limited to the eastern hemisphere the Company showed almost from the beginning that it realized the full extent of its privilege and would not allow it to be infringed in any particular without protest and resistance.

In 1567 Humphrey Gilbert addressed a memorial to the Queen announcing his intention to attempt the discovery of a passage to Cathay by the northwest, and asking for a special grant of privileges.[92] These were to include the right to press mariners for the first four voyages, the payment of lower customs for forty years, the right to hold one-tenth of all lands that might be discovered, to have half of all fines and forfeits taken from those who should make use of the northwest route without authorization, and to have all ships employed in the traffic freed forever from imprest for any common service of the realm. This memorial was directly in conflict with the privileges

91 Cal. S. P. (Domestic) 1581-1590, p. 587.
92 Cal. S. P. (Colonial) 1513-1616, pp. 6-7.

of the Muscovy Company. Accordingly, under date of June 24, 1567, the governors of the Company drew up a formal remonstrance which they sent to Secretary Cecil. In this document the Company announced that ''since they have made attempts for the discovery of Cathay and are determined to do so again,[93] either by the northeast or northwest, they claim the ordering of all such discoveries according to their privileges, but will not refuse Mr. Gylberte's advice and help if he will assist them.'' [94]

Where its own privileges were clearly recognized, however, the Company does not seem to have stood in the way of explorations to the northwest. Michael Lok, for example, procured from it a privilege for the discovery of Cathay by a northwest route.[95] A few years later the ore brought back by Frobisher from his voyage was smelted at Muscovy House.[96]

A final instance under date of 1602 will indicate the Company's tenacity in asserting its claims. In that year Captain George Waymouth was employed by the two-year-old East India Company to take charge of a voyage of exploration to the northwest. All arrangements were concluded when the Muscovy Company called a halt by asserting its exclusive right to the navigation of the northern seas. The East India Company appointed a committee to secure permission from the rival organization to undertake the voyage.[97] In this they failed. They then made another attempt, resolving this time that if the Muscovy Company would not undertake the voyage itself or join with the East India Company for that purpose the latter would lay the case before the Privy Council.[98] On December 22 the Muscovy Company ''having received let-

[93] The following year came the Bassendine project.

[94] Cal. S. P. (Colonial) 1513-1616, p. 8.

[95] Cal. S. P. (Colonial) 1513-1616, p. 22.

[96] Cal. S. P. (Domestic) 1547-1580, p. 586; p. 605.

[97] Cal. S. P. (Colonial) 1513-1616, p. 128.   [98] *Ibid.*, p. 129.

ters from the Privy Council" agreed to join the East India Company in the discovery.[99]   The latter Company, however, finally undertook the venture alone.   This victory of the East India Company may in a sense be considered symbolic of the part which that organization was to play thenceforth in English commerce and colonization.   The Muscovy Company no longer occupied the center of the stage.

.   .   .   .

The history of the Muscovy Company in the 16th century is of significance, first of all, because of the large part it played in the evolution of English commerce. When we consider that this company was the first of that large group of trading and colonizing organizations which entered as so large a factor in the expansion of English trade in the seventeenth and eighteenth centuries it is indeed difficult to overstate its historical importance.   Modeled in many respects on the still earlier Company of Merchant Adventurers, the Muscovy Company by the introduction of a Joint Stock system adapted its organization to the needs of a more distant field of activity. It must be regarded as the prototype of many of those later companies whose more successful careers have tended to prevent due recognition being given to their great predecessor of the sixteenth century.

Of no less importance for the historian is the large influence of the Muscovy Company in the development of the political relations of the English government.   The trading companies probably did more than any other one agency to bring the nations of Europe into that close interdependence which characterizes the last three centuries of European history.   The significance of the Muscovy Company for Russia is that it brought that country into the family of civilized European nations and introduced

[99] Cal. S. P. (Colonial) 1513-1616, p. 130.

to it the higher civilization, culture and arts of the West. For English history one of the Company's chief contributions consists in the large part it played in the expansion of the political and diplomatic outlook of the future world-empire.

THE MUSCOVY COMPANY

APPENDIX

List of members of the Muscovy Company, May 1 (?), 1555. This MS. is preserved in the Public Record Office, London. C. S. P. (Dom.) Addenda, Mary, 1553-1556, Vol. VII, No. 39.

The Lord High Treasurer.
The Lord Howard.
The Earl of Pembroke.
The Lord High Admiral.
The Lord Pagett.
The Lord Savay (?).
The Lord Chamberlain.
Sir Robert Rochester Knight Comptroller.
Sir Henry Fernegam Knight Vice chamberlain
Sir Edward Hastings Knight Mr of Horses
Sir Thomas Whartom Knight
Sir Thomas Cornwalis Knight
Sir William Pitts Knight
Sir John Bo . . . Knight
Sir Edward Walgrave knight
Edwarde Griffith Esquire
William Cordall Esquire
Sir William Cecill knight
Sir Henry Sidney knight
Sir Thomas Wrothe knight
Sir Richard Blunt knight
Sir Richard Sackvyle knight
Sir John Cleve (?) knight
Sir William Woodhouse, knight
Sir Thomas Woodhouse knight
Sir William Dansell (?) knight
Mr. Nicolas Wotton Clerke.

Sir John Gressham
Sir Andrew Judde
Sir George Barne ⎫ knights and Aldermen
Sir Thomas White
Sir John Yorke, knight ⎭

Mr. Davy Woodrooff
Thomas Osley Gelder
Thomas Curtis
William Garrarde ⎫ Aldermen
William Chester
Thomas Lodge
Mrs. Margaret Kyrtom
Henry Herdsom ⎭

116

Sebastian Caboto
Thomas Gresham
Anthony Hussey
John Marsh Jun (?)
John Southcott
Henry Brinker } Esquiers
Thomas Egerton
John Dymock
Wm. Clystom
Clement Throgmorton
Edmond Somner (?)

James Pagett
Thomas Gravesende
Bernarde Randolphe
James Marshe
William Ha . . try } Gentlemen.
Thomas Colshill
Richard Yonge
William Wotton

Antony Hickman
Alexander Carlisle
Antony Gamage (?)
Antony Pargetar (?)
Alexander Mather
. . . Edwardes
Blase Saunders
Christopher Marler
Clement Clarke
Davy Appowall (?)
David Saunders.
Edmonde Stille
Edwarde Jackman
Edwarde Cashlyn (?)
Edwarde Garthe
Edmonde Roberts
Edmonde Linste (?)
Evan Luoge (?)
Edmonde Hasolpott (?)
Edwarde Gilbarte
Elizabeth Wilforde
Edwarde Prynne
Frannas Lambarde
Frannas Robynsom
Frannas Burnam (?)

George Heson (?)
Goffrey Walkden
Goffrey Langhen
George Hoploy
George Ca . . .
George Bursom
George Myffe (?)
Henry Richardes
Henry Bithar
Henry Grother (?)
Humfrey Baskerfelde
Henry Fallowfelde
Henry Fissher
Henry Flainack (?)
Henry Lynar
John Hart
John Brooke
John Le . . . Notary
John Crynus (?)
John Harysom
John Amioll (?)
John Elyott
John Ryvers
John Quarles
John Wilferde (?) Inn
John Hopkyns.
John Heathe
John Traves
John Brai . . he
John Wilkinson
John Sparke
John Cotton
John Stark (?)
John Campany
John Femposen (?)
John Mylner
John Midley.
John Bucklande
John Stantonn
John Harshe
Lyonell Inckett
Laurence Glasner (?)
Martyn Trevener
Miles Mordynge
Nicolas Bacon
Nicolas Burton
Nicolas Fuljambe

Phillippe Ennter
Phillippe Bolde
Phillippe K . . er
Katherin . . .
Richarde Malory
Richarde Poynter
Richarde Chamberlyn
Richarde Foulke
Roger Marten
Richarde Spryngham
Richarde Barne
Robert Dai . . berey
Robert Woolman.
Richarde Duckett
Richarde Elkin
Roberte Browne
Roberte Spenser
Richard Wills (?)
Rowlande Heywarde
Raulf Grenway
Roberte Dowin Inn
Roberte Crockhey
Roberte Dorne (?)
Richarde Patricke
Richarde Chaimalour (?)
Richarde Taillour
Stephaine Abowroughe (?)
Thomas Godman
Thomas Wilke
Thomas Luke (?)
Thomas Chamber
Thomas Banester
Thomas Palleysten (?)
Thomas Nicolls thilder niker
Thomas Heton (?)
Thomas Langley
Thomas Casfell
Thomas Heigham
Thomas Browne
Thomas Smythe
Thomas Sparke'
Thomas Anderson
Thomas Allen
Thomas Moore
Thomas Stanbridge
Thomas Starke Drap
Thomas Atkynsone Notary

Thomas Sares (?)
Thomas Unoffe (?) Goldsmythe
Thomas Ffranncis
William Watsone
Walter Yonge
William Allenne
William Gifforde
William Lincknor (?)
William Mericke
William Streete
Walter Levesone
William Knyght
William Malory
William Rosse
William Bully
William Billingston
William Monnstowe (?)
William Bonde
William Tucker
Walter Marler
William Dawke (?)
William Humfrey
Walter Garwan
William Levison
William Cholmelen
Xtofer Danntisey (?)
Xtofer Draper

LIST OF CHIEF SOURCES USED

Hakluyt, Richard. *The Principal Navigations Voyages Traffiques and Discoveries of the English Nation.* 12 Vols. Glasgow, 1903. —Volumes II and III contain more than six hundred pages of documentary material more or less directly connected with the commercial relations of England and Russia. Of particular value are the two charters of the Company (II, 304-316 and III, 83-91), the correspondence of the Company with its agents in Russia, and the contemporary accounts of the explorations undertaken by the Company (*passim*).

Tolstoy, George. *The First Forty Years of Intercourse between England and Russia.* St. Petersburg, 1875.—This is a collection of eighty-two documents covering the period from 1553 to 1593 and devoted almost exclusively to diplomatic correspondence. Each document is given in both English and Russian, with the exception of eighteen which, originally in Latin, are printed in Latin and Russian only. Many of the documents included in this volume are not elsewhere accessible in print.

Russia at the Close of the Sixteenth Century. London, 1856. This volume of the Hakluyt Society Publications contains two valuable contemporary works, Dr. Giles Fletcher's *Of the Russe Common Wealth*, and *A Relacion or Memoriall Abstracted owt of Sir Jerom Horsey His Travells*, etc. The five appendices (pp. 267-381) contain valuable contemporary material on the missions of Fletcher and Horsey.

Early Voyages and Travels to Russia and Persia. 2 vols., London, 1886. This volume of the Hakluyt Society Publications, edited by E. Delmar Morgan and C. H. Coote, while chiefly of value for the Persian trade, contains material on the Muscovy Company not easily accessible elsewhere.

Calendars of State Papers, Domestic, Foreign, Venetian and Colonial (East Indies). The Calendars contain numerous references to the Muscovy Company and to Russian relations. Unfortunately most of the references are fragmentary and a few are enigmatical. The originals in the Record Office have in most cases been consulted but have not, as a rule, furnished much additional information. Perhaps special mention should be made of S. P. (Dom.) Addenda Vol. VII, No. 39, which contains a list of the members of the Company in 1555. (See Appendix, pp. 116-120.)

Reports of the Historical Manuscripts Commission. Hatfield House MSS., Rutland MSS., Calvetti Correspondence. Much of the correspondence of both the older and younger Cecil throws an interesting light on the relation of the English government to Russia and to the Muscovy Company. No material of prime importance, however, has been gathered from these sources.

Records of the Court of Husting. Roll 341, No. 29. MS. preserved in Guildhall, London. Interesting as helping to locate Muscovy House.

Wright, Thomas. *Queen Elizabeth and Her Times, A Series of Original Letters, etc.* 2 Vols. London, 1838. Its chief value for our purpose consists in a letter written by William Smith, May 15, 1572, giving a definite picture of Russian conditions and the state of the Company.

The Diary of Henry Machyn, Citizen and Merchant-Taylor of London, from A. D. 1550 to A. D. 1563. London, 1848. (Camden Society). Contains a few interesting notes on the first Russian embassy and makes occasional mention of members of the Muscovy Company.

Wriothesley, Charles. A *Chronicle of England during the Reign of the Tudors.* 2 Vols. London, 1875. Like the above this is chiefly of interest for its incidental description of the embassy of Napea in 1556-7.

English Trading Expeditions Into Asia Under the Authority of the Muscovy Company (1557-1581)

Thesis presented to the Faculty of the Graduate School of the University of Pennsylvania in partial fulfilment of the requirements for the degree of Doctor of Philosophy, 1910.

By EARNEST V. VAUGHN, Ph.D.

CONTENTS

CONTENTS

ENGLISH TRADING EXPEDITIONS INTO ASIA UNDER THE AUTHORITY OF THE MUSCOVY COMPANY (1557-1581)

CHAPTER I

THE SEARCH FOR AN OVERLAND ROUTE TO CATHAY

During the sixteenth century Englishmen were engaged in a search for a route to Cathay that would not conflict with the claims of the Spaniards and the Portuguese. Beginning with the voyage of John Cabot and extending to the establishment of the East India Company, many attempts were made to solve the problem, and though all such attempts previous to the close of the century were destined to fail in their ultimate purpose, they derive great significance from the fact that they really laid the foundations for the commercial and colonial empire of England. The first half of the century was largely a period of discussion and of tentative effort, during which the theory of the northeastern as well as of the northwestern passage was very clearly outlined.[1] But it was not until the second half of the century that England definitely awakened to her opportunities and began to take her place in discovery, exploration, and trade expansion.

The new epoch may be said to have begun for Englishmen when Willoughby and Chancellor set sail, on May 20, 1553, to seek out unknown lands which might serve as an

[1] Robert Thorne, in 1527, suggested sailing northward to the pole and thence southwest or southeast to Cathay. Hakluyt, *Voyages*, II, 161-163, 176-178. A little earlier Paulo Centurione, an Italian, outlined a route overland from Russia, similar to that later followed by the Muscovy Company, except that its terminus was the Baltic instead of the White Sea. Eden, *First Three English Books on America*, 286-7, 308-310. According to Beazley, *The Cabots*, 181, Centurione in 1525 offered his plan to Henry VIII.

outlet for English merchandise.[2] This voyage is of further significance in that it inaugurated a period of remarkable activity in the endeavor to find an independent
northern route to China or India.   In the fifty years following this voyage to the northeast efforts were made in
various directions to reach the coveted markets of the East,
either by sea to the northeast or the northwest, overland
by way of Russia and the countries beyond the Caspian,
or eastward through the Mediterranean and the Levant,
until finally success was achieved along the forbidden route
to the southward which the Portuguese had monopolized
for a century.

The earliest developments, however, followed Richard
Chancellor's arrival in the White Sea, his journey to Moscow, and his friendly reception by Ivan IV.[3] In answer
to a letter of Edward VI addressed to all kings and poten-
tates to the northeast toward the empire of Cathay, Chancellor received from the Czar a promise that English merchants should have freedom of movement and of trade
throughout his realm, and to that end it was suggested
that an ambassador be sent from England to settle all details in regard to these privileges.[4] Apparently this letter of the Czar's, together with Chancellor's reports concerning Russia,[5] made considerable impression in England,
for in the spring of 1555 three factors, Richard Chancellor,
George Killingworth, and Richard Gray sailed for Russia
with letters from Philip and Mary and with instructions
to negotiate with the Czar.[6] Upon the occasion of a third

[2] The motive for the voyage is clearly expressed in Clement
Adams's account and also in Cabot's Ordinances, arts. 20 and 21.
Hakluyt, II, 200-202, 239-240.

[3] Ibid., II, 244-251.

[4] Ibid., II, 209-211, 271-272.

[5] Chancellor's own account is merely a description of Russia.
That of Clement Adams, based on information obtained from Chan-
cellor, gives also an account of the journey. Both are given in
Ibid., II, 224-270.

[6] Ibid., II, 278-281.

voyage the following year, the English merchants sent to their factors detailed instructions as to how the new Russian trade should be conducted.[7] Thus trading relations were established with Russia along the line of a practicable sea route around Norway and Sweden which made the English merchants independent of the Baltic cities.

On February 6, 1555, Queen Mary granted a charter to these "Marchants adventurers for the discoverie of lands, territories, Iles & seigniories unknowen" which gave them the exclusive right to trade with Russia and with all other lands lying to the "Northwards, Northeastwards, or Northwestwards," not heretofore frequented by her subjects.[8] This was the beginning of the well-known Muscovy or Russia Company. Favored by this charter and by a grant of privileges from Ivan IV,[9] this Company devoted itself to the development of its trade to the White Sea and to the interior of the country, and thence beyond the Caspian Sea. Factories were established in various parts of Russia—Kholmogory, Novgorod, Vologda, and Moscow—and a considerable trade resulted which seems to have been to the advantage of both countries concerned, or at least of their governments.

However, the development of the Russian trade was not permitted to obscure the search for a passage towards Cathay. The vague and general terms of the original sailing instructions gave place, upon the second voyage in 1555, to fairly definite suggestions towards the carrying out of this ultimate purpose; the factors sent out to Russia were told to "use all wayes and meanes possible to learne howe men may passe from Russia, either by land or sea to Cathaia, . . . and to what knowledge you

[7] Hakluyt, II, 281-289.
[8] *Ibid.*, II, 308, 315.
[9] *Ibid.*, II, 297-303.

may come, by conferring with the learned or well travailed persons, either naturall or forrein, such as have travailed from the North to the South.''[10]   In the same year, a clause was inserted in the charter of privileges granted by the Czar which gave the English merchants freedom to pass at their pleasure into other countries, either by sea, by land, or by fresh water, thus preparing the way for such an attempt.[11]   The next year the Muscovy Company sent out the *Searchthrift,* under Stephen Burrough, to continue the temporarily delayed search for a sea passage to the northeast. Departing from Gravesend, April 29, 1556, Burrough rounded North Cape and passed beyond the Pechora as far as the island of Waigatz; but he was prevented from renewing his explorations in the following spring.[12]   Though by no means lost sight of in the succeeding years, it was not until the Pet and Jackman expedition, in 1580, that the northeastern passage was again attempted.

With the year 1557 the interests of the Muscovy Company turned more strongly to the interior of Russia, and especially to the alternative overland route through that country to the East. Presumably the factors, according to their instructions, had made inquiries concerning the possibilities of such a route, and the result is to be seen in the fact that Anthony Jenkinson was now placed in charge of the ships for Russia, with a further commission to undertake the search for an overland route to Cathay. To that end the Company wrote to their factors in Russia to furnish him with the men, money, and supplies, that he should regard as necessary for the undertaking.[13]   The choice of the English merchants was an excellent one, as

[10] Hakluyt, II, 285.
[11] *Ibid.,* II, 299.
[12] *Ibid.,* II, 322-344, 363.
[13] *Ibid.,* II, 390. There seems to be no evidence that Jenkinson deserves the credit of originating the plan.

Jenkinson was an admirable type of the Englishman of the period, bold, indefatigable, ready for any adventure; in the course of his varied career in the service of the Muscovy Company he was to prove himself equally able as explorer, merchant, and diplomat.[14] The inauguration of this plan marks the beginning of those expeditions into Asia under the authority of the Muscovy Company which are to form the subject matter of this and the following chapters.

Departing from Gravesend with four ships, on May 12, 1557, Jenkinson reached St. Nicholas on July 13, and from thence proceeded to Moscow, where he was well received by the Czar. He tarried there during the winter, and then in the following spring petitioned Ivan IV for a royal license to depart on his mission beyond the Caspian Sea. Not only was this permission granted, but in addition the Czar graciously gave "his letters under his great seale, unto all princes through whose dominions master Jenkinson should have occasion to passe, that he might the sooner and quietlier passe by meanes thereof."[15] As this overland voyage of Jenkinson was a deliberate attempt to solve the great problem of a route to Cathay by combining the new sea-route around the North Cape and the river systems of Russia with the northernmost of the mediæval trade routes from East to West, it was an undertaking of considerable magnitude as well as of great interest.

At this time the situation in Russia was very favorable to such an undertaking on account of her recent conquests towards the east and south. Following the liberation from the Tartar yoke towards the close of the fifteenth century, Ivan the Great had done much to consolidate the kingdom

[14] He had had considerable previous experience as a traveler. At Aleppo, in 1553, he had obtained from the Sultan a trading privilege. Hakluyt, III, 195, V; 109-110.

[15] Ibid., II, 436. Jenkinson's own briefer account of the journey to Moscow and his reception there is given, Ibid., II, 413-421.

and to put down internal dissensions. His policy was con-
tinned by his son, Vassili III, and by his grandson, Ivan
IV, known in history as Ivan the Terrible. In 1552 the
latter conquered Kazan, an important Tartar fortress on
the Volga, and two years later the capture of Astrakhan
near the mouth of that river extended the power of Russia
to the Caspian Sea.[16] Thus, not only did the Volga become a Russian river but also communication with Persia
and other lands beyond the Caspian was made comparatively safe and easy. These developments, therefore, were
of the greatest advantage to Jenkinson and to the Muscovy
Company.

On April 23, 1558, Jenkinson left Moscow, accompanied
by Richard and Robert Johnson and also a Tartar interpreter.[17] He proceeded by way of the rivers Moscow
and Oka to Nijni Novgorod and from there down the
Volga to Astrakhan, which he reached by July 14. His
description of the journey down the Volga includes an
account of the Krim and Nogay Tartars, who, thanks to
the Russian conquests, were held somewhat under control. Astrakhan, however, was the outpost of the Russian
authority to the southeast; consequently for the rest of
his journey the traveler had to depend largely upon his
own tact and resources. Though it was a mart town for
Russian, Tartar and Persian merchants, Astrakhan does
not seem to have impressed Jenkinson very favorably, as
he expressed the opinion that its trade was hardly worth
following.[18]

After some delay in order to provide and equip a boat

16 Howorth, *History of the Mongols*, II, 355-357, 422; Rambaud,
History of Russia, I, 252-256. Jenkinson, in Hakluyt, II, 451, 454,
seems to have the dates wrong.

17 Jenkinson's account of the expedition, sent to the merchants
of the Muscovy Company upon his return, is given in *Ibid.*, II,
449-479, and is the basis of the following pages.

18 *Ibid.*, II, 456.

for the next stage of the journey, Jenkinson and his companions, in company with certain Tartars and Persians, embarked at Astrakhan on August 6, and successfully overcoming the dangers of navigation at the mouth of the Volga they entered the Caspian Sea four days later, the first Englishmen perhaps to sail upon its waters. Turning northward after leaving the Volga, the course followed the coast-line somewhat closely as they sailed around the northern end of the Caspian Sea and down its eastern coast as far as the port of Mangishlak, which evidently was a point of departure for caravans to the eastward. On account of a storm, however, it was necessary to land at a less desirable haven on Koshak bay just opposite Mangishlak. Here on September 3 Jenkinson disembarked, and he and his company were "gently intertained of the Prince, and of his people," that is, presumably by the Turkomans of that region.

It was with these people that arrangements had to be made regarding camels and provisions for the caravan journey through Turkestan. In fact, before a landing was made, negotiations had been begun for camels to carry the merchandise of the travelers to Vezir, a twenty days' journey from Mangishlak,[19] and the messengers had returned with encouraging words and fair promises in all things. However, Jenkinson was really at their mercy and before his departure he "founde them to bee very badde and brutish people, for they ceased not dayly to molest us, either by fighting, stealing or begging, raysing the prise of horse and camels, and victuals double, that the wont was there to bee, and forced us to buy the water that wee did drinke: which caused us to hasten away, and to conclude with them as well for the hier of camels, as for

[19] Twenty-five days from their landing place. Hakluyt, II, 459, 461.

the price of such as wee bought, with other provision, according to their owne demaunde.''[20]

On September 14 a caravan of one thousand camels set out from this place.[21] Several days later, upon reaching the country of Mangishlak, it was waylaid by certain armed Tartars in the name of their master, Timur Sultan, the governor of that region, whereupon the wares were opened and those things that were wanted were taken without any pretense of payment. Evidently the ruler of Mangishlak did not intend to lose his tribute because the caravan started elsewhere. Unlike the other merchants, Jenkinson was not willing. to submit to such treatment, and so· he presented himself before Timur Sultan to protest most vigorously against being robbed and to request the Sultan's favor and passport while traveling through his country. The request was granted, but Jenkinson was able to recover only a part of his loss.[22] He says, however, that if he had not thus sought out the ruler he would probably have been killed and his merchandise seized, as he understood that commands had been given to that effeet. After answering the many questions of the Sultan and giving his reasons for coming into that region, Jenkinson was permitted to depart and rejoined the caravan. Now began the long march through the Turkoman country, during which the travelers suffered greatly for water and were driven by necessity to kill some of the horses and camels for food. October 3, they came to ''a gulphe ot the Caspian sea,'' probably Lake Sarikamish, where they

[20] For each camel's weight, four hundred pounds, they gave three Russian hides and four wooden dishes, besides various gifts. Hakluyt, II, 459.

[21] There is no reason for saying all these camels were Jenkinson's, as Tolstoy, p. XIV, Howorth, *Mongols*, II, 972, and others do. There were forty travelers in the caravan, while on his second expedition Jenkinson had only forty-five camels and a few horses. Hakluyt, II, 467, III, 21.

[22] *Ibid.*, II, 460.

found fresh water and paid toll to the Turkoman king.[23] Four days later they arrived at Vezir, the dwelling place of Hadjim Khan, the king, and three of his brothers.[24] Here the usual procedure took place; Jenkinson presented his gift to the Khan and delivered the Czar's letters, whereupon he was permitted to dine in the royal presence. In a second audience on the following day the Khan asked concerning the affairs of England and Russia, and then at his departure gave him letters of safe conduct.

When Urgendj was reached, on October 16, it was again necessary to pay custom, this time for each person as well as for the camels and horses. While Jenkinson was there Ali Sultan, brother of Hadjim Khan, returned from a campaign in Khorassan, thus affording a glimpse of the almost continual warfare that existed between the Persians and the Tartar chieftains to the north.[25] Once more the Czar's letters were presented, the usual questions were asked, and the all important letter of safe conduct was granted. Though it was a walled town, Urgendj was then in a state of decay, due perhaps to the recent period of civil strife which had driven most of the merchants from the place, while those remaining were so poor that Jenkinson was able to sell them only a few kersies.[26] The chief commodities sold there were such as came from Bokhara or Persia, and of these he says the quantity was small.

After remaining at Urgendj for nearly six weeks the

[23] Hakluyt, II, 461; post 136, note 27, and authorities there cited.

[24] "All the land from the Caspian sea to this Citie of Urgence is called the lande of Turkeman, & is subject to the said Azim Can, and his brethren which be five in number." Hakluyt, II, 463. See also Howorth, *Mongols*, II, 886.

[25] Jenkinson says the town of "Corozan," but there seems to be no such place. Anthony Jenkinson and other Englishmen, *Early Voyages and Travels*, I, 70, note 3. For the raids see Howorth, *Mongols*, II, 888.

[26] "It hath bene wonne and lost 4. times within 7. yeeres by civill warres." Hakluyt, II, 463.

caravan proceeded eastward along the Kunia Daria for a hundred miles, crossed the Amu Daria,[27] and on December 7 arrived at Kait, a city under the authority of still another brother of Hadjim Khan. This Sultan, it seems, had designs upon the Christians in the caravan, but fear of his brother at Urgendj kept him from carrying them out. It is quite characteristic, however, that the councilor who imparted this information "willed us," as Jenkinson says, to make the Sultan a present, which he took and delivered to his master. That was not the only payment expected, for at this place the merchants paid as custom one red hide of Russia for each camel, besides petty gifts to the officials.[28]

Shortly after the departure of the caravan from Kait an event occurred which throws the strongest possible light upon the dangers of travel among the wild and predatory tribes of Turkestan. The whole region seems to have been infested with bands of robbers, but the stretch of desert country from Kait to Bokhara was the worst that Jenkinson had to traverse in the course of his long journey. On the night of December 10 four horsemen were taken as spies, from whom it was ultimately learned that three days' journey ahead there was a band of forty men lying in wait for the caravan, and that they themselves were of that company. The Sultan thereupon furnished a guard of eighty soldiers to accompany the caravan. On the third day these soldiers, after scouting for a time, came running back, declaring that they had found traces of the robbers and that a meeting with them was imminent. So they at once "asked us what we would give them to conduct us further, or els they would returne. To whom we offered

[27] It hardly seems necessary here to give the arguments on the vexed questions of Aralo-Caspian geography. For Jenkinson's connection therewith see Hakluyt, II, 461, 465; Howorth, *Mongols*, II, 972-977; Huntington, *The Pulse of Asia*, 347-350.

[28] Hakluyt. II, 465.

as we thought good, but they refused our offer, and would have more, and so we not agreeing they departed from us, and went backe to their Soltane, who (as wee conjectured) was privie to the conspiracie.''[29]

Within three hours after the departure of the soldiers, horsemen were seen approaching and the travelers, forty in number, drew together for defense. The fight that ensued lasted nearly all day, with losses on both sides, and had it not been for four hand guns used by Jenkinson and his company the robbers would have been successful. As it was, a truce was agreed on until the following morning. During the night a parley was held, in which the leader of the robbers demanded the surrender of the Christians in the caravan, promising that the rest might depart in peace, but this proposition was rejected. When morning came, however, neither side wished to risk a renewal of the conflict, and so an agreement was reached, by the terms of which the thieves were to withdraw after receiving a specified amount of plunder, together with a camel to carry it away.[30] Thus the struggle was ended satisfactorily; but the fear of this and of other bands of robbers followed the travelers to the end of their journey.

Finally, on December 23, the caravan entered Bokhara, a large, walled city in Bactria, commercially important because its central location made it a meeting place for the merchants of the East and of the West for the interchange of their wares. It had been just eight months since Jenkinson and his companions set out from Moscow and four months and a half since they entered the Caspian Sea; and later Jenkinson estimated that the remainder of the journey to Cathay would have occupied nine months more.[31] Three days after his arrival Jenkinson dined with

[29] Hakluyt, II, 466.
[30] Soldiers sent out from Bokhara later broke up the band and recovered part of the goods. *I*bid., II, 471-472.
[31] *Ibid.*, II, 473.

Abdullah Khan, the ruler of Bokhara, and presented to
him the letters of the Czar of Russia. On various occasions the Khan sent for him to discuss the power of the
Czar and of the Great Turk, as well as other subjects.
However, their relations were not in all respects so satisfactory, as Jenkinson wrote that "before my departure
he shewed himself a very Tartar; for he went to the warres
owing me money."[32] It became necessary for him to remit
part of the debt and to take wares in payment of the rest.

During the three months and a half that he was at
Bokhara, Jenkinson had ample opportunity to study the
commercial situation in detail. Apparently local conditions were not very favorable to trade, although one of
the quarters into which the city was divided was set apart
for merchants and markets. The revenues of the Khan
were small and depended largely upon his impositions
on trade: he is said to have taken the tenth penny in all
sales made within the city, either by craftsmen or merchants, to the great impoverishment of the people; also
when in need of money he sent his officers to the shops
to seize the wares of the merchants, as was done to pay
Jenkinson for some kersies. Besides he seems to have
manipulated the coinage to his own advantage.

Every year great numbers of merchants resorted to Bokhara, traveling thither from India, Persia, Balkh, Russia,
and various other countries, and also from Cathay until the
closing of the passage shortly before Jenkinson's arrival.
To the Englishman these merchants seemed beggarly and
poor and the wares they brought small in quantity, while
often two or three years were necessary to dispose of
them. It is not surprising, therefore, that he regarded
the trade as hardly worth following.[33] However that may
have been, there are certain features of the trade centering

[32] Hakluyt, II, 471.
[33] Ibid., II, 470-473.

in Bokhara that undoubtedly had an important bearing upon Jenkinson's mission into central Asia. For one thing the existence of commercial relations with Russia seems to show how fully Jenkinson had been proceeding along well-known and established lines of trade. Furthermore, it is clear that Bokhara was not a promising market for English cloths; the Persian merchants themselves brought thither various sorts of cloth, part of which at least they obtained at Aleppo or through the Turkish merchants, while the merchants from India refused to barter their commodities for Jenkinson's kersies. Besides, it was seen that the latter did not bring to Bokhara any gold, silver, precious stones, or spices, as all such trade now passed by way of the sea, the markets being under Portuguese control. But the most discouraging fact of all was the knowledge that for three years the passage to the eastward had been closed on account of wars in the region of Tashkend and Kashgar, thus not only shutting off the commodities that usually came from Cathay but also making it impossible for Jenkinson to continue his quest for an overland route to that country, which was the primary reason for undertaking his journey.[34] Under these conditions, therefore, Jenkinson and his companions had to content themselves with collecting at Bokhara what information they could in regard to Cathay and the various routes by which it might be reached.[35]

In the spring, when the caravans began to depart and when it seemed probable that Bokhara would be besieged as a result of the renewal of the war with Khorassan, Jenkinson determined that it was time to set out on the return journey. At first he thought of returning by way

[34] Hakluyt, II, 473; *Early Voyages and Travels*, I, 107-108.

[35] As Jenkinson reserved his discussion of Cathay until his return his opinions are not definitely known. His companion, Richard Johnson, collected information concerning the various routes to Cathay. Hakluyt, II, 474, 480-482.

of Persia in order to investigate its commercial possibilities more thoroughly than he had been able to do at Astrakhan and Bokhara. But for various reasons he was unable to carry out this plan, among them being the closing of the routes in that direction by the renewal of the war with the Shah and the action of the "metropolitan" of Bokhara in seizing the letters of safe conduct the Czar had given him, without which, he says, he could not have traveled in any safety. Furthermore, he had become convinced that the wares he had received in barter or in lieu of money due him were not suitable for the Persian trade.[36] Thus it became necessary to return by the same route that he had come.

On March 8, 1559, the return journey was begun, in company with a caravan numbering six hundred camels.[37] In due time Urgendj and Vezir were reached: near the former the caravan fortunately escaped a large band of rovers who were lying in wait for its return, at the latter the preparations were made for the final stage of the journey to the Caspian Sea. The voyage by sea to Astrakhan lasted from April 23 to May 28 on account of storms and other difficulties. After a long, monotonous trip, by water to Murom, thence by land, Jenkinson early in September appeared before the Czar at Moscow, presented to him several ambassadors who had been sent to Russia under his care from the rulers of Bokhara, Balkh, and Urgendj,[38] and answered his various questions touching the countries that had been visited. The following February he went to Vologda, remained there until the

36 Hakluyt, II, 474.

37 This calls for the same comment as ante, p. 134, note 21. The statement in *R. H. S. Trans.*, VII, 69, that he returned with six hundred camel loads of Oriental merchandise may be given as a further example of such statements.

38 This is significant as a recognition of Russian influence. However, Jenkinson was probably mistaken in regarding it as the first of such embassies. *Early Voyages and Travels*, I, 94, note 2.

opening of navigation, and then proceeded to Kholmogory to await the embarkation for England.

Such is the history of Jenkinson's attempt, under authority of the Muscovy Company, to solve by a direct overland route from Russia the problem of reaching the markets of Cathay. Though he failed in his endeavor to open such a route, his actual achievement is such as to entitle him to a high place in the list of Elizabethan explorers. The first of his nation to penetrate into Asia, he had traveled through a dangerous and little known region as far as Bokhara, and had explored and described the Volga and eastern and southeastern Russia, the northern portion of the Caspian Sea, and the various Tartar kingdoms eastward as far as Bactria. In a word, he had added much to the geographical knowledge of his time.[39] However, he was always mindful of the interests of the English merchants, and thus was especially concerned with the possibilities of trade in the different countries he entered. Though his conclusions were not very flattering, still they do not seem to have discouraged further activity beyond the borders of Russia, as his return was followed by a succession of voyages into Asia for purposes of trade. The only reference to the immediate pecuniary results of the undertaking is Jenkinson's statement that, in spite of dangers, losses, expenses, and disappointments, he had brought back merchandise sufficient "to answere the principall with profite." [40]

[39] A full discussion of Jenkinson's services to geography may be found in *Early Voyages and Travels*, introd. pp. CXIII-CXLVIII. The map attributed to him is given opp. p. CXX.

[40] *Ibid.*, I, 108.

CHAPTER II

THE ESTABLISHMENT OF TRADING RELATIONS WITH PERSIA

As the voyage of Richard Chancellor laid the foundation for the English trade with Russia, so that of Anthony Jenkinson over the Caspian Sea pointed out the way from Russia to the countries of western Asia and determined the direction of all further efforts of the Muscovy Company in that region. It was evident, as a result of the journey to Bokhara, that a route overland to Cathay was not only dangerous and difficult but under existing conditions actually impossible, and so, probably upon Jenkinson's advice, the activities of the English merchants were turned towards Persia. As has been pointed out, Jenkinson had made inquiries concerning the Persian trade and perhaps at both Astrakhan and Bokhara had come in contact with the merchants from that country, and, when he found further progress eastward effectually blocked, he had for a time thought of going there. Also, upon his return to Moscow he definitely expressed the belief that the regions adjacent to the Caspian Sea offered a good field for the activities of the Company.[1] Thus in 1561, the year following his arrival in England, the Muscovy Company determined to attempt the establishment of trading relations in the region suggested by him.

There were at this time several advantages to be derived from the development of the Persian trade. In the first place, the fact that the best silk producing provinces, Shirvan, Ghilan, and Mazanderan, were in northern Persia, in immediate proximity to the Caspian Sea and thus easily accessible from Russia, promised to the English merchants

[1] *Early Voyages and Travels*, I, 108.

an advantage over the Portuguese whose harbors for the exportation of that valuable commodity were several hundred miles distant from the source of supply. In the second place, the advantage of such trading relations was enhanced by the ever-present possibility of war between Turkey and Persia, the two rival Mohammedan states, and of the consequent closing of the usual lines by which European wares reached the latter. And finally, with Persia as a new base of operations, it was hoped that the English merchants might push on by caravan towards the Persian Gulf and India and thus divert the much-desired products of the south from the Portuguese to the Russo-Caspian route. As Ormuz was so much nearer than Cathay, the advantages of this plan over the previous one were very evident. That such an overland route towards India now became an ultimate aim of the Muscovy Company will clearly appear in the course of the narrative of the successive expeditions from Astrakhan southward over the Caspian Sea.

During the period from 1561 to 1581 there were six of these "voyages" or expeditions sent out by the English merchants and the Persian trade was prosecuted with courage and perseverance in the face of the most serious difficulties and discouragements. It is believed that these expeditions are worthy of being better known, especially as they illustrate so well the exploring and commercial activities of the age, and it is the purpose of this and the following chapters to describe them as clearly as possible, though primarily from the economic rather than from the geographical point of view.

As was most fitting, Anthony Jenkinson, now in the service of the Queen as well as of the Muscovy Company,[2] was commissioned to carry out the new project. Once more Elizabeth wrote to the Czar in his behalf, requesting

[2] Hakluyt, III, 5.

for him freedom and safe conduct in passing through the Russian dominions. She also made request that the Czar commend Jenkinson to other foreign princes and especially "to the Great Sophie, and Emperor of Persia, into whose Empire and Jurisdictions, the same our servant purposeth with his for to journey chiefly for triall of forreine merchandizes."[3] At the same time Elizabeth sent a letter to the Shah, in which she announced Jenkinson's purpose, assured him that the enterprise was grounded only upon the honest intent of establishing trade with his subjects and with other strangers trading in his realm, and requested that he give passports and protection to the traveler for himself, his servants, and his merchandise, so that he might go about freely in the Persian dominions. She concluded with the hope that, if friendly relations were established between them, these small beginnings would lead to great results, to the honor as well as to the profit of both kingdoms.[4]

The instructions[5] issued by the Muscovy Company furnish an excellent view of the preparations, the necessary procedure, and the purposes of the expedition. According to these instructions, Jenkinson was to proceed to Russia, present the Company's gift and the Queen's letters to the Czar, and then make request for license and safe conduct to pass to and from Persia, or other lands, with whatever merchandise he desired to carry with him. Furthermore, if considered advisable by Jenkinson and the factors in Russia, an agreement was to be made with the Czar concerning the payment of a certain amount of duty upon all goods thus passing through Russia, in order better to secure the imperial favor. This did not prove necessary, however, as the same object was served by the Czar's pe-

3 Hakluyt, III, 5.
4 Ibid., III, 7-8.
5 Ibid., III, 9-14.

cuniary interest in the voyage. Freedom of passage once obtained, Jenkinson should select such servants and apprentices of the Company as he desired for the expedition, and these were to be strictly subject to his orders.

The wares proposed for the Persian market were not the same as those intended for Russia. To the latter country the Company sent cloth of gold, plate, pearls, sapphires, and other jewels, and these, even if not disposed of to advantage in Russia, were not to be taken to Persia, at least to any great value. In addition to these, however, there were placed on the ships eighty fardels, containing four hundred kersies, packed for the Persian trade, though it was considered desirable, if the market were favorable, to dispose of part of these in Russia, as the market in Persia or neighboring lands was as yet quite uncertain. Also Jenkinson was to take from Russia such kersies and other cloths as seemed to him suitable for Persia, and furthermore any desirable Russian commodities were to be provided for him by the agents of the Company.

When Persia was reached, Jenkinson's instructions required that he should proceed to the Shah's court to procure letters of privilege which would serve as a basis for the future development of trade in that country. It was desired that this grant should include permission to the factors of the Muscovy Company to pass with their merchandise through Persia into India or adjacent countries, and in like manner to return.

There are two characteristics of these instructions that are worthy of special mention. In the first place, they gave to Jenkinson great power and discretion in the selection of wares and of servants, in the choice of routes, in the disposal of merchandise, and in other matters, thus showing a wise dependence upon the judgment of an experienced and trusted agent. In the second place, the instructions reflect some uncertainty in regard to the passage into Persia and the possibilities of the trade there. Thus, on the question of the passage, it is provided that, in case the journey proved impossible the following summer, Jenkinson should try to dispose of the kersies and other wares in Russia and then employ himself in the search for a passage around Nova Zembla,[6] or else return to England. If the Russian market should prove to be poor and a passage to Persia in 1563 should seem to be reasonably sure, then he was to wait for a year and proceed to Persia as planned. If both alternatives failed, he was then to carry his wares to Constantinople or wherever the market appeared most promising.

On May 14, 1561, Jenkinson embarked at Gravesend, just two months later he reached St. Nicholas, and by August 20 he was in Moscow.[7] It was only after some delay and considerable dispute that he was permitted to present in person his letters to the Czar, and then his request concerning passage into Persia was denied.[8] He disposed of the greater part of the wares intended for Persia and was on the point of returning to England when the intervention of Osep Napea[9] secured for him a reconsideration, with the result that he received not only free-

[6] They also suggested that Richard Johnson be employed in the same direction: "because the Russes say that in travelling Eastwardes from Colmogro thirty or forty dayes journey, there is the maine sea to be found, we thinke that Richard Johnson might employ his time that way by land, and to be at Mosco time enough to goe with you into Persia." Hakluyt, III, 14.

[7] This is the eighth of the voyages to Russia under the auspices of the English merchants. Ibid., III, 9.

[8] The ostensible reason for refusal was a proposed military expedition to Circassia, but Jenkinson suspected other motives. Ibid., III, 17.

[9] In 1557 Osep Napea had been Russian ambassador to England and had returned with Jenkinson on the latter's first voyage. For an interesting account of his reception in England, see Ibid., II, 354-357. See also Machin, Diary, 127, 130, 132, and Acts of Privy Council, (1556-8), 27, 52, 55-57.

dom of passage and letters of commendation to foreign princes but also certain commissions from the Czar himself. Again preparing for the expedition, he departed from Moscow on April 27, 1562, in company with the ambassador of Persia.[10] Upon reaching Astrakhan, the ship for the Caspian voyage was prepared, and on July 15 Jenkinson and his company set sail, for a time under convoy of two Russian brigantines as a protection against pirates. This time the course was to the southward along the western shore of the Caspian. Successful in surmounting the usual dangers of navigation, shoals, storms, and robbers, Jenkinson landed at Derbend, an important port and frontier fortress of the Persians. The final landing place, however, was at Shabran, midway between Derbend and Baku, which was reached two days later. Here the ship was unloaded and the preparations made for the inland journey, during the course of which the governor at Shabran showed his friendliness to Jenkinson by appointing a guard of forty armed men for his protection against rovers. On August 12 word came from the ruler of Shirvan that Jenkinson should be permitted to proceed on the journey to Shemakha. He reached that place August 18, and two days later was admitted to the presence of Abdullah Khan at his court twenty miles outside the city, being there well received and invited to dine in the royal presence.[11]

During the dinner Abdullah Khan questioned him concerning his country and religion, the relative power of the Emperor, the Czar, and the Great Turk, and various other things, and then demanded to know the cause of his com-

[10] Jenkinson's account of the expedition, including the voyage from England to Moscow, is given in Hakluyt, III, 15-38, or in *Early Voyages and Travels*, I, 121-156. The latter gives in the notes a few instances of different readings in the *MSS.* in the Hatfield and the Helmingham Hall collections.

[11] Hakluyt, III, 21-22. To dine in the royal presence was a mark of favor, both in Russia and Asia. Various other instances might be given, as *Ibid.*, II, 227-229, II, 420, 421, III, 47, etc.

ing and his ultimate destination, all of which he apparently answered to the Khan's satisfaction. In the end he was promised not only freedom of passage but also a bodyguard to conduct him to the Shah at Kazvin, a thirty days' journey distant. Before dismissing Jenkinson the Khan showed him further favors, the most important of which was freedom from custom for all of his merchandise.[12] Thus, the beginning of the Persian venture was all that Jenkinson could desire, and his success seemed to promise well for a favorable reception from the Shah.

While at Shemakha Jenkinson outlined the arguments by which he hoped to win the favor of the Persian ruler. That these arguments were based squarely upon the idea of common hostility to the Turks is clearly shown by the following statement of the case. The English, not being friendly with the Turks, are not permitted to pass through Turkish territory into Persia, while the Venetians, in league with them and enjoying certain privileges, are able through them to supply the Shah's dominions with English goods. If it should please the Shah to grant to the English merchants privileges similar to those granted by the Turks to the Venetians, a great and profitable trade would in all probability result; the Persians would be supplied with the English commodities and also have a market for their own products, '' although there never came Turke into the land.''[13] Abdullah Khan, it is said, was so well pleased with the policy thus outlined that he wrote to the Shah

[12] Hakluyt, III, 22.

[13] Ibid., III, 28. It is hardly necessary to point out that Jenkinson's argument does not accurately represent the situation. Venice had made peace with the Turks in 1540, and for the next thirty years tried to avoid warfare as a means of self-protection. Soon after 1566 the Turks began to plan the capture of Cyprus, which was actually taken in 1571. Thus, though the two countries were at peace at the time Jenkinson went to Persia, the Turk was nevertheless the greatest enemy of the Venetians. Brown, Venice, 362-371.

in regard to it, and at the same time he assured Jenkinson that his request would meet with a satisfactory answer. .

The province of Shirvan, which was destined for the next few years to be so closely connected with the activities of the Muscovy Company in western Asia, was ruled over by Abdullah Khan, though in subordination to the Shah of Persia. It is described as being in a state of decline, due largely to its subjection and to the many wars fought between the Turks and Persians for its possession. Shemakha, though still the most important town, was much decayed, while Arrash was becoming a wealthy trading center and the chief mart for raw silk, being resorted to by Turkish, Syrian, Russian, and other foreign merchants. The most important commodities of Shirvan were gall nuts, cotton, alum, and especially raw silk, and, in addition, small quantities of drugs, spices, and other products, brought thither from India.[14]

After providing camels, horses, and other necessaries for his journey, Jenkinson on October 16 left Shemakha to seek the Persian ruler. His route to Kazvin was by way of Jevat and Ardebil and thence for ten days through the Elburz mountains. Upon his arrival, November 2, 1562, he was given lodgings near the royal palace and in due time was entertained by a son of Abdullah Khan at the command of the Shah. However, his request for an opportunity to present Elizabeth's letter met with the response that great affairs were in hand and that he must wait until they were finished, though in the meantime he could get his present ready for the Shah.

The "great affaires" proved to be negotiations between the Sultan and the Shah for a permanent peace, the Turkish ambassador having reached Kazvin four days before Jenkinson's arrival, and shortly thereafter the peace was duly sworn to,[15] a result that had disastrous conse-

[14] Hakluyt, III, 24.
[15] Ibid., III, 27, 28; Malcolm, History of Persia, I, 332. ·

quences for the English mission to Persia. For one thing
it was a serious obstacle to the further presentation of the
arguments given at Shemakha. Moreover, the Turkish
merchants in Persia at once began to insist that Jenkinson's arrival was inimical to their trade and consequently
they demanded that the Shah should refuse to show him
any favor, apparently making this question a test of the
new treaty of friendship and alliance.[16] Evidently the
Turkish merchants saw that their exclusive control of the
northern outlets of the Persian trade was threatened by
the English movement through Russia.

When, on November 20, Jenkinson was finally admitted
to an audience with the Shah,[17] the result of the hostile
influences at the court was very clearly shown. Following Jenkinson's presentation of his gifts and letters and
the statement of the object of his mission to Persia the
usual questioning began, in the course of which the Shah
finally turned to the question of religion and demanded
of him whether he was an unbeliever or a Mussulman.
Upon his admission that he was a Christian, the Shah
repudiated all thought of friendship with a confessed unbeliever, and so commanded him to depart from his presence. Thus matters stood for a time. Finally, it was
decided that Jenkinson should neither be received with
friendliness nor dismissed with favor; inasmuch as he was
a ''Frank'' and of a nation hostile to the Turks, it was
feared that any other treatment might displease the Sultan
and lead to the breaking of the lately concluded peace.
Furthermore, it seemed to the Shah that there was no ad-

---

16 Hakluyt, III, 29, 31.

17 Eden, *History of Travayle*, 323, 324, says it was Abdullah Khan's
influence alone that obtained even this much attention. It was
argued that Christians were mortal enemies of the Turks and Persians and their religion. Abdullah Khan himself stated that both
the merchants and the holy men (?) were opposed to Jenkinson.
Hakluyt, III, 33.

vantage in friendship with unbelievers whose country was so far away, and that the best thing to do was to send Jenkinson to the Great Turk as a present.[18] Fortunately for Jenkinson, however, his friend Abdullah Khan interfered in his behalf, with the result that on March 30, 1563, he was permitted to withdraw from Kazvin in safety.

Thus it was brought home to the sanguine pioneer of trade that the difficulties with which he must contend were much more numerous and varied than merely those of a physical and economic nature. Religion, political affiliations, the complications of distant international alliances, the exigencies of war and the intrigues of rival merchants, all entered into the intricate problem and made more difficult its solution.

On the return journey from Kazvin to Shemakha Jenkinson met Abdullah Khan at Jevat and received from him letters of safe conduct and a grant of privileges for the English merchants, together with other marks of that ruler's favor. While delayed at Shemakha to provide camels for the journey to the sea, he sent men on before to repair the ship and have it in readiness. Also he sent his companion, Edward Clark, to Arrash, with a commission to proceed from there into Georgia for the purpose of establishing trading relations with that country. When Clark was approaching the Georgian frontier, however, the discovery that he was a Christian threatened to prevent the success of the undertaking, and so he returned to Shemakha.[19] Jenkinson arrived at Astrakhan with his merchandise on May 30, and at Moscow nearly three months later, where he spent the following winter, that of 1563-1564.

In accordance with the Czar's command, all the merchandise from Persia was taken to the imperial treasury

[18] Hakluyt, III, 31.
[19] Ibid., III, 34.

to be opened. Fortunately those wares purchased under commission from the Czar, that is, precious stones and wrought silks of various sorts and colors, proved satisfactory to him. Those belonging to the Company, coarse linens, raw silks, and other merchandise, were either stored in their warehouse in Moscow or sent to England. As the Czar seemed especially well pleased with Jenkinson's conduct of "the princes affaires" that had been committed to his charge, the latter took advantage of the situation to ask in behalf of the Company for a new and fuller grant of privileges, which was immediately promised and later obtained under his Majesty's seal.[20] During the winter, also, Jenkinson organized a second expedition for Persia to be sent out under another representative of the Company the following spring. On June 28, 1564, he himself left Moscow, and on September 28 reached London after an absence of nearly three years and a half.[21]

On the whole, this second voyage of Jenkinson must be regarded, like the first, as failing in its purpose, for the two main objects of his mission, the establishment of a trade with Persia and of a route to India, had not been accomplished and apparently their attainment had been made improbable by the treaty between the Shah and the Sultan. There are some indications, however, that at heart the former was favorably disposed towards Jenkinson and the English merchants. Aside from the open and ef-

[20] Hakluyt, III, 33, 37. There seems to be no further record of any such privileges, though Jenkinson here speaks of two copies being made.

[21] Arthur Edwards, Jenkinson's chief successor, thus wrote to the Company regarding him: "Master Anthonie Jenkinson hath deserved great commendation at all your worships hands; for the good report of his well and wise doings in those parts [Persia], was oftentimes a comfort to me to heare thereof, and some good help to me in my proceedings." *Ibid.*, III, 63. The grants of the Czar and Shah in 1567 show that Jenkinson shortly became a member of the Company. *Ibid.*, III, 64, 93.

fective friendship of Abdullah Khan, reference may be made to the fact that after Jenkinson's dismissal from Kazvin orders had come from the Shah to entertain him well, and further to Jenkinson's belief that the Shah himself intended to receive him favorably and would have done so except for the conclusion of the treaty.[22] The conditions surely were not as discouraging to the Company as they seem to a later student, for the next year another agent of the Muscovy Company made the journey to Kazvin on a similar mission.

The voyage itself, however, was by no means a complete failure. For one thing Jenkinson brought back a much fuller knowledge of the lands to the south of the Caspian Sea and of the political and commercial conditions prevailing there. It was something, also, that Ivan IV was favorably disposed to the undertaking and even committed to it through his interest in its results. Then, too, in spite of unfavorable conditions, considerable merchandise had been brought back from Persia, though it is impossible to say whether or not the expedition proved financially profitable. But after all, although the English merchants had not received permission to enter Persia itself they had obtained from Abdullah Khan, a valuable grant of privileges for trade in the province of Shirvan, as a result of which they were assured of an excellent starting point for future expeditions. This grant of privileges, obtained April 14, 1563, is brief though comprehensive.[23] It gave to the "companie of merchants Adventurers of the Citie of London" the following privileges: license and safe conduct to trade in Shirvan with both the Persian and the foreign merchants, freedom from the payment of custom on any wares bought or sold in that country, and finally, assurance that, if any of their wares were taken for the

[22] Hakluyt, III, 33.
[23] *Ibid.*, III, 39, 40.

Khan's treasury, the treasurer would pay full value for them, either in ready money or in raw silk.

As a result of these privileges, therefore, the expedition organized by Jenkinson upon his return to Moscow was enabled to set out with certain definite advantages over the preceding one. For this second Persian "voyage" Thomas Alcock, George Wren, and Richard Cheinie, were appointed as factors, the first named being placed in charge.[24] Starting from Jaroslav, May 10, 1564,[25] they arrived at Astrakhan on July 24 and at Shemakha on August 12. Abdullah Khan received them with the same friendliness that he had shown to Anthony Jenkinson. At Shemakha Alcock sold some of his merchandise and then, on October 20, proceeded to Kazvin, leaving Cheinie to collect the various sums due for the wares. The latter, however, was unable to recover very many of these debts, and so Alcock, upon his return, made earnest suit at court for their recovery. But Abdullah Khan was displeased because of the murder of a Mohammedan by a foreign merchant and there seemed no hope of any favor from him. Hearing that the Russians were sending their goods to the seashore for fear that the Shah should hear of the murder, Alcock ordered Cheinie to take charge of the goods brought from Kazvin to Shemakha, while he remained at court. Three days later the news reached Shemakha that Alcock had been killed on his way to that

[24] They were chosen by Jenkinson and Thomas Glover, the agent of the Muscovy Company in Russia. Hakluyt, III, 37, 38, 40. The account of the voyage was written by Richard Cheinie, though later than 1565, as the reference to Richard Johnson, *Ibid.*, III, 43, proves. Strangely enough this and the later voyages have all been attributed to Jenkinson's own leadership by various writers from Anderson, *History of Commerce*, II, 105, to Cawston and Keane, *Early Chartered Companies*, 36.

[25] Cheinie, as quoted by Hakluyt, says 1563, but there is little doubt that 1564 is correct. See Jenkinson's statement, Hakluyt, III, 37-38.

place.[26]   Being now responsible for the safety of the merchandise, Cheinie immediately followed the example of the Russian traders by sending his merchandise to the sea and thence to Russia, while he remained at Shemakha for six weeks in an endeavor to collect the debts due him, in which he was only partly successful.

Though impressed with the possibilities of the Persian trade and recommending that it be followed up,[27] Cheinie felt called upon to criticize certain abuses that revealed themselves in the conduct of the expedition. For one thing he complained because information in regard to the preparations for the journey was withheld from him; also he was unable to tell what stock the Company had, as " the bookes were kept so privilie that a man could never see them."   But his greatest indignation was reserved for the practice of private trading, by means of which, as he claims, others reaped the fruit of his labor.   Thomas Glover had in the venture over a hundred roubles, Thomas Pette fifty roubles, Richard Johnson twenty roubles, and a certain Tartar seventy roubles, all of whom got their returns before Cheinie got back from Persia. Besides, the Czar was interested in the voyage; though it is not known how much money he furnished, Cheinie expresses the opinion that he received double, and perhaps treble, on his investment. It is his opinion also that neither Ivan IV nor the private traders paid any part of the expense of the expedition.[28] From these statements, therefore, it is clear that the Persian venture was not exempt from the quarreling and the private trading that proved to be the bane of the Muscovy

[26] The reason for his murder is not known. According to Arthur Edwards, some thought it due to a debtor he was pressing for payment, others attributed it to robbers. Later the Company apparently without foundation, attributed it to quarreling with the people. Hakluyt, III, 49; *Early Voyages and Travels*, II, 216, 217.

[27] Hakluyt, III, 43.

[28] *Ibid.*, III, 40, 42, 43.

Company in Russia as well as of most of the other early commercial companies in the various countries with which they traded.

In the spring of 1565, under the direction of Thomas Glover, preparations were under way for a third expedition, whether the result of a now settled policy on the part of the Company or due to the favorable reports of Richard Cheinie there seem to be no indications. Edward Clark was first chosen as the agent for Persia, but upon his death Richard Johnson, a much less satisfactory man, was appointed to the place, and with him were associated Alexander Kitchin and Arthur Edwards.[29] At Jaroslav, the starting point, wares were collected from Vologda and Moscow, and other necessary preparations were made. A small bark of thirty tons burden had been built at that place for the voyage on the Volga and the Caspian Sea; it was built after the English fashion, but proved to be too small for the purposes of the Persian trade.[30]

The three factors, leaving Jaroslav on May 15, 1565, and Astrakhan on July 30, reached the desired port in Shirvan, August 23, where they anchored their bark in a small river and secured camels for the journey to Shemakha. Upon reaching that place, on September 11, they met with an even more friendly reception from Abdullah Khan than the last year. They were given a house for their use, and were told to put all their requests in writing so that he might further understand their desires.[31] But unfortunately Abdullah Khan died on October 2, 1565; by his death, not only did the English merchants lose a good friend but also the province of Shirvan was thrown

[29] Hakluyt, III, 44-46. In letters to the Company Arthur Edwards gives an account of the expedition. Four of these letters are printed in Hakluyt's collection, while two others, dated June 24 and 29, are lacking, judging from the statement, *Ibid.*, III, 61.

[30] *Ibid.*, III, 45.

[31] *Ibid.*, III, 47.

into great confusion. This situation explains why it was impossible, at least for a time, to collect the debts due the Muscovy Company, and also why the trade did not prove as profitable as was expected. To add to the misfortunes of the expedition, Alexander Kitchin died on October 3; and previous to that the loss of one of the three mariners had also severely crippled the undertaking.

It was the hope of the factors, however, that they might obtain privileges from the Shah, which, once granted to them, would enable them quietly and without hindrance to develop a considerable trade in raw silks, spices, drugs, and other commodities. Some influential though not disinterested Persian friends having agreed to help Richard Johnson obtain the privileges and collect the debts, he ordered Arthur Edwards to go with them to Kazvin upon this double mission. On April 26, 1566, the latter set out for the Persian capital. His reception was in striking contrast to that of Jenkinson several years before: the Shah received him most graciously, granted him a long conference in which various topics bearing on trade were discussed, and, having heard his requests, promised the desired letters of privilege. In addition, the Persian ruler made known his desire that the English merchants should send him various sorts of cloths. After the conference Edwards hastened to put his requests in writing so that they would be ready to submit at the next audience with the Shah. Thus, on June 29, he received a formal grant of privileges "sealed and firmed with the Shaugh's owne hand," with the promise that if it was not satisfactory it would be amended.[32] As a result of these marks of the Shah's favor, the position of Edwards and of the English merchants in Persia seemed greatly improved; and in his letter to the Company, written upon his return to Shemakha, Edwards said, "I doubt not but we shall live here

[32] Hakluyt, III, 56.

from hence foorth in quietnes, for now in all places where
I come I am friendly used with the best.''[33]

That the grant of privileges gave important trading advantages to the English merchants is clearly shown by an
enumeration of its provisions.   In the first place, it was
decreed that they should have freedom of passage to and
from Persia and neighboring countries, that they should
enjoy the right to buy and sell all sorts of wares and to
trade with both foreign and native merchants, and that
they should not be required to pay any toll or customs
duties upon their merchandise.   In the second place, they
were promised protection from the officials, justice regarding the recovery of debts due them, immunity from the
arbitrary seizure of their goods, exemption from liability
for the misdeeds of individual merchants or servants, freedom from the annoyance due to the repudiation of bar-
gains once made, and aid when needed in the landing of
their wares.[34]

Probably the explanation of the changed attitude of the
Shah towards the English merchants is to be found in his
relations with the Turks.   It is evident that he was much
interested in the crushing defeat suffered by the Turkish
army at Malta in the preceding year.[35]   Also it is very
probable that the treaty of peace with the Sultan had
not been successful in maintaining friendly relations between the two powers, as it is reported that the year before
Edwards came to Kazvin the Turkish ambassador ''did
put the Shaugh in despaire, saying that the Turke would
not permit any cloth to be brought into his Countrey.''[36]
In addition to his resentment at this action, the Shah

[33] Hakluyt, III, 56.
[34] These privileges, given in Edwards' letter from Astrakhan,
June 16, 1567, were to be followed by further grants on the formal
demand of the Company. *Ibid.*, III, 56, 64, 65.
[35] *Ibid.*, III, 54, 143.
[36] *Ibid.*, III, 57.

would be inclined to welcome the English merchants as a means to offset any possible loss of merchandise through the closing of the customary route.

However, the favor shown the English merchants did not by any means end the troubles of their factors in carrying on the Persian trade. For one thing, as the succession in Shirvan was still unsettled, the disorder became such that men feared to travel on account of robbers. In the face of this confusion, also, the Shah's grant of privileges does not seem to have greatly facilitated the collection of debts at Shemakha; nor, in fact, did it suffice to prevent the recurrence of similar difficulties at Kazvin, as is amply shown by Edwards' own experience.[37] Furthermore, in their relations with each other the factors were not at all harmonious, the trouble apparently being due either to the inefficiency of Richard Johnson or to his neglect of his duties. The bills of debt that Johnson left with Edwards were very carelessly made out, two of them being without either the amounts or the names of the parties, while others, made payable to Johnson only, could not have been collected at all by Edwards had not the charter of privileges provided for such cases. In other respects Edwards found fault with Johnson's conduct of affairs; he claimed that the latter, contrary to the intentions of the Company, had kept him in ignorance of certain details regarding both the preparations for the voyage. and the wares bought and sold in Persia; he urged upon the Company the necessity of employing in Persia only servants who were honest and free from vice and who were able to govern themselves.[38] The following year the Muscovy Company upheld these various contentions of Edwards. They criticized Johnson's action in withholding information and suggested that orders be given that all

[37] Hakluyt, III, 59-61.
[38] Ibid., III, 45, 52, 59, 60.

factors sent to Persia should have access to the accounts and reckonings; and they expressed surprise that he should have been chosen as chief, as his own letters and report were sufficient to prove his unfitness for the charge.[39]

Arthur Edwards, like Anthony Jenkinson, labored earnestly in behalf of the interests of the Muscovy Company, studying the commercial possibilities of different regions, reporting in some detail upon the commodities most desirable for the Persian trade, and pointing out possible improvements in trading methods. He was very optimistic concerning the prospects at Shemakha, and expressed the wish that the Company had a market for the half of the merchandise there obtainable. After his favorable reception at Kazvin his enthusiasm naturally became greater and his views of the Persian trade were considerably expanded, the Shah apparently exerting himself to make the situation seem as attractive as possible.[40] In carrying out this prospective trade he thought it possible to shorten the time required to send merchandise from Persia to England. To that end he suggested that by early sales and a prompt collection of the silk that commodity might be sent to Astrakhan by April 1, and from thence to Kholmogory in time to be loaded on the ships along with the wares sent from Russia.[41] Perhaps here, as in other matters, Edwards was over-sanguine.

Both Richard Cheinie and Arthur Edwards recommended the establishment of trading relations with Ghilan, a province on the southwestern coast of the Caspian, with which so far the English merchants had not come in contact. The former pointed out its commercial possibilities,

[39] *Early Voyages and Travels*, II, 218, 219.
[40] For instance, the Shah asked Edwards if he was able to furnish yearly one hundred thousand pieces of cloth. Also the latter sent home a long list of wares desired by him, but it is somewhat doubtful whether he took them ultimately. Hakluyt, III, 56, 66, 67, 140.
[41] *Ibid.*, III, 62.

its nearness to the Persian capital, and its advantage as a base for the advance towards Ormuz. In addition to these advantages, the latter suggested its situation in the very heart of the Persian trade and also its direct communication with Astrakhan. As a result of a conference at Kazvin with an ambassador from Ghilan, Edwards believed that at small expense trading privileges could be obtained in that province. But more than that, his conclusion seems to have been that Ghilan should be made the center of English activities.[42]

It is evident from the account of the third Persian expedition that in several respects it marks an important stage in the development of the plans of the Muscovy Company. Not only were the English merchants re-established in Shirvan, following Cheinie's enforced withdrawal, but also the task undertaken by Jenkinson now seemed accomplished through the successful negotiation of a grant of privileges at Kazvin. Though too optimistic in his expectations Arthur Edwards might reasonably feel that he had laid the foundations for the Persian trade and that the Company would profit greatly by his labors. Once established in Persia the next step, namely, the opening of a route to Ormuz and India might well seem to be only a matter of time. As far as Persia is concerned, therefore, the affairs of the Muscovy Company, by 1566, promised well for the future success of the English trade.

[42] Hakluyt, III, 43, 51, 61, 62.

CHAPTER III

While the factors of the Muscovy Company were laying the foundations for trade in Persia, there were certain developments in England and Russia which had an important bearing on that undertaking as well as on the position of the Company itself. In the history of the Company, the year 1566 is marked by two noteworthy events: first, the grant of privileges by the Shah which seemed to put the Persian trade on a reasonably firm footing and, second, the obtaining of an act of Parliament reincorporating the group of English merchants and adding to their privileges. As the Shah's grant has already been considered, it remains only to notice the new act of incorporation and the circumstances leading to its passage.

It seems that the demands of the trade in Russia and the development of the overland route through Persia proved to be a severe strain upon the resources of the Muscovy Company, especially as a greater number of ships were needed to keep pace with their activities. As a consequence it was desired to make a considerable increase in the stock, but on account of discouragment due to private trading through Narva the Adventurers could not be persuaded to make this increase. Therefore, on November 20, 1564, a petition was presented to the Council requesting that William Bond and all other private traders be restrained from trading within the Russian dominions, and the following month the Council made an order to that effect.[1] In the following year the profitable

[1] *Cal. S. P. Dom.*, 1547-1580, p. 246; *Acts of Privy Council*, 1558-1570, under date of Dec. 14 and 16, 1564.

trade enjoyed by the Company through Narva was being further affected by such straggling merchants, and so the request was made that that port be definitely included within the sphere of the Muscovy Company in order to prevent "the like pedlarlike kinde of dealing ever after." [2]

To a considerable degree at least the Parliamentary act of incorporation, passed on December 17, 1566,[3] was an answer to the demands for the restraint of private trading in Russia. After reviewing the earlier history of the Muscovy Company, its expenses and losses, and its achievements, the act declared for one thing that the official title of the Company was too long, and also that certain subjects of England, contrary to letters patent, had been trading in the Russian dominions, to the great injury of the trade of the fellowship. In regard to the first point, it was enacted that henceforth the Company should be known only by the name of "the fellowship of English merchants, for discovery of new trades," and that as such it should exercise its corporate functions.[4] Concerning the second point, the act provided that no lands unknown or unfrequented by Englishmen before the first Russian voyage, either in Russia or the "countries of Armenia major or minor Media, Hyrcania, Persia, or the Caspian sea," should be open to the trade of English subjects, unless by the consent of the said fellowship of English merchants.[5] Private traders with ventures in the forbidden region were given until 1568 to withdraw. Thus, in form at least, the monopoly of the Muscovy Company was duly asserted.[6]

[2] Wheeler, *Treatise of Commerce*, 55. Narva became Russian in 1558, and remained under Ivan's control until 1581.

[3] D'Ewes, *Journal*, 133. *Statutes of the Realm*, IV, part 1, p. 483, shows that it was merely a private bill. The Act is printed, Hakluyt, III, 83-91.

[4] *Ibid.*, III, 87.

[5] *Ibid.*, III, 88.

[6] See Gerson, *The Organization and Early History of the Muscovy*

Meanwhile, Anthony Jenkinson was again in Russia in the service of the English merchants in order to meet other dangers that threatened their privileged commercial position. Two years previously, Raphael Barbarini, an Italian, had received from Queen Elizabeth letters commending him to the Czar. He was well received and shown much favor, and in 1565 he obtained trading privileges in Russia. Consequently the Muscovy Company felt it necessary to attempt his overthrow. In addition to this task Jenkinson was instructed to request the Czar to confirm the monopoly of the Company by excluding all foreign merchants except the English from the trade to the White Sea.[7] In both respects he seems to have been very successful; Barbarini withdrew from Russia, and a provision for the exclusive control of the northern trade was included in the new grant of privileges obtained by Jenkinson in the following year.[8]

This new and fuller grant of privileges, signed by the Czar on September 22, 1567, contains a passage which definitely outlined and extended the privileges actually enjoyed by the English traders in the prosecution of the Persian trade. It was provided that, if the English merchants desired to pass from Astrakhan to Bokhara, Shemakha, or elsewhere, the Russian officials should permit them to do so, without delay, without payment of custom, and without opening their goods, even when they did not have the Czar's merchandise with them.[9]

As a result of the various grants of privileges obtained by them, the Muscovy Company, by 1567, occupied a much

Company, for a strong statement of the view that Narva really was included in their sphere under the terms of the original charter.

[7] Tolstoy, *England and Russia*, Nos. 6-8; Hamel, *England and Russia*, 170-176, and appendices K to R; *Early Voyages and Travels*, II, 183-186.

[8] Hakluyt, III, 97.

[9] *Ibid.*, III, 94, 95.

stronger position than heretofore. According to the **Parliamentary** charter of incorporation the members of the Company were upheld in their monopoly of the Russian and Persian trade as far as Englishmen were concerned; according to the Czar's grant of privileges they were confirmed in their exclusive use of the northern ports of Russia, not only against other Englishmen but against all other foreigners as well, and, in addition, they were formally given the right of passage through Russia to Persia and other countries; and finally, through the privileges secured from Abdullah Khan and later from the Shah himself, they seemed prepared to develop a trade in Persia and to open the way to India.

That the English merchants were strongly interested in Persia and India at this time is well shown by the instructions sent out to their agents in Russia a few months after the granting of the second act of incorporation. These instructions [10] are somewhat detailed and cover a wide range; it is sufficient, however, to note that they seem to imply an attempt to reorganize and strengthen the management of affairs in both Russia and Persia and to do away with many abuses that had revealed themselves therein as well as to direct the usual operations of the trade. In regard both to Persia and Russia it was ordered that a just statement of weights and measures be sent home for purposes of comparison with those of England, that a uniformity of apparel be prescribed for the servants of the Company in order to put an end to their extravagance in dress, that all Englishmen in their service be advised against giving offense in regard to any question of religion or government, that wares delivered to servants for apparel or to strangers for gifts be truly valued and charged to the proper account, that private traffic be prevented, especially between Russia and Persia,

[10] *Early Voyages and Travels*, II, 206-227.

that as soon as possible the factors send to the Company a
statement concerning the value and location of the property and goods then in Russia and a similar statement concerning the wares belonging to the Persian account, and
that thereafter an annual report be rendered for the Persian trade. In regard to the Persian voyage it was
further ordered that all the factors should have access to
the accounts and reckonings, both for the avoidance of
false dealing and for the gaining of experience, and that
each year a true report of the trade should be sent to the
Company. Still other provisions had as their object the
greater safety of the Persian route; charts were to be
made of the Volga and the Caspian Sea and written reports were to be made both in regard to the outward and
the homeward voyages so that by comparison from year to
year the dangers of navigation might be lessened.[11]

It is further shown by the instructions that the Muscovy
Company were already planning two Persian expeditions
for the following year, one of them to start from England
and the other from Russia. In regard to the latter the
Company expressed the wish that Arthur Edwards, who
had been recalled from Persia, should be retained as the
chief factor for that country, though the matter was left
to the discretion of the Russian agents.[12] It was also desired by the English merchants that this expedition should
pay considerable attention to the development of a trade
in drugs and spices. When they obtained their charter
from Parliament the merchants had taken upon themselves
the obligation to furnish those commodities to England,

[11] Articles 15, 23, 28, 32, 38, 41, 46, 57, 58, and 60. In the
middle of the eighteenth century Englishmen actually did considerable work in charting the route in connection with an attempted
revival of the Persian trade. See, for example, the chart of the
Caspian and the description and map of the Volga, given in Hanway, *Historical Account of the British Trade over the Caspian Sea*,
1, 87, 93-95.

[12] Articles 16, 51.

and consequently they exhorted their factors to use all care and diligence in furthering such a trade.[13] As a means to that end they adopted two recommendations made by Edwards during the preceding voyage: they proposed to enter into negotiations with the ruler of Ghilan in the hope of obtaining the desired commodities as well as a grant of trading privileges for that province; they also suggested a journey to Ormuz to investigate its trade and to attempt the establishment of commercial relations with its merchants. For the latter purpose John Sparke was designated as a suitable man on account of his ability to speak Portuguese.[14]

The Persian expedition of 1568 was organized at Jaroslav and placed in charge of Arthur Edwards, as the English merchants had requested, with John Sparke, Lawrence Chapman, Christopher Faucet, and Richard Pringle, as his associates.[15] Leaving Jaroslav in July, they reached Bilbil on August 14. At this place, contrary to the Shah's grant, the people were unwilling to aid in unloading the merchandise; also they began their customary practices of extortion when they saw the travelers at their mercy. Upon reaching Shemakha, the Englishmen found there no opportunities of trade on account of their late arrival, and because of their delay for a month other merchants, who had left Russia later, were able to get the advantage of them elsewhere. Finally it was decided that the factors should separate for the better sale of the goods; consequently Edwards, Sparke, and Chapman went to Kazvin with the greater part of the merchandise, while Faucet and Pringle were left behind with the rest, which

[13] Article 52.

[14] Articles 54, 55, 63.

[15] Lawrence Chapman, in his letter of April 28, 1569, gives an account of the earlier part of the voyage. This is supplemented by Edwards' account as given in the notes of Richard Willes in Eden, *History of Travayle*. Both are printed in Hakluyt, III, 136-149.

was intended for the market at Shemakha and Arrash.

At Ardebil Edwards was able to do some trading. As the important commercial city of Tabriz was not far distant, Chapman was sent to make trial of the market there. He found that his kersies would not bring a good price, as the cloth trade was well supplied by Armenian, Turkish, and native merchants. However, he succeeded in bartering the kersies for spices, a transaction which he thought to be a fairly good bargain, especially in view of the closing of Ormuz by war and the strong desire of the Company for such commodities. As for drugs, he says that he found an abundance at Tabriz, but that they were very high and not as good as those brought to England from other places. While there Chapman also made an excellent sale of one hundred pieces of cloth to a merchant representing the ruler of Georgia, who not only offered payment in money or silk upon their delivery but also held out the prospect of trading privileges in that country similar to those enjoyed in Persia. Chapman sent his interpreter to Shemakha to see to the carrying out of this agreement, but unfortunately the merchant repudiated the bargain without any regard to that provision of the Shah's grant of privileges which forbade such practices.[16]

After joining Edwards at Kazvin, Chapman was sent to Ghilan to look for a good harbor and also to determine what commodities would be best for the proposed trade in that region. He visited Lahijan, the chief town, Langerud, and Rudisser, and reported that that portion of the province had recently been overrun and despoiled by the Shah, so that the people were not able to buy a single kersey. However, his statements regarding the abundance of alum and raw silk amply confirmed the earlier reports about the resources of Ghilan.[17]

[16] Hakluyt, III, 138, 139.
[17] Ibid., III, 141.

The further plan of the Company to send a factor to Ormuz was not carried out. Though John Sparke presumably was sent out especially with that purpose in view, and though Chapman announced his purpose of going there as soon as the way was open,[18] there seems to be no record of any such attempt. Probably the fact that Ormuz was closed during the whole period of this expedition is at least a partial explanation of the failure to take this important step in advance.

Meanwhile Arthur Edwards presented himself before the Shah at Kazvin with a request for further privileges for the English merchants. The latter demanded of him what sort of merchandise he could furnish, whereupon Edwards claimed to be able to supply him directly from England with all the wares that came to his country from there indirectly by way of Venice, Aleppo, and Tripoli, namely, kersies, broadcloths, and other kinds of cloth.[19] Furthermore, he declared that, if given freedom of passage and such other privileges as were deemed necessary, he would furnish all such merchandise, and other commodities as well, more cheaply and with less delay than they were now furnished through the Venetian and Turkish route. The Shah, it is said, was well pleased at this, and shortly afterwards he granted to Edwards a second letter of privileges, " all written in Azure and gold letters, and delivered unto the lord keeper of the Sophie his great seale," later to be sealed and turned over to Lawrence Chapman.[20]

This grant of privileges was mainly concerned with various details of the Persian trade, being clearly intended as a supplement to the grant originally received from the Shah. The first article gave specific authorization to the

[18] Hakluyt, III, 142.
[19] Ibid., III, 144.
[20] Ibid., III, 146-147; Eden, History of Travayle, 334-335.

plan of the English merchants of developing trade with Ghilan. Then there followed provisions regarding Persian assistance in case of shipwreck, the custody and delivery of the merchandise upon the death of any of the English traders, the right to procure without hindrance such camel men as were desired, the prohibition of extortion by the Persians and the responsibility of the owners of camels for their contracts and for the merchandise committed to their care, the privilege of a guard for protection when traveling was considered dangerous, the duty of all Persian subjects in the towns along the highway to furnish the merchants with "honest roume and vitails for their money," and, finally, the privilege of buying or building houses for their own use wherever desirable. It is very probable also that there was a provision designed to protect the Company against dishonest servants who hoped to avoid punishment or restitution of goods by becoming Mohammedans, though such an article is not to be found in the formal list of privileges as printed.[21]

In concluding the account of the fourth voyage it seems worth while to compare the views of Arthur Edwards and Lawrence Chapman in regard to the commercial possibilities in Persia. The latter missed no opportunity to point out that Edwards had greatly exaggerated the advantages of the Persian markets, and furthermore, he indulged in considerable criticism of the latter's management of the present venture. He called attention to the reported failure to sell the goods left at Shemakha, to the overstocked condition of the market at Tabriz, to the secret enmity of the Turkish merchants and the methods by which they sought to hinder the English trade, to the failure of the Shah to take off Edwards' hands the merchandise he had

---

[21] Eden, *History of Travayle*, 334; Hakluyt, III, 145. For further explanation of the practice itself, see *Ibid.*, III, 148, or Eden, 335.

ordered on the previous visit to Kazvin, and to the great disadvantages of travel, the scarcity and execrable quality of the water, and the danger of robbery or murder at the hands of the people. ''Better it is, therefore, in mine opinion, to continue a begger in England during life than to remaine a rich merchant seven yeeres in this countrey, as some shall well finde at theyr comming hither.''[22] Yet after all Chapman seems to admit that the trade in time would greatly improve.

On the other hand Edwards seems to be as enthusiastic as he was on the previous expedition. His account was given after the return to England, while that of Chapman was written in the midst of the undertaking, and therefore it may be that the ultimate results of the venture were much more favorable than for a while seemed probable, though at the same time it is undeniable that the attitude of the two factors was fundamentally different. In addition to the further privileges obtained from the Shah, it is reported that in return for his wares Edwards brought from Persia all sorts of raw and wrought silks, carpets, spices, drugs, pearls and other precious stones, and various other kinds of rich merchandise. Unfortunately, however, there is no hint as to whether the expedition was financially a success. It is further reported that Edwards in his enthusiasm thought the Persian trade would prove greater than the Portuguese trade to the East Indies. He argued that the return might be made to England each year, whereas the Portuguese voyage took two years; consequently the merchandise of India could be carried more advantageously by way of Persia and Russia than by way of the Cape of Good Hope.[23] This

[22] Hakluyt, III, 141.

[23] Ibid., III, 147, 148. Somewhat similar views were held by Michael Lok, London Agent of the Muscovy Company, and by Bannister and Duckett. Russia at Close of Sixteenth Century, introd. XII-XIV; Early Voyages and Travels, II, 260. For an even more

is practically the same argument that he had already used in regard to the Levantine trade.

While Edwards and his associates were seeking for trade in Persia the situation in Russia was rapidly becoming critical for the Muscovy Company and consequently for the proposed expedition from England to Persia. There were two main sources of trouble, namely, the difficulties arising out of the trade at Narva and the insistence of the Czar upon an offensive and defensive alliance with Elizabeth, and out of these questions grew the necessity for the Randolph mission and the request for a new grant of privileges for the Russian and the Persian trade.

Of most importance perhaps was the diplomatic situation. Upon his return to England in 1567, Jenkinson brought a secret message from the Czar to the Queen which seems to have been the beginning of the trouble. Offering perpetual friendship to Elizabeth, the Czar asked that she join him in an offensive and defensive alliance against all enemies, and especially against Sigismund II, King of Poland. He also requested that she send him sailors and shipwrights and that she permit him to export from England various sorts of military supplies. And furthermore, he demanded the giving of assurances that either of them would grant refuge and protection to the other in case misfortune should make such exile necessary. Finally he required that the Queen's answer be given by the middle of the following year.[24]

About the time of the Czar's secret message the affairs of the Muscovy Company were reaching a crisis on account of the developments at Narva. Though by 1567 the Company had established a considerable trade at that place,[25]

extravagant statement regarding both Persia and Cathay see *Cal. Cecil MSS.*, No. 1119.

[24] *Early Voyages and Travels*, II, 236-238.
[25] *Ibid.*, II, 218.

it seems to have been very unfortunate in its choice of factors, as the latter not only engaged in trade on their own account but also joined with outside English traders and with certain other foreigners, to the great injury of the White Sea trade.[26] Thomas Glover, one of these irregular traders, was especially troublesome because of his refusal to render an accounting for the period during which he had been in charge of the affairs of the Company in Russia.[27] To make matters much more serious Glover and his associates were upheld by Ivan IV and received from him special privileges of trade in his dominions.[28] At the solicitation of the now thoroughly alarmed Company Elizabeth dispatched messengers to the Czar demanding the seizure of these dishonest factors, but the Czar, dissatisfied at the subordination of his political schemes to commercial questions, had the messengers seized and detained at Narva.[29]

Though Elizabeth was not interested in an alliance with the Czar, she was much concerned about the fortunes of her merchants in Russia, and consequently the attitude of the Russian ruler forced her to meet the embarrassing situation created by the proposal of alliance and mutual asylum. Therefore, it was determined to send Thomas Randolph, an experienced and able diplomatist, to ward off the threatened danger. Randolph's instructions required him to temporize regarding the question of asylum and to avoid committing himself to any very definite propositions of alliance. On the other hand he was informed that the only possible treaty relation with Russia was that of a grant of privileges for the English merchants and that

[26] Tolstoy, introd. XX-XXII; *Early Voyages and Travels*, II, 284.

[27] *Ibid.*, II, 278.

[28] Post, 174, note 32, and 202, note 10.

[29] Letter of Elizabeth (Sept. 16, 1568), Hamel, *England and Russia*, 189, 190, appen. U. and W.; *Early Voyages and Travels*, II, 281, 282.

this was the special reason for sending him to Moscow. In the proposed negotiations two members of the Muscovy Company, Thomas Bannister and Geoffrey Duckett, were associated with him, and in all commercial matters he was to be guided by the instructions they received from the Company.[30]

Upon their arrival at Moscow late in September, 1568, Randolph, Bannister, and Duckett, were not left in doubt regarding the Czar's displeasure; none of their countrymen were permitted to meet them, and for over four months they were kept practically as prisoners in their lodgings. Finally, on February 20, 1569, Randolph was summoned before the Czar to deliver his message. Except for a secret conference a few days later there was a further wait of six weeks, and then he found the Czar ready to accede to his requests. On June 20 a new charter of privileges was signed by Ivan IV, whereupon Randolph departed for England, accompanied by Andrew Saviena, who was sent to confirm the grant of privileges and to continue the negotiations with Elizabeth.[31]

The new grant was a confirmation and extension of the rights previously enjoyed by the Company. The monopoly of the northern ports was upheld, all Englishmen save members of the Company were forbidden to trade at Narva, though the merchants of all other nations were to be freely admitted to that port as before, and finally the privileges of trade granted to Glover, Rutter, and others, were to be revoked.[32] The privilege of passage through Russia to Asia was again stated and was now declared to belong to the English merchants exclusively, their only obligations being to take the Czar's merchandise with

[30] *Early Voyages and Travels*, II, 241, 242.

[31] Randolph's own account is in Hakluyt, III, 102-108. See also *Early Voyages and Travels*, II, 277, 278, 283, 284.

[32] Hakluyt, III, 109, 116-118; *Early Voyages and Travels*, II, 283.

them to Persia and on their return to bring their wares
first to his treasury.[33]   The Czar further agreed that the
Persian expedition now under way should not only have
freedom of passage but also letters from him bespeaking
the favor of the Shah, and that whenever the Company
desired to send out an expedition to seek Cathay it would
be granted permission to repair to Russia to make all
necessary preparations.[34]

In addition to aiding Randolph in these negotiations,
Bannister and Duckett had been chosen by the merchants
as their factors for the Persian voyage. As they had
necessarily to await the outcome of the negotiations with
the Czar before carrying out the second part of their
instructions, it was not until July 3, 1569, that they left
Jaroslav for Persia.[35]   They were accompanied by Lionel
Plumtree and twelve other Englishmen, together with
forty Russians that they had employed. About forty
miles above Astrakhan they were attacked by a large band
of Nogay Tartars, but after a fierce two hours' struggle
they were able to drive off their enemies, though their own
losses were very heavy. Consequently it was necessary to
remain for a time at Astrakhan for the recovery of the
wounded as well as for the equipment of their vessel; and
before they were ready to depart a large army of Tartars
and Turks besieged that place. According to Bannister's
statement the Englishmen were compelled to unload their
goods, sink their ship, and do their part towards the defense of the town.[36]   Apparently finding the place stronger

[33] Hakluyt, III, 109, 110, 117.

[34] Among special grants, under date of July 10. *Ibid.*, III,
118, 119; *Early Voyages and Travels*, II, 275.

[35] The account of this expedition given in Hakluyt, III, 150-157,
is well supplemented by a number of letters of Bannister and Duckett.
These have not been printed but fortunately they are fully abstracted
in the *Calendar of State Papers.*

[36] For details of these misfortunes see Bannister to Cecil, *Cal. S.
P. For.*, 1570, pp. 221, 222.

than had been anticipated and fearing an attack by the Russian army, the besiegers withdrew in confusion and with great loss.[37]   It was not until the middle of October that the factors were able to continue their journey to Bilbil and thence to Shemakha, where the whole company spent the winter.

Proceeding to Ardebil the following spring, the two factors separated.   Being unable to travel on account of sickness, Duckett with half of the men and part of the merchandise remained at Ardebil for five or six months. He not only found the place torn by internal dissensions but also rather unsatisfactory from a commercial standpoint.   Upon leaving Ardebil he seems to have spent the next two years and a half at Tabriz.[38]

Meanwhile, in answer to a summons to the English merchants from the Shah, Bannister had proceeded to Kazvin, where for a time he met with considerable trouble and opposition in the prosecution of his suit for trading privileges.   He complains of the evil behavior of the servants of the Company and of their great enmity to himself; he points out that he also had as enemies all who had purchased goods from him, as by keeping him from the Shah they hoped to avoid making payment; and finally, he states that he was compelled to meet the opposition of the Armenian and other merchants who traded between Aleppo and Persia.   Becoming convinced that it would be useless to appeal to the Shah or to his advisers, Bannister made earnest suit to Hyder Mirza, a younger son of the Persian ruler whom the latter had designated as his successor, and fortunately he was able to win the favor of that prince. As a result he was shortly summoned to the court and permitted to deliver the Queen's letters and messages, and all of his requests with a single exception were granted

[37] Hakluyt, III, 150, 151; Rambaud, *Russia*, I, 268.
[38] Hakluyt, III, 151-153.

and embodied in letters of privilege.[39] For one thing a letter was issued to Hyder Mirza which authorized him to dispense justice in all cases where the English merchants were concerned. Also it was agreed that one of the Shah's servants should be licensed each year to collect all debts due the merchants anywhere in the Persian dominions. Furthermore, a formal grant of trading privileges was given by the Shah to his "greatest and best merchants," which declared that they might trade at their will and pleasure throughout his dominions. To this general statement of privilege there were attached several articles providing for the further regulation of the trade in that country. In addition to these grants the Shah further showed his good will towards Bannister by purchasing considerable merchandise from him and what is more to the point, paying him ready money for the same.

Bannister had also made request for permission "to transport and carie through his dominions certaine horses into India," but the Shah, it is said, "seemed loth to yeeld thereunto, and yet did not altogether denie it, but refused it to some further time." [40] This is interesting as the first definite attempt to carry out the instructions of the Company in regard to such an overland route, and its success would have meant the completion of the plans originally outlined by Jenkinson in connection with the first Persian voyage. As nothing more was done, it is very probable that the Shah was opposed to the undertaking, especially in view of the attitude taken towards a somewhat similar movement to the eastward in the following year. Lionel Plumtree, persuaded he says by certain men from Bokhara, made preparations for a journey to Cathay, and when everything was ready he secretly joined a caravan.

[39] Bannister to Cecil, *Cal. S. P. For.*, 1571, pp. 439, 440; *Cal. S. P., East Indies*, I, 89; Hakluyt, III, 152.
[40] *Cal. S. P. For.*, 1571, p. 439; Hakluyt, III, 152.

But after a six days' journey he was overtaken and brought back by horsemen sent after him by one of the Shah's lieutenants. According to Plumtree's account, he was not permitted "to passe on so perillous and dangerous a journey for feare of divers inconveniences that might follow." [41]

On November 9, 1570, Bannister departed from Kazvin, accompanied by a "sergeant of arms" sent by the Shah for the apprehension of the debtors of the English merchants. Escaping a band of robbers that was lying in wait for him, he rejoined Duckett at Tabriz, succeeded in collecting the debts owing him, and then proceeded to Shemakha to see to the transportation of his merchandise for England. At the same time he prepared for the Company the required statements regarding his sales and the goods remaining in his hands.

It seems to have been the intention of Bannister and Duckett to return from Persia in the spring of 1571, but at that time and again in 1572 this was made impossible by the acute situation that had arisen in Russia out of the further demands of the Czar for an alliance with Elizabeth.[42] The Persian as well as the Russian trade was thrown into great confusion and even demoralization; the ship intended for Persia was detained, merchandise from that country was seized and held at Astrakhan and Kazan, and certain wares belonging to the Company were taken outright by the Czar's officials.[43] Confronted by this sit-

[41] Hakluyt, III, 153, 154. The horsemen were procured by Humphrey Greensell; probably the Englishmen feared the Shah's displeasure, as Plumtree seems to suggest.

[42] Cal. S. P., East Indies, I, 8, 10.

[43] Hakluyt, III, 181, 182, 190. The utter demoralization of arrangements at Astrakhan is best shown by a letter of William Smith, who had been sent to meet Bannister and Duckett in 1571. The writer was very frank in his criticisms of the trade and of Company's service. Wright, Queen Elizabeth and Her Times, I, 416-420. See also Cal. S. P., East Indies, I, No. 19. Queen Elizabeth

nation, Bannister determined to occupy himself further in trade, and to that end he went to Arrash in order to purchase raw silk. The stay at that place proved disastrous to the expedition, as Bannister, Lawrence Chapman, and three other Englishmen fell victims to the unwholesome climate. As two others were robbed and slain, the loss was seven persons in the course of five weeks.[44] Without delay Duckett took steps to get control of the merchandise at Arrash, which had been at once seized and sealed by the Shah's officials, but it was only after a long journey to Kazvin for letters from the Shah to the ruler of Shemakha that he succeeded in obtaining possession of the goods. If this had not been done, the merchandise would have fallen into the hands of the Shah, according to the custom of the country.

As a result of negotiations between Elizabeth and the Czar, the way was opened in the spring of 1572 for the return of Duckett and his associates, but too late for them to take advantage of it before the following year, thus still further prolonging the Persian voyage. After his return from Kazvin to Shemakha, therefore, Duckett made a journey to Kashan, an important commercial town of the interior of Persia, frequented by the merchants of India. Remaining there for two months and a half, he brought some spices and a considerable quantity of "Turkie stones" and of various sorts of wrought silks. During the rest of the year he visited other places for the purchase of raw silk and other commodities.[45] Finally, in the spring of 1573 he came to Shabran, loaded his merchandise, and on May 8 embarked for Astrakhan.

However, the misfortunes of this remarkable expedition
felt it necessary to write to the Czar in behalf of Bannister and Duckett. *Early Voyages and Travels*, II, 303.

[44] Hakluyt, III, 153; Duckett to Cecil (April 4, 1572), Cal. S. P., East Indies, I, 10.

[45] Hakluyt, III, 154, 155.

were by no means at an end. Because of the winds and the dangerous shoals of the Caspian Sea, the ship beat about for twenty days and then on May 28, while riding at anchor, it was attacked by a band of Russian outlaws. After some very severe fighting the Englishmen were forced to give up their ship in return for promises of personal safety, whereupon they were cast adrift in the ship's boat and compelled to make their way to Astrakhan as best they could. From that place the Russians sent out an expedition against the robbers, but it bungled matters so badly that nothing was accomplished. A second expedition did considerably better; it came up with a part of the outlaws, killed them, and recovered merchandise to the value of £5000 out of the £30,000 or £40,000 that had been lost, but the rest of the goods together with the ship was apparently never heard of again.[46]

After delaying two months at Astrakhan for the recovery of their strength the Englishmen began the long voyage up the Volga. Somewhere between Kazan and Jaroslav the ice in the river crushed their boats and so once more they were threatened with loss of life and goods. As much of the merchandise as was saved they conveyed overland in sleds to Vologda and thence to St. Nicholas for shipment to England. However, Duckett, Plumtree, and Amos Riall took some wares to Moscow and there made sales to the Czar, receiving the money therefor. The following summer they embarked for England and after a severe passage of over nine weeks they reached London in October, 1574, thus ending the longest and most unfortunate of all the Persian ventures.[47]

[46] Hakluyt, III, 155, 156.

[47] Upon his return Duckett had trouble with the Company over the terms of his agreement with it. *Acts of Privy Council,* 1581-2, pp. 378, 379. An intimation of the nature of the trouble is given in one of Bannister's letters to Cecil. *Cal. S. P., East Indies,* I, 8, 9.

Judged by the number of men engaged, by the length of time spent in Persia, by the amount of territory covered and the number of towns visited, and especially by the various glimpses of the trade afforded here and there, the fifth voyage to Persia was considerably the largest and most important of the expeditions of the Muscovy Company beyond the borders of Russia. In order to take advantage of the important Persian and Russian grants of 1566 and 1567, the Company carefully prepared for this expedition, they placed it under competent leadership, and apparently they expected much from it. Unfortunately in this as in the other voyages no formal statement of the amount or the profits of the trade either to or from Persia is to be found, but scattered references in the letters of the agents seem to indicate clearly enough that, under the Shah's protection, the trade in both respects offered excellent possibilities.[48] Also, after recounting the various misfortunes and losses of the expedition, Lionel Plumtree exclaimed that "if it had pleased God to prosper that all things had come home as safely as they were carefully provided and painfully laboured for, it had proved the richest voyage and most profitable returne of commoditie that had ever bene undertaken by English merchants."[49] He furthermore added that, in spite of those misfortunes, the merchants did not lose any of their principal, but only the interest and the profit due them upon their stock. These statements being true, the volume of the trade and its profits as well must have been such as to justify the great risks taken by the Muscovy Company in its prosecution.

[48] For example, on his way to Kazvin Bannister sold a thousand pieces of kersies, and later he took to Shemakha for shipment two hundred camel loads of merchandise and money; Duckett thought the Company might make £10,000 on a consignment of his, while on his return in 1573 it has been seen that his cargo was valued at £30,000 to £40,000. *Cal. S. P., For.*, 1571, p. 439, 440; Duckett to Cecil, April 4, 1572, as quoted in *Voyages and Travels*, II, 427, note 1.

[49] Hakluyt, III, 157.

CHAPTER IV

Upon the return of Geoffrey Duckett to England in 1574 after his long absence in Persia there followed an interval of five years in which nothing further was done in the attempt to develop the trade beyond the Caspian Sea. When, in 1579, conditions became such as to permit a renewal of the venture, an expedition was sent out which was destined to be no more successful than previous ones, and which proved to be the last of that remarkable series of voyages across Russia into Asia under the authority of the Muscovy Company. This comparatively long period of inaction between the fifth and sixth voyages does not seem to have been the result of discouragement following Duckett's misfortunes while returning from Persia; apparently his losses did not by any means destroy the faith of the English merchants in the advantages of their commercial relations with that country, as is well shown by the renewal of their efforts when the situation again appeared favorable. Though it is admitted that the available sources do not justify one in giving a definite explanation of this inactivity, still it may be well worth while to point out certain facts that seem to have an important bearing on the question. Of these undoubtedly the most significant are the probable condition of the Muscovy Company, the enthusiasm of Englishmen for rival interests and the changes in political conditions in Russia, and especially the breaking of diplomatic relations with England as a result of further negotiations concerning an Anglo-Russian alliance.

In no other way perhaps can some of the essential characteristics of the Russian and Persian trade be so well explained and emphasized as by the story of these negotiations between the Queen and the Czar. To all appearances Thomas Randolph had been successful in his mission to the Russian court; the grant of privileges obtained by him for the Muscovy Company not only covered the questions in dispute but also was the fullest grant of trading privileges that the English merchants ever enjoyed in Russia. Unfortunately for the merchants, however, Randolph did not fully succeed in putting aside the troublesome question of an alliance, the one thing above all else in which the Czar was interested. Thus, on his return to England in 1569, Randolph was accompanied by Andrew Saviena, who was to continue in that country the negotiations for a secret treaty. Though the ambassador remained in England for nearly a year, it proved impossible to obtain the desired treaty; he had to content himself with Elizabeth's offer of a strong league of amity as far as other treaties and alliances would permit, together with promises of mutual aid against their common enemies.[1] At the same time a secret letter signed by a number of important English nobles and officials was sent to the Czar promising him a safe retreat in England if at any time he found it needful.[2] With these letters Saviena departed for Russia about the middle of May, 1570.

The Czar, angry at the outcome, wrote a somewhat insulting letter to Elizabeth,[3] in which he declared that her kingdom was ruled by merchants and that she preferred their interests to great affairs of state. He had already seized the goods of the English merchants,[4] and now he

[1] Elizabeth to Ivan (May 18, 1570), *Early Voyages and Travels*, II, 288; Tolstoy, No. 25.

[2] *Early Voyages and Travels*, II, 290-292.

[3] Tolstoy, No. 28; *R. H. S. Trans.*, VII, 86-90; *Early Voyages and Travels*, II, 292-297.

[4] *Ibid.*, II, 299.

proceeded to revoke all the privileges that he had granted
to them. Consequently the Muscovy Company was confronted with the grave danger of losing its trade with
Russia and of seeing the destruction of its hopes in regard to Persia and the East. As other means failed to
ward off the danger, it was finally decided that Anthony
Jenkinson should be sent to cope with the extremely critical situation that had thus developed. Though Jenkinson arrived at St. Nicholas on July 27, 1571, it was not
until the following March that he was permitted to present himself before the Czar and not until the middle of
May that he obtained the final reply of Ivan to his requests in behalf of the English merchants. In regard to
the treaty the Russian ruler announced that for the present he would cease to importune the Queen. He further
stated that he would forgive the Company for its misdeeds
and restore its privileges.[5] Upon receipt of the answers to
his various requests Jenkinson at once departed, and later
the grant of privileges was written out for the formal approval of the Czar. Throughout the whole proceeding,
however, it seems clear that the Company had suffered
severely as a result of the Czar's recent displeasure and
also that Jenkinson had lost much of his former favor.

It was, however, this relatively fortunate ending of Jenkinson's negotiations that opened the way for Duckett's
return from Persia and the restoration of the previous
conditions underlying the trade with that country. Furthermore, it was promised that a plan proposed by Jenkinson for the establishment of the whole trans-Caspian trade
at Astrakhan should be given due consideration and the
Czar's pleasure therein made known later.[6] This last
point is significant as an indication of a possible abandon-

[5] Hakluyt, III, 187, 189.

[6] Ibid., III, 183, 190. Christopher Burrough later advised that
the Russian trade be thus centered at Kholmogory. *Early Voyages
and Travels*, introd., CXI-CXII.

ment of the Persian voyages and a suggestion that 'perhaps better results might be obtained by attracting Persian trade to Astrakhan than by seeking it at Shemakha or Kazvin. Though such a plan offered certain obvious advantages, it does not seem to have received any further attention, and the next voyage followed the established lines of trade.

The friendly relations between England and Russia continued for a time, but on August 20, 1574, two years after Jenkinson's mission, the Czar reopened the whole question of the secret treaty. Daniel Sylvester brought word to England of the Czar's angry complaints and the situation seemed to show that the treaty was necessary in order to avert the ruin of the trade.[7] After his return to Russia in the following year Sylvester had two audiences with the Czar, in which Ivan IV explained his desire for a place of refuge, reiterated his grievances, and declared that the messages brought by Sylvester were as unsatisfactory as those brought by Saviena and Jenkinson. He threatened to take away all privileges from the English merchants if his demands were not acceded to, though he agreed to wait for the Queen's final decision before resorting to such extreme measures.[8] When this was made known in England it was seen that further delay or temporizing was out of the question, and consequently Sylvester was again sent back with letters from the Queen, but at Kholmogory he was killed by lightning and all of his letters and papers were burned, with the result that the real nature of his mission is not known. For three years thereafter the negotiations apparently were allowed to drop and as far as the Company is concerned the period is lacking in documentary explanation of any kind.[9] Though it seems clear

[7] Czar to Elizabeth (Aug. 20, 1574), *R. H. S. Trans.*, VII, 96-100.

[8] For Sylvester's account of these audiences of Nov. 29, 1575, and Jan. 29, 1576, see *Ibid.*, VII, 107-111.

[9] Tolstoy, introd. XXXIII; *R. H. S. Trans.*, VII, 111.

enough that the Muscovy Company continued to carry on its Russian trade, there is very little to suggest the character of its actual position or the scope of its privileges during that time.

As has been pointed out, this diplomatic situation and the consequent uncertainty in regard to the future of the Muscovy Company seems to offer a plausible explanation of the temporary abandonment of the Persian venture. During the period from Duckett's return to England in 1574 to the sending out of the final expedition in 1579 the Company undoubtedly found itself in the midst of the confusion and disorder that characterized the latter part of the reign of Ivan the Terrible, and without the Czar's positive sanction and protection it may well have hesitated to send more merchandise into Russia for the Persian market. Besides, since the closing of Astrakhan and the Volga to the return of Bannister and Duckett, nothing further was needed to emphasize the risk of the Persian venture when its base in Russia was not secure. Furthermore, the growing frequency of wars in the region through which it was necessary to pass may have had an important bearing upon the interruption of the Persian trade. It was to this cause that Elizabeth, in her letter to the Shah in 1579, attributed the break in the commercial relations between England and Persia,[10] though manifestly she would not desire to make any mention of the Czar's unfriendliness.

There is another fact which from the English side may also have had its influence on the interruption of the Persian trade. In that suggestive shifting of attention from one route to another during this period, it may be that the hope of passage by way of Russia and Persia was over-

[10] Hakluyt, III, 213. Wars were almost constant from 1569 to the end of the period of the Persian voyages. Howorth, *Mongols*, II, 503, 504, 507-509, 511, 515, 516, etc.

shadowed by the enthusiasm for the voyages of Frobisher to the northwest in 1576, 1577, and 1578, in search of another solution of the same problem, and that further activity was suspended to await the outcome. If that be so, then the reaction from Frobisher's failure will explain the great activity of the Muscovy Company in the next two years, namely, the Persian expedition of 1579-81 and the voyage of Pet and Jackman to the northeast in 1580.

And finally, mention may be made of the fact that at this time the Muscovy Company had suffered great losses and had assumed burdensome debts, for the payment of which a levy was made on the Adventurers. There was trouble, however, in regard to its collection, and as a result the Privy Council appointed a committee to look into the matter.[11] If the records of the Company were in existence, possibly they would show that this phase of the situation offers a real explanation of the period under consideration.

The influences underlying the Anglo-Russian trade proved strong enough to overcome the strained relations between the two countries resulting from the Czar's displeasure towards Elizabeth. On the one hand the English merchants were anxious to maintain their position in Russia and Persia; on the other hand Ivan's struggle with the King of Poland to the west served to emphasize his need of commercial relations with a country able to supply the much-desired military stores independently of the Baltic route. In the years following the death of Sylvester, Ivan is said to have been in desperate straits, and so it is not surprising to find that in 1580 he determined to send Jerome Horsey, one of the agents of the Muscovy Company in Russia, overland to England for the purpose of negotiating for military supplies. Horsey was well re-

[11] *Acts of Privy Council*, under dates Dec. 2, 1578, and Mar. 7, 1579.

ceived by the Queen and by the merchants and the latter
supplied him with everything the Czar had desired from
them.[12]

· Meanwhile the English merchants had organized and
sent out another Persian expedition, under Arthur Edwards, William Turnbull, Matthew Tailbois, and Peter
Garrard as agents. It was eleven years since Bannister
and Duckett had sailed from England on the preceding
venture, and now as then Elizabeth besought the Shah to
receive her merchants with favor and to grant them trading privileges.[13] In view of the interruption of the trade
and the change of rulers in Persia it was felt that such
new grants were highly desirable.[14] The factors with
their merchandise reached St. Nicholas on July 22, 1579,
and by October 16 they were at Astrakhan where they
found their ship in readiness.[15] However, the approach
of winter and reports of Turkish conquests in Shirvan led
the Englishmen to remain in Astrakhan until the following spring. During the winter that place was besieged
for a short time by an army of Nogay and Krim Tartars,
a fact that well illustrates the altered conditions prevailing in those regions that border on the Caspian Sea.

With the spring there came news that the Persians had
won a victory over the Turks but that the latter still held
Derbend and the greater part of Shirvan. Upon consultation, therefore, it was decided that Arthur Edwards with

[12] Copper, lead, powder, saltpetre, brimstone, and other things, to
the value of £9,000. *Travels of Jerome Horsey* (*Russia at Close
of Sixteenth Century*), 194.

[13] Hakluyt, III, 212-214.

[14] *Cal. S. P., East Indies*, I, 61. On the death of Shah Tahmasp
three of his sons came to the throne in rapid succession, Hyder
Mirza, Ismail II, and Mohammed Mirza. Malcolm, *Persia*, I, 334-
338.

[15] This the sixth Persian voyage is described by Christopher Burrough, the account in Hakluyt, III, 214-247, being gathered from
his various letters.

half of the goods should remain at Astrakhan [16] while the
other factors proceeded with the rest to the coast of
Shirvan to see what might be done there. In case no trade
was found, it was the intention that they should go on to
the province of Ghilan with their merchandise. Meantime two men were sent back to Jaroslav with letters of
advice for England and with orders for the detention in
Russia of all the goods coming that year from England
for the Persian market.[17]

On May 1 the three factors left Astrakhan and on the
27th they anchored at Bildih in Shirvan, a port between
Bilbil and Baku. The reports concerning the Turkish conquests were now fully confirmed, and besides it was said
that Shemakha was almost desolated. In fact the situation seemed so unpromising that the factors were almost
persuaded to return to Russia.[18] However, receiving permission and aid from the Turkish officer at Baku they
determined to go to Derbend to request a grant of privileges from the Pasha whereby they might trade in safety
in any part of his dominions. This official declared his
willingness to give them the privileges, and yet, knowing
the disturbed state of the country and perhaps not un-
mindful of his own profit, he advised the bringing of their
ship to Derbend, which was accordingly done. Here, on
June 29, they unloaded their merchandise, paying the
Pasha one kersey out of each twenty-five as toll.

From Derbend goods to the value of £1000 were sent to
Baku in charge of three servants of the Company. Though
the Englishmen were well received, their sales were small;
and besides, an attempt of one of their number to re-
establish trading relations with Shemakha very nearly re-

[16] Edwards died at Astrakhan somewhat later. Hakluyt, III, 231,
232.
[17] *Ibid.*, III, 220.
[18] *Ibid.*, III, 225.

sulted in the loss of his goods and his life.[19]   Their ship having proved unseaworthy, another was obtained in its place, but this unfortunately was wrecked on the return from Baku and a chest of money and a portion of the merchandise were lost.   Meanwhile, at Derbend itself the trade was somewhat better, though raw silk was the only commodity to be had, and this was obtained only through the Pasha's hands.   Though the dealings of the latter were not always equitable and his prices for the English wares were rather low, the country was in such confusion and travel so dangerous that it was only through him that the English merchants were able to obtain any merchandise at all.[20]

On October 2 the factors were suddenly ordered by the Turkish governor to leave Derbend.[21]   The next day, just as they were ready to return to Astrakhan, they received the news of the mishap to those who had been sent to Baku.   Their voyage to the southward to pick up these men caused some delay, and it was not until the 16th that the return voyage began.   On account of the lateness of the season their ship was caught in the ice near the islands off the mouth of the Volga and both ship and cargo had to be abandoned, while the merchants made their way on the ice towards Astrakhan.   Lost for a time and suffering privation, they finally met a rescue party that had been sent out.   A little later the goods were loaded on sleds and after escaping capture by a band of Tartar horsemen they also were brought in safety to Astrakhan.[22]   After spending the winter at that place, most of the English merchants on April 9, 1581, set out for Jaroslav, leaving three men behind for a time to attempt the disposal of more of the

[19] Hakluyt, III, 230.
[20] Ibid., III, 234.
[21] Ibid., III, 232.
[22] Ibid., III, 239-245, gives the story in detail.

merchandise. In due time the merchants and also the wares brought from Persia reached England in safety.

Thus, this attempt of the Muscovy Company to reëstablish its commercial relations with Persia proved to be a hopeless task; not only did the factors fail to enter Persia proper, but what little encouragement they at first received from the Turks was soon withdrawn and clearly nothing remained except to abandon the undertaking. The realities of the situation form a striking contrast to the hopes and plans of the merchants in England, who evidently were counting heavily on a renewal of the trade. It was thought by them that a ratification of the privileges formerly granted by Shah Tahmasp I would be sufficient reason for sending an ambassador to Persia, and it was suggested that a "gentleman bred in the Court" should be chosen for this mission. Also it was proposed to send out with him experienced men of different trades to learn the methods of manufacture of saltpeter, Turkey blades, plates for armor, carpets, and other things.[23] A beginning along this line had been made in 1579 when Morgan Hubblethorne, a London dyer, was sent with the Persian expedition at the expense of the city in order to make a study of dyeing substances and methods of dyeing in the countries to be visited, with a view to introducing improvements at home in this branch of the cloth industry,[24] but unfortunately this phase of development as well as the hope of a profitable trade in Persia was ended as a result of the Turkish advance to the Caspian Sea. With the failure of their expedition the English merchants seem to

[23] *Cal. S. P., Dom.*, 1581-1590, p. 587; *Cal. S. P., East Indies*, I, 50, 61. The former gives 1589 as the date of these documents, the latter 1580?; the reference to a voyage to the northeast points to 1580 as probably correct.

[24] Hakluyt, III, 245, 249-251. In *Acts of Privvy Council*, Last of May, 1579, may be found the letter to the warden of the Dyers which led to this action.

have made the best of the situation by wisely deciding to
abandon so hazardous a field of commercial activity,
though they kept somewhat in touch with eastern merchants through their trade at Astrakhan.[25]

Although no more trading expeditions were sent to Persia by the Muscovy Company for over a century and a
half, the right of passage through Russia to that country
continued to be a matter of interest and retained its place
in the various grants or renewals of privileges obtained
from successive Czars. Early in 1587, for example, when
Jerome Horsey obtained a letter of privileges from the
successor of Ivan IV, provision was made that English
merchants should be permitted to cross the Caspian into
Persian or other countries without payment of duty.[26]
Another grant made in the following year at the solicitation of Giles Fletcher went further than this, as it declared that the Company should have the sole right to
trade through Russia "into Media, Persia, Bogharia, and
other East countries." [27] Other letters of privilege, such
as those of 1596, 1605, and 1621, continued to mention this
right of passage.[28] That it was a privilege not lightly
valued is shown by the negotiations of 1617-8, in which the
Czar's desire for a large loan was used in an attempt to
obtain from him this along with other concessions.[29] Furthermore, it was regarded as of sufficient importance to be
given full expression in the treaty of alliance and trade
entered into by Russia and England in 1623.[30] Even as

[25] See Elizabeth to Theodore (April 30, 1589), Tolstoy, No. 66,
for the conditions existing in 1583.

[26] Hakluyt, III, 350, 351; Horsey, *Travels*, 227, 228.

[27] Hakluyt, III, 355, art. 11; Fletcher, *Russe Commonwealth*, in
Russia at Close of Sixteenth Century, 80.

[28] Hakluyt, III, 442; Purchas., XIV, 154, 170, 288.

[29] *Cal. S. P., East Indies*, II, Nos. 307-310, 312, 467; *Cal. S. P.,
Dom.* Add., 1580-1625, pp. 639, 640; Hamel, *England and Russia*,
390, 391.

[30] Rymer, *Foedera*, VII, pt. IV, p. 73.

late as 1697, fifty years after the loss to the English merchants of all their privileges in Russia,[31] it is interesting to find that the Committee of Trade and Plantations considered this freedom of passage and of trade to Persia as one of the more important of the old-time privileges that if possible it was desirable to regain.[32]

In addition to these treaties and grants of privileges there were various plans proposed for the Persian trade which likewise show a continuance of interest. Apparently an expedition was under consideration in 1601, provided the necessary concessions could be obtained from the Czar.[33] Twelve years later some stir was created by a project for the extension of the trade not only to Persia but also to India. Although James I was sufficiently interested to have Sir Henry Neville discuss the matter several times with the Council, the thoroughly unsubstantial character of the project is perhaps enough to explain why nothing more is heard of it.[34] Much more promising in character was the proposal to revive the transit trade through Russia that followed the temporary amalgamation of the Muscovy and East India companies in 1618 for this and other purposes.[35] The next year they sent out Giles Hobbes to go over the route from Jaroslav to Ispahan by way of Astrakhan, the Caspian Sea, and Shemakha, and to report on the situation. After discussing in his report the possibilities of the trade, the rivalry of the Turks, the Arabs, the Armenians, and especially the Portuguese, and the practicability of the various routes from

[31] *Cal. S. P. Dom.*, 1653, No. 149.

[32] *Cal. of MSS. of Marquis of Bath* (*Hist. MSS. Comm.*), III, 148-151.

[33] *Salisbury MSS.*, Pt. XI, pp. 347, 348.

[34] Winwood, *Memorials*, III, 453; *Cal. S. P., Dom.*, 1613, p. 182, and *Ibid., East Indies*, I, No. 644; *Report on MSS. Duke of Buccleugh and Queensberry*, (*Hist. MSS. Comm.*), I, 124.

[35] *Cal. S. P., East Indies*, II, Nos. 306, 314.

Moscow to Persia, Hobbes concluded by recommending the reopening of this northern route through Russia.[36] However, the only actual exploitation of Persia in the seventeenth century was destined to be that by the East India Company from the opposite direction, but that development lies outside the limits of the present discussion. It was not until the time of Peter the Great that Englishmen were again afforded extensive opportunities in Russia, and not until towards the middle of the eighteenth century that English merchants once more sent their factors and their merchandise from Russia over the Caspian Sea to make trial of the Persian trade, though unfortunately with no better or more permanent results than they had achieved in their earlier attempts during the reign of Queen Elizabeth.[37]

[36] Purchas, V, 257-262.

[37] One of these factors, Jonas Hanway, has told the story in great detail, in his *Historical Account of British Trade over the Caspian Sea*, Vol. I.

CHAPTER V

THE STRENGTH AND WEAKNESS OF THE PERSIAN VENTURE

A study of the successive voyages of the Muscovy Company into Asia reveals how fully they were characteristic of the new epoch of adventure, of exploration and of expanding commercial activity. The twofold purpose of the founders of the Company, namely, exploration and trade, had been kept constantly in mind and had been prosecuted with courage and persistence in the face of great difficulties. To that end the voyage of Chancellor had been followed without delay by the development of the Russian trade and particularly at the same time by a series of voyages to the south and east for the purpose of still further extending the markets for English goods and of bringing the English merchants in touch with the commodities of the East. Between 1557 and 1581 seven such expeditions were equipped and sent out under the authority of the Company, the first one striking boldly for Cathay along the line of the northernmost of the great mediæval trade routes, while the later ones settled down to the somewhat less ambitious project of developing the Persian trade and thereby opening the way to Ormuz and India. With the history of these expeditions in mind it is now possible in a concluding chapter to notice the more important points concerning the movement as a whole. Among these probably the most significant are the extent and value of the actual achievements of the English factors, the character and possibilities of the Persian trade and the method of conducting it, the extent of the indebtedness to Russia, and finally the reasons for the failure to establish such an overland trade with Asia.

195

Persia should not be regarded as an inaccessible country, as it may easily be approached either from the north or from the south. Though Englishmen have made use of the Persian Gulf route since early in the seventeenth century, the earliest approach as has been seen was by way of the Caspian Sea. It has also been pointed out how the English merchants had been brought in touch with Astrakhan and the Caspian by combining the newly discovered sea route to the White Sea with the inland waterways of Russia. The Caspian Sea in turn afforded comparatively easy communication with the caravan routes eastward towards Bokhara or with the maritime provinces of northern Persia, and thus the Muscovy Company was enabled to tap the resources of the East independently of the Spanish or Portuguese routes. Such at least was the hope of the English traders, and it was only by the successive expeditions and their accompanying misfortunes that they were made fully to realize the almost insuperable obstacles in the way of its attainment. But meanwhile the merchants and their factors persevered, believing that success was near and that they would divert the commerce of Persia from the Turks, Venetians, and Portuguese.

Unfortunately, however, this magnificent plan fell far short of actual accomplishment. When Jenkinson's first voyage proved the futility of the central Asian route to Cathay, the Muscovy Company turned at once to a second possible line of advance to the East, and with varying degrees of success Jenkinson and his successors strove to make Persia a basis of further advance as Russia had been before. Luckily for the merchants they were permitted to make Shemakha a starting point for expeditions to the interior very much as they had made use of Kholmogory for Russia itself. When they proceeded to Kazvin they met at first with rebuff, but later they gained the favor of the Shah and received from him several grants of trading privileges. From Shemakha and Kazvin their activities spread to various other commercial centers, though they confined themselves mostly to the region immediately to the west and southwest of the lower Caspian, that is, between the towns of Shemakha, Tabriz, and Kazvin. Kashan, visited by Duckett in 1572, marks the greatest advance to the southward. Though it is somewhat surprising that the sphere of their activities was not greater, especially in view of the boldness and scope of the earliest voyages, still it should be remembered that the cities named above had more or less widely extended trade connections and thus the significance of the Russo-Caspian route should not be measured by the nominal limits of the English voyages. And besides, in addition to the need of developing a new base, the opening up of this region in the course of a few years was in itself no mean achievement and will stand comparison with the progress made elsewhere during the Elizabethan era.

The fact remains, however, that the Muscovy merchants failed in their endeavor to establish overland connections with the Persian Gulf and India. Though for a time it seemed as if their hopes would be realized, the refusal of the Shah to permit Bannister to proceed to India practically marked the end of the movement in that direction. Meanwhile, the factors had continued their efforts in Persia itself, and it is in the opportunities of the Persian trade that one must look for the chief element of strength in the expeditions into western Asia.

As viewed by the Muscovy Company the possibilities of the Persian trade were twofold; on the one hand the markets of that country were expected to supply an outlet for English cloth and other wares, while on the other hand the highly prized commodities of Asia were to be furnished to western Europe by the English merchants. It is very noticeable that through all the accounts of the voyages it is

English cloth, especially kersies, that formed the staple article of the Persian trade and often nothing else is mentioned. The charter granted the Muscovy Company in 1566, apparently taking for granted that cloth was the one important English export, provided for the further encouragement of the industry by declaring that no one should take out of England "any maner of cloths or karsies" for the lands to which the Company traded unless the same had been dressed and for the most part dyed within the realm.[1] From these facts it is clear that the Persian venture is merely representative of the characteristic features of Elizabethan trade as a whole. However, the lists of wares desired for the Persian market, such as those sent by Edwards, make mention of various other commodities as well.[2]

From the other side the success of the Persian venture depended upon the resources and commercial possibilities of that and of neighboring countries. At that time the chief cities of Persia were Shemakha, Arrash, Ardebil, Tabriz, Kazvin, and Kashan, already mentioned, together with Meshed and Herat further to the east and Yezd in central Persia.[3] Besides, Ormuz should be mentioned, though not a part of Persia, because it had important trade relations with that country just as Aleppo did to the westward. The immediate interest, however, is with that group of cities to the northwest, along the coast of and inland from the Caspian Sea, that is, the region already mentioned as indicating the extent of English activity. This region may be said to correspond roughly with the provinces of Shirvan, Azerbaijan, Ghilan, and Kasvin, and with Mazanderan it embraced the most important silk-producing sections of Persia.[4]

[1] Hakluyt, III, 90.
[2] Ibid., III, 53, 66, 67.
[3] Ibid., III, 35.
[4] The best map of Persia is probably that in Curzon, *Persia*, Vol.

That these provinces offered a fair variety of commodities is shown by the accounts of the various factors and by travelers who have described the resources of the country.[5] But after all the greatest importance seems to have been attached to the spices and drugs that came from India by way of Ormuz and to the alum, dye-stuffs, and raw silks of the northern Persian provinces. Upon these, and especially upon the silk trade, depended the prospect of a permanent and profitable commerce and the hope of rivaling the Venetians and Turks and the Portuguese. It was the silk trade, mentioned by Marco Polo [6] and many later travelers, that urged on the English traders and later became the object of rivalry between English, Dutch, and Russian merchants. Furthermore, additional strength was given to the Persian venture by the ever-present possibility of establishing direct trading relations with the merchants of India, especially for the drugs and spices so much desired by the Company. In passing judgment on the Persian trade as a whole, Jenkinson was inclined to be rather conservative,[7] Chapman was very critical, and Edwards was remarkably enthusiastic and retained his enthusiasm through at least two expeditions into that country. Perhaps the latter did not sufficiently distinguish between actual conditions and hopes for the future, and yet the general impression one derives from the whole movement is that Persia did offer good opportunities for trade and that in spite of serious disadvantages the English merchants might have been reasonably successful in their undertaking if commercial considerations alone had determined the mat-

I, end. Shirvan corresponds to the present Russian province of Baku, but at that time it extended as far as Derbend.

[5] For a list of travelers to Persia from early times down, see Curzon, *Persia*, I, 16-18. Ample bibliographies for the different provinces are given in connection with the various chapters.

[6] Yule, *Marco Polo*, 51.

[7] Hakluyt, II, 474, 478.

ter. On the whole, perhaps, the estimate of the trade that has been given in connection with the expedition of Bannister and Duckett will serve in a measure at least as a general statement of the case for the entire series of voyages.[8]

In all essential features the Persian trade seems to have been organized and conducted in the same way as that of Russia and usually in close conjunction with it. The factors and merchandise for Persia were brought to St. Nicholas by the usual Russian fleet sent out in the spring or early summer, and instructions were issued which applied both to the Russian and the Persian voyages. The latter voyages nevertheless were apparently regarded as entirely separate expeditions, though in some degree under the supervision of the agent of the Company in Russia, especially in case the English merchants themselves did not assume authority. It would be a mistake, however, to consider this agent as being in full control, as there was always a chief factor for Persia just as there was for Russia. Sometimes the appointment of the Persian factors was left to the Russian agent or to a special representative of the Company, but usually the merchants themselves designated the men to lead their ventures over the Caspian Sea, and especially is this true of the more important voyages, which were organized and sent out from England itself. Of at least equal significance is the fact that the letters and reports were sent by the Persian agents directly to the Company itself and not to the Russian agents. Furthermore, the Company insisted that separate accounts be kept for the two countries. Thus, on the whole it may be said that the direction and control of these voyages resided in the officials in London, and so was practically independent of the organization in Russia, though making use of it in the furtherance of the trans-Caspian trade.

From St. Nicholas the merchandise for Persia was trans-

[8] Ante, p. 181.

ported to Jaroslav, which, on account of its nearness to Vologda and its situation on the Volga, became the point of final preparation and departure for all the expeditions after the first. At this place were collected the wares from England, from Vologda, or from Moscow, that were considered desirable for the voyage, together with provisions and other necessary supplies. When once in Persia the procedure was much the same as in Russia. Usually the factors separated for the better carrying on of the trade; part of the merchandise would be retained at Shemakha for that and the Tabriz markets, while the rest would be taken to Kazvin, some sales often being made along the way. From these centers other places were visited in the effort to open up new markets for the English cloths or to purchase raw silk and other desired commodities for the home market. Various other duties fell to the lot of the Persian factor, such as the seeking of new privileges, the collection of debts, the collection of information in regard to the resources of neighboring countries or provinces, and the guarding of English interests against Turkish and other rivals. The wares were always brought to Shemakha for the return voyage.

In the conduct of the Persian trade certain evils and difficulties soon made themselves felt. Here, as was the case in Russia, discord at times threatened the success of the undertaking, due either to the character and mistakes of the leaders or to the jealousies of subordinates. Another great source of trouble was the prevalent evil of private trading,[9] though this did not become anything like as serious as in Russia, where it threatened for a time to disrupt the Company. Furthermore, although no advantage seems to have been taken of the fact, it is interesting to note that the Czar's special grant of privileges to Thomas Glover and

[9] Wright, *Queen Elizabeth and Her Times*, 419; *Early Voyages and Travels*, II, 213; ante, 155, 162, 173.

his associates included the right of trading to Persia.[10] Probably the most persistent difficulty confronting the factors was that of collecting the debts due them from the sales of their merchandise. Some debts were lost, others were compromised, while many were collected only with great difficulty, as a result of an apparently strong effort on the part of the Persian to escape his obligations. Though the Shah's grant of privileges met this situation, his authority does not seem to have been strong enough to make it thoroughly effective. Still another drawback to the trade arose from the fact that the native merchant might in the end repudiate his bargain. The unhealthy climate of northern Persia in summer, the enmity of the Mohammedan for the Christian, the danger from bands of robbers, the lack of suitable accommodations and of wholesome food, and the scarcity and poor quality of the water, all these added to the difficulties of the English factor beyond the Caspian Sea.

Before leaving the subject of the English trade in Persia, one may well delay long enough to emphasize the influence of Russia upon the movement. That its success and its very existence depended upon the good-will of the Czar has perhaps been made sufficiently clear. But it should be further noted that the debt of the English merchants to the Russian ruler goes much beyond that of mere acquiescence in their trading ventures to the south of Astrakhan; not only did he grant them freedom of passage and exclusive enjoyment of the trade to Asia but also through his conquests and the extension of his authority he made the route possible to them. Even more than that, the growing influence of Russia in western Asia [11] was exerted in behalf of these foreign traders. It was always consid-

---

[10] *Cal. S. P., For.*, 1566-1568, pp. 492, 493.

[11] Hakluyt, II, 475, 478, III, 33, 37; Ramband, *Russia*, I, 75; ante, 140, etc.

ered necessary to get letters from the Czar to the rulers of the lands to be visited, and even as far away as Bokhara Jenkinson is found placing his dependence upon such letters. Though this protection sometimes proved to be slight, still there was little else to fall back upon except the travelers' own resources.

From another point of view the Russian influence may be said to have formed the basis of English activities in Asia. In addition to the fact that it was the knowledge gained in Russia which revealed to the merchants the possibility of making connections with the Asiatic trade routes, it is very probable that Anthony Jenkinson in both of his voyages was merely following in the track of other traders to and from Russia, though this should not be allowed unduly to detract from the boldness of his achievement. Situated advantageously near the mouth of the Volga, Astrakhan was and for a long time had been a sort of mart town for Asiatic merchants, while from it Russian traders crossed the Caspian Sea for merchandise.[12] Jenkinson himself, as has been seen, met Persian merchants at Astrakhan, and somewhat later Giles Fletcher described the Russian trade to Persia for silks and other commodities, especially to Derbend and Shemakha, the latter of which he calls the staple for raw silk.[13] Furthermore, it is said that the people of Bokhara trafficked with Moscow, their commodities being spices, musk, ambergris, rhubarb and other drugs, and Siberian furs.[14] Taken in this connection it was very significant that on his journey to Bokhara Jenkinson undoubtedly followed a well established caravan route in company with Tartar and other merchants. It is quite reasonable to conclude, therefore, that both the Bokhara and the Shemakha routes were at least fairly well known

[12] Hakluyt, II, 473, 476; *Russe Commonwealth*, in *Russia at Close of Sixteenth Century*, 96; Eden, *First Three Books on America*, 314.
[13] Hakluyt, II, 478; *Russe Commonwealth*, 96.
[14] Hakluyt, II, 427.

in Russia and that this information furnished the starting point for further advance on the part of the Muscovy Company.[15]

As was suggested at the beginning of this chapter, there were elements of weakness as well as elements of strength in the Persian venture. With the latter now in mind, it is desirable to consider the former in some detail in order to explain the ultimate and complete failure of the commercial advance into Asia. In following the history of the different voyages there appeared certain phases of the situation which seemed to make the advanced position of the Muscovy Company a very difficult one. Among these may be mentioned the absolute dependence of the merchants upon the favor of the Shah and the Czar, the competition that everywhere met the English from Tartar, Turkish, Armenian, and Venetian merchants, and finally, the great length, complexity, and danger of the route that had been established. Even in the short period under consideration these aspects of the movement made themselves felt in a very positive way.

Whenever the Shah or the Czar made a grant of privileges to the English merchants, it was done voluntarily and as a matter of favor, and thus in the same way that it was made it might suddenly be changed or abrogated entirely. Therefore, it is hardly possible, at least under the then existing conditions, to regard such grants as giving a sufficiently fixed and durable basis for the newly developed English commerce. Perhaps sufficient proof of this from both the Persian and the Russian side has been given in the preceding pages, and so it is enough to recall that the whole story of English negotiations with the Czar centered around this danger of an abrogation of privileges and that

[15] The references to Russian jealousy of the English merchants are slight, the only two noted being *Early Voyages and Travels*, II, 390, and *Ibid.*, I, introd. CXII.

apparently the only thing that saved the situation was the Czar's military necessities. The Czar's good-will, of course, was even more important than that of the Shah, as both the Russian and Persian trade depended upon it.

Furthermore, the Persian trade had to be conducted in the face of competition from long-established and resourceful merchants, and the letters of the English factors contain many references to these competitors. Apparently the Turks were the strongest, because of their control of the routes leading to the Mediterranean ports, and perhaps because of the fact that the Persians were their fellow religionists. At first they were able to thwart Jenkinson's plans, but later a change in the Shah's attitude towards them enabled Arthur Edwards to obtain trading privileges. Later still, together with the Armenians and Venetians, they were found trying to block Bannister's negotiations as they had those of Jenkinson. In various other ways they did what they could to injure the English position in Persia.[16] The Armenians also were strongly intrenched in that country; they brought kersies and other cloths from Aleppo or were supplied with them in their home markets by Venetian traders, and, as has been seen, they were a strong factor in the markets of Shemakha and Tabriz. Thus by way of the Levant both Turks and Armenians were supplied by the Venetians with European and perhaps even English wares and passed them on to the Persians. Arthur Edwards, for instance, found that considerable Venetian cloth was sold at Kazvin.[17] But possibly of most importance are the indications that these competitors were probably able to undersell the English merchants or pay more for native products.[18] It may be added that Edwards clearly recognized that the Mediterranean

[16] Hakluyt, III, 141, 142.
[17] Ibid., III, 55.
[18] Ibid., II, 478, III, 52, 62, 63, 137, 142, etc.

was shorter than the Russian route, while Jenkinson from the beginning pointed out that the outlet through Syria was a serious drawback to the designs of the Muscovy Company in Persia.[19] Taking all these facts together it is evident that the existence of the Levant routes should be given considerable emphasis as an element of weakness in the position of the Muscovy Company.

Another important source of weakness is to be found in the character of the route upon which the trade depended. For one thing its great length and complexity should be considered. As has been seen, it involved the sea voyage around the North Cape to St. Nicholas, thence up the Dwina and Sugana in boats to Vologda, where the Company had one of its factories, and from there overland to Moscow or Jaroslav. This ended the first great stage of the journey, as at Jaroslav the expeditions were finally fitted out for Persia. But after the long trip down the Volga to Astrakhan some further preparations were also necessary for the sea voyage. From here the merchants entered the Caspian and sailed southward to some convenient port in Shirvan, from whence the merchandise had to be transferred by caravan to Shemakha. And finally, it has been seen that Shemakha in turn became the point of departure for all expeditions to Kazvin or elsewhere in Persia. The mere description of the route makes comment superfluous as regards its length and the number of stops and changes that were necessary.

Such a route evidently required much time and considerable expense. The earlier stages of the voyage of course were the same as those for the Russian trade. It seems that at least from one to two months was needed to make the trip from Gravesend or Harwich to St. Nicholas, the fleet usually sailing in May or June and reaching port sometime during July. The journey from Kholmogory,

[19] Hakluyt, II, 473, 478.

near St. Nicholas, to Jaroslav or Moscow occupied the time from late in July to the latter part of August or early September. With the actual Persian voyage from Jaroslav to Astrakhan and Shemakha greater differences appear. For example, the number of days taken up by the voyage down the Volga varied from twenty-eight to seventy-six, while from Astrakhan to Shirvan much depended upon propitious conditions, the second expedition occupying only nine days, though the most of them took three weeks or more. Also the earlier expeditions left Jaroslav in April or May, after spending the winter in Russia, while the last two got started considerably later and had to remain either in Astrakhan or Shemakha for the following winter. Several days were usually consumed in the overland journey from the port of entry to Shemakha. The quickest voyage of all was that of Arthur Edwards in 1568, which left Jaroslav in July and landed at Bilbil on August 14. Usually the merchants arrived in Shirvan anywhere from August to October. Thus, it took considerably over a year to make the voyage from England to Persia, while that from Russia to Persia could hardly be made with any reasonable expectation of being able to return the same year.

In addition to its length and complicated character, the route was subject to various hazards and was in the main quite open to attack. For one thing, there were the risks arising from the navigation of the Volga and the danger from storms and shoals when sailing upon the Caspian. If the return journey were delayed too long there was the further risk of being caught in the ice. However, greater actual loss was suffered at the hands of robbers, fear of whom was nearly always present both in Persia and in southern Russia as well as on the Caspian Sea. Of these and other dangers there has been ample illustration in the narratives of the different voyages, and undoubtedly they added their part to the great burden laid upon the trade by the character of the route.

The disadvantages of the Persian venture so far pointed out were very real and important, but they did not preclude the possibility that the Muscovy Company might be able to cope successfully with them and thus bring about a reasonably permanent and profitable trade with the countries bordering on the Caspian Sea. Moreover, such a result does not seem at all improbable when one considers how much the Company had accomplished in Asia in the short period of twelve years from 1561 to 1573. And besides, when the downfall of the Persian trade came, it was not due primarily to any of the influences discussed above, but rather to changing political conditions in the region of the Caspian Sea, on both the Russian and the Persian side, which were rapidly making its further prosecution exceedingly dangerous and in fact practically impossible.

Shortly after the appearance of the English in Russia Ivan IV had reached the height of his power, but soon a great change came over him, which made the latter part of his reign as great a failure as the earlier part had been a success. On both the west and the east his enemies pressed him so closely that many of his earlier conquests were lost, while at home his people were alienated. His struggle with the Tartars of the lower Volga continued throughout the period of the Persian voyages, and at times it threatened serious consequences to those expeditions, as has been shown in the preceding chapters. As long as these wars continued there was constant danger that the line of communication with Persia would be broken, possibly by the capture of Astrakhan itself.

As bad as conditions became in Russia they will hardly compare with the confusion and civil strife in Persia that followed the death of Shah Tahmasp in 1576. Dynastic troubles led to such disorder that the country seemed rapidly disintegrating as a result of the weakness of the central authority, and these conditions continued for several years, that is, until Abbas the Great succeeded in establishing his undisputed sway. Meanwhile, the enemies of Persia made haste to take advantage of the situation; the Uzbeg Tartars again poured into Khorassan, other Tartar tribes entered Shirvan, and the Turks began to prepare for a renewal of their struggle with the rival Mohammedan state.[20]

After various successes in 1578 the Turkish army took and fortified Tiflis in Georgia, and then marched towards Shirvan. Entering that province they occupied Shemakha and Derbend and reduced the whole region to submission. Following the withdrawal of the main Turkish force, however, the Persians returned and regained Shemakha, whose inhabitants they punished for their submission by destroying their city. Thereupon they withdrew to Kazvin, leaving the Turks in possesion of Derbend and Baku. When peace was concluded in 1587 the Turks retained these places, together with Tabriz, Arrash, and other towns.[21] It was this advance of the Turkish power to the Caspian Sea that deprived the English factors of their base of operations, checked the expedition of 1580 and expelled the merchants from the country, and severed the line of communication between England and Persia, thus, for the time being at least, effectually preventing any further activity in that direction.[22]

Important developments along other lines of approach to the coveted trade of the East soon made the further

[20] Malcolm, *Persia*, I, 333,338; Howorth, *Mongols*, II, 730. For internal conditions in 1586 see report of Giovanni Battista Vechietti to the Pope, printed in *English Historical Review*, VII, 314-321.

[21] Hakluyt, III, 224, 234; Knolles, *Historic of the Turks*, 376-395, 432.

[22] Camden, *Annals of Queen Elizabeth*, 124; Hanway, *Historical Account*, I, 6. The former adds as a second cause the losses through robbery.

prosecution of the Persian trade by way of Russia and the Caspian much less attractive and desirable to Englishmen. The Turkey or Levant Company, founded in 1581, brought English merchants in touch with southern Persia and India by a more direct and practicable route than that of the Muscovy Company. Furthermore, just at the close of the century the foundation of the East India Company led to the successful establishment of English trade in the East by way of the sea and made the southern extremity of the Persian Gulf the center of English activity in the development of the Persian trade, while the northern route by way of the Caspian Sea ultimately fell to Russia. Though they had failed in their purpose, the factors of the Muscovy Company are worthy of remembrance for their struggle of twenty years to found such an Asiatic trade. It was a struggle that called for the same qualities that Englishmen were showing elsewhere and to its leaders belongs a place in the list of those explorers and traders who have made the epoch so noteworthy.

BIBLIOGRAPHY

CONTEMPORARY SOURCES

Calendar of State Papers, Colonial Series. Edited by W. Noel Saints-
bury, by the Hon. J. W. Fortesque, and by C. Headlam. 19
vols. London, 1860——.
————*Domestic Series*, of the Reigns of Edward VI, Mary, Eliza-
beth, and James I. Edited by Robert Lemon and by Mary
Anne Everett Green. 12 vols. London, 1856-1872.
————*Foreign Series, of the Reign of Elizabeth.* Edited by Rev.
Joseph Stevenson, by Allan James Crosby, and by Arthur
John Butler. 15 vols. London, 1863-1907.
> A considerable number of documents bearing upon the
> Persian expeditions are given in these Calendars, but most
> of this material has been printed in full in the collections
> named below. In the Colonial Series the first volume for
> the East Indies calendars all the papers on the subject from
> the Public Record Office, the British Museum, and the India
> Office. The letters of Bannister and Duckett are fully ab-
> stracted in the Cal. S. P. For., and have not been printed
> elsewhere.

Eden, Richard. *The History of Travayle in the West and East Indies.* Arranged and augmented by Richard Willes. London, 1577.
> Eden gives a brief account of Jenkinson's Persian voyage,
> prints the privileges granted by the Shah in 1566 and 1569,
> and gives some further information. However, the chief
> contribution is Richard Willes' notes on the fourth voyage,
> which were later printed in Hakluyt.

Fletcher, Dr. Giles, and Horsey, Sir Jerome. *Russia at the Close of
the Sixteenth Century.* Comprising the treatise, "*Of the
Russe Commonwealth,*" by Dr. Giles Fletcher and the "*Travels of Sir Jerome Horsey.*" Edited by Edward A. Bond.
Hakluyt Society Publications. London, 1856.
> Both works treat of the period following that under con-
> sideration, but they furnish some points of information on
> the earlier period. Of most interest is the memorial of
> Michael Lok on the Russian and Persian trade, printed in
> full in the Introduction.

Hakluyt, Richard. *The Principal Navigations Voyages Traffiques
& Discoveries of the English Nation Made by Sea or Overland to the Remote and Farthest Distant Quarters of the
Earth at any time within the compasse of these 1600 yeeres.*
12 vols. Glasgow, 1903-1905.

The great collection of Elizabethan voyages, indispensable for the subject in hand, as we are dependent upon it for most of the narratives of the Persian expeditions and for other important material, as, for example, the Parliamentary charter of 1566. The large number of documents, letters, and descriptions, made use of in this account of the Muscovy Company's activities in Asia is fully brought out by the footnotes.

Jenkinson, Anthony, and Other Englishmen. *Early Voyages and Travels to Russia and Persia.* Edited by E. Delmar Morgan and C., H. Coote. Hakluyt Society Publications. 2 vols. London, 1886.

While primarily giving documents illustrative of the life and travels of Anthony Jenkinson, these volumes also include the narratives of other English factors who were sent to Persia. They include some important material not found in Hakluyt, and form the fullest and best collection for the study of the voyages into western Asia.

Purchas, Samuel. *Hakluytus Posthumus or Purchas His Pilgrimes Contayning a History of the World in Sea Voyages and Land Travels by Englishmen and others.* 20 vols. Glasgow, 1905-1907.

Contains some material already printed in Hakluyt, as, for example, the account of Jenkinson's first voyage and Christopher Burrough's notes on the sixth Persian voyage.

Queen Elizabeth and Her Times. A Series of Original Letters, selected from the inedited Private Correspondence of the Lord Treasurer Burghley and others. Edited by Thomas Wright. 2 vols. London, 1838.

Contains a letter of William Smith to James Wodcoke (May 15, 1572), which gives an excellent glimpse of the troubles of the fifth Persian voyage from the point of view of the factor sent to Astrakhan to meet the expedition.

Tolstoy, George. *The First Forty Years of Intercourse between England and Russia.* St. Petersburg, 1875.

A collection of documents given both in English and Russian. Of much less value for the Persian than for the Russian activities of the English merchants, but indispensable for the study of Anglo-Russian diplomatic relations.

Warner, William. *Albion's England.* London, 1602. An interesting metrical account of Jenkinson's travels may be found in this work.

MODERN WORKS

Anderson, Adam. *An Historical and Chronological Deduction of the Origin of Commerce.* 4 vols. London, 1787-1789.

In this work there are brief and scattered references to the successive voyages to Persia. MacPherson, *Annals of Commerce*, merely incorporates for this period the work of Anderson.

Casimir, Nicholas. *The English in Muscovy in the Sixteenth Century.* Transactions of the Royal Historical Society (Vol. VII). London, 1878.

A fairly good account of the diplomatic relations between England and Russia, made up largely of documentary material.

Cawston, George, and Keane, A. H. *The Early Chartered Companies.* London and New York, 1896.

Very brief and hardly satisfactory on the Persian phase of the activities of the Muscovy Company.

Curzon, Hon. George N. *Persia and the Persian Question.* 2 vols. London and New York, 1892.

These volumes contain much information on Persia. Chapter XXIX, Part 1, briefly sketches the Anglo-Persian trading relations from their beginnings to the latter part of the nineteenth century. The map and the bibliographies in the footnotes are most useful.

Dictionary of National Biography. Edited by Leslie Stephen. 63 vols. 3 vols. supplement. New York, 1885-1901.

Articles on Anthony Jenkinson, Thomas Alcock, and Christopher Burrough.

Hamel, Joseph. *England and Russia.* Translated by J. S. Leigh. London, 1854.

Of value for the period it covers, but its value is much lessened by the failure to give references. Its allusions to the Persian voyages are slight and only incidental.

Hanway, Jonas. *An Historical Account of the British Trade over the Caspian Sea.* Second edition. 2 vols. London, 1754.

The author also includes an account of his travels and a history of the revolutions in Persia, especially in the eighteenth century. Though dealing with a period later than the one under consideration, this work discusses in detail some of the same difficulties and problems that confronted the Elizabethan traders in Persia, and thus indirectly it throws considerable light on the earlier movement. Hanway's references to his predecessors are neither extensive nor valuable.

Howorth, Henry H. *History of the Mongols from the 9th to the 19th Century.* Two parts, 3 vols. London, 1876-1880.

Useful for the history of the Tartars during the period of the Anglo-Persian venture.

Huntington, Ellsworth. *The Pulse of Asia.* Boston and New York, 1907.

Chapter XVII gives a summary of the arguments and conclusions regarding the Caspian Sea and the Oxus River from the earliest times down. This chapter, somewhat modified, may be found in the American Geographical Society Bulletin, vol. 39, pp. 577-596, under the title "Historic Fluctuations of the Caspian Sea." These geographical questions have a close connection with the subject of Jenkinson's route to Bokhara.

Jurien de la Gravière, J. B. E. *Les Marins de XV*e *et XVI*e *Siècle.* 2 vols. Paris, 1879.

———*Les Marins de XVI*e *Siècle.* Révue des deux Mondes. Paris, 1876.

This French work covers in detail the two eastern voyages of Anthony Jenkinson as well as the earlier work of Cabot, Chancellor and the English merchants in Russia. However, it merely follows Jenkinson's own account of these voyages almost without variation of plan. The five articles in the Révue cover practically the same ground as the book.

Malcolm, Sir John. *The History of Persia from the Most Early Period to the Present Time.* New edition, revised. 2 vols. London, 1829.

Though an old book, Malcolm's is still recognized as the best history of Persia.

Milton, John. *A Brief History of Moscovia, and of other less known Countries lying Eastward of Russia as far as Cathay. Gathered from the Writings of Several Eye-witnesses.* In Prose Works (Bell), Vol. V. London, 1884.

Though based upon the sources indicated, the portions bearing on Persia are very brief and annalistic in character, and do not give much idea of the movement.

Origin and Early History of the Russia or Muscovy Company (The). London, 1830.

Compiled from Hakluyt and Purchas, but carelessly done. Brief and of little value.

English Trade in the Baltic During the Reign of Elizabeth

Thesis presented to the Faculty of the Graduate School of the University of Pennsylvania in partial fulfilment of the requirements for the degree of Doctor of Philosophy, 1911.

By NEVA RUTH DEARDORFF, Ph.D.

CONTENTS

NGLISH TRADE IN THE BALTIC DURING THE REIGN OF ELIZABETH

CHAPTER I

THE ELEMENTS OF THE EASTLAND TRADE, 1550-1603.

By the middle years of the sixteenth century England ad already entered upon a period of marked commercial expansion. By that time the English nation had become conscious of distinct commercial desires and ambitions. Englishmen talked of the trade of England and compared it with that of other national states in existence at that time. They were eager to advance their economic interests. But in entering the race for economic power they were handicapped in many ways. On account of the lethargy in these matters which had characterized the generations just preceding them, they now found themselves circumscribed by rather narrow territorial limits. Lack of exact geographical knowledge seems to have rendered North America only a somewhat hazy conception, suggesting little more to the minds of the early Elizabethans than the chagrin caused by finding such a stubborn barrier lying in the way of their reaching the Indies by sailing west. As for Spanish America as a place in which to develop a settled trade, it was out of the question. It took a bold Englishman even occasionally to break through the Spanish monopoly on a half piratical venture. Portugal was doing her best to hold western Africa as a field for her own exclusive trade. India and the far East were known to Englishmen only through the accounts of men of other nationalities until far into Elizabeth's reign and English commerce with that country belongs to the seventeenth century. So that, so far as opportunities for colonial trade were concerned, the outlook must have seemed far from encouraging to the Englishmen of 1550.

It is true that England had numerous trade connections with the Netherlands, France, Spain and Portugal, but these countries were as anxious as she for commercial supremacy. Englishmen could scarcely hope to establish themselves so firmly or to make themselves so indispensable to these nations that their trade would flourish in spite of political and religious conflicts and in the face of local jealousy and opposition. The Merchant Adventurers, the strongest English trade organization of the time, could hold its position in Antwerp but a few years after it became evident that England and Spain would eventually take up arms.

But there were places where the English merchants of this time thought they saw opportunities for trade. A northeast route to China had never been tried, so now they decided to lose no more time. Growing out of their attempt to find such a route came the opening of trade with Russia. And then, ever keeping the goal of the Orient before their eyes, they pressed on until they reached Persia and established commercial relations between England and that distant land.

Although the English were eagerly taking up the "search of newe trades "[1] they were by no means losing sight of the possibilities that lay in certain old familiar ones. If they had failed to make their way to China and the far East, they at least knew the Levant where they could tap the flow of commerce as it passed along the ancient trade routes leading from eastern Asia to the Mediterranean. They were also keenly aware of the rich commercial opportunities offered by Germany. There the Merchant Adventurers could depend upon the lack of cohesion among the political units to afford them a chance to use local ambitions and jealousies to further their interests and secure protection and concessions for trade. Besides the Levant

[1] Hakluyt, Principal *Navigations, Voyages, Traffiques and Discoveries of the English Nation*, Glasgow, 1903-1905, II, p. 240.

and Germany there still remained the old trading connection with the Baltic countries, Prussia, Poland, Livonia and Esthonia—regions known in England at this time as Eastland—and it is this trade that is the subject of our special and detailed inquiry.

In considering the trade between two countries one must inquire into the productions of each and ascertain whether either produces goods likely to be in demand in the other. Such an inquiry directed toward the Baltic country in its relation to England shows that the former region yielded goods of vital importance to the English.

Foremost among the productions of Eastland come ship stores. For an island people with depleted forests, scarcely anything outside the absolute necessities of life could be of greater importance. England's political and economic salvation, then as later, depended upon her having an adequate navy. But for much of the material out of which to construct the ships of this navy, she had to go abroad. Since the resources of North America were practically unknown to the Englishmen of the sixteenth century, almost the only place from which they could procure naval supplies was the Baltic countries. In 1547 the King of England dealt with the Hanse Towns through the Steelyard "in suche merchandise and wares as his Majeste is woute as the case requireth to have owte of those partes for the furniture of his Navie, as cables, mastes, ankers, pyche, flaxe and such other" to the value of 50,000 crowns.[2] During the years 1551, 1553 and 1554 the Hansards were bringing pitch, tar, flax, hemp and iron into England.[3] The next year the English were evidently engaged in somewhat extensive trade in those commodities, for in February of that year the Privy Council wrote to the Eng-

[2] *Acts of the Privy Council*, New Series, London, 1890—, II, p. 61.
[3] Schanz, *Englische Handelspolitik gegen Ende des Mittelalters*, Leipzig, 1881, I, p. 223 note.

lish merchants "being presentlie in the citie of Dansick, and thier factours, that where it is enfourmed . . . that dyvers of them have bought upp all the hempe and cable yarne that is in the said citie, and have also gotten a graunte of all the rope makers there to spynne for them untill midsomer next, they are charged to desiste from thiese thier doinges untill suche tyme William Watson, presently sent thither to make provision for cable for the Quenes Majesties Navye, be furnisshed of the same."[4] A few years later (1558) permission was given by Sigismund Augustus, King of Poland, to this same William Watson to purchase materials in Dantzig for her Majesty's Navy.[5] In the next decade Thomas Allen was sent five times to Dantzig for this purpose.[6] Indeed, in doing this the English seem to have been only following the traditional line of trade for these goods. As the officials of the Muscovy Company said in 1564, "suche wares haue beene allwaies brought out & from the East Seas as from Danske and other places adioyninge."[7]

How dependent England was on the East Countries for naval supplies is illustrated by a letter, dated August 22, 1568,[8] sent to Cecil by Thomas Bannister and Geoffrey Duckett. In this communication these merchants enlarged upon the advantages that were to be gained by encouraging the Muscovy Company; and among these advantages they maintained that this company would furnish the Queen's navy with cables, cordage, masts, sails, pitch and tar whereby her Grace would be "delivered out of the bondage of the King of Denmark and the town of Dantzick."[9]

[4] A. P. C., V, p. 236.

[5] *Calendar of State Papers, Foreign*, 1553-1558, p. 375.

[6] C. S. P., For., 1561-1562, p. 81; *Forty-fifth Report of the Deputy Keeper of the Public Records*, App. II, pp. 23-24.

[7] S. P., Dom., Eliz. 35, f. 23.

[8] The new style of dating has been used in this essay.

[9] C. S. P., For., 1566-1568, p. 518.

In the year 1581 Thomas Allen was again engaged in securing naval stores in the East Countries.[10]   Some years later in 1590 his purchases there must have been somewhat extensive, for he mentions having advanced £3000 [$75,000 in modern values] from his own money to purchase masts.[11]   In the same year Ralph Querneby and Robert Savage shipped for the navy Norway masts costing over £337 [$8,000].[12]   Apparently the Queen purchased in all over £5,600 [$130,000] worth of cables, masts and oars in the East Parts during the autumn of 1589 and spring of 1590.[13]   In fact these things were of so much importance that the English ambassador at the Porte persuaded the Sultan to postpone an attack upon Poland which he was planning.   Understanding that ''her Majesty had great need of many things from the country necessary for her navy, he withdrew his force, though he was assured of victory, only for her Majesty's sake, who received great thanks from the King of Poland.'' [14]

In the latter years of the century when the struggle with Spain had grown so acute and so much depended upon England's power on the sea, it became still more important for England to have some place where she could constantly replenish her supply of naval stores.   The situation was still further complicated by the fact that Spain was also in the market for these goods.   This state of things is reflected in the Spanish ''advertisements'' of Robert Savage of February, 1598.   At that time he wrote: ''Last year I disappointed the King of Spain's factors of 24 great masts that were in Dantzig, 18 of which I

[10] C. S. P., Dom., 1581-1590, pp. 24 and 26.
[11] C. S. P., Dom., 1581-1590, p. 701.
[12] S. P., Dom., Eliz. 233, f. 81.
[13] S. P., Dom., Eliz. 225, f. 62 and Eliz. 233 f. 24.
[14] Lodge, *Illustrations of British History*, London, 1838, II, p. 414.

brought thither, for Her Majesty, but the rest are lying at Dantzig.''[15]

At the beginning of the seventeenth century the East Countries remained the principal source of supply for this kind of goods. Wheeler, whose "Treatise of Commerce" appeared in 1601, gives a list of all the goods imported into England from all the countries with which she had trading relations. In the list for Eastland the ship stores are especially conspicuous—flax, hemp, pitch, tar, deal-boards, oars, cables and cable yarn, ropes and masts for ships.[16] In 1603 James I appointed Simeon Furner his agent in the East Countries for supplying the navy with "pitch, tar, hemp, flax, oakum, sailcloth, cables, ropes, masts, iron, firs, deals, etc."[17]

We can hardly over-estimate the importance of these goods for England at this time. These were the instruments which she used to assure her position in relation to the other powers, particularly Spain. These were the tools with which she worked in laying the foundations for two of the greatest elements in all of her subsequent history, colonial empire and its complement, power on the sea.

Of scarcely less importance was the import of grain from Eastland. At this time English agriculture was still in the state of transition from tillage in open fields to grazing in enclosures.[18] This occasioned much uncertainty as to the grain supply and the country was haunted throughout the sixteenth century by constant apprehensions of a dearth. In such a condition of things it was vastly important to have some definite place to which to go in order

[15] C. S. P., Dom., 1598-1601, p. 29.

[16] Wheeler, A *Treatise of Commerce*, London, 1601, p. 23.

[17] C. S. P., Dom., Add., 1580-1625, p. 423.

[18] Cheyney, *Social Changes in England in the Sixteenth Century*, Part I, *Rural Changes*, 1895. University of Pennsylvania Publications, Series in Philology, Literature and Archeology, IV, No. 2.

to replenish the supply of bread stuffs.   In 1551 (February 8) the Privy Council wrote to Thomas Watson to provide 12,000 quarters of rye and 4000 quarters of wheat "in Estelande or Danske, to be brought into this realme, parte for the Northe Parties, parte to London, Portesmouthe and the South."[19]   In August, 1558, William Burnell brought to London 300 quarters of wheat "W^{ch} he broughte and pvydyd in dansyk for the vse of the saide cytye";[20] and at about the same time we hear of "Willm Frankelande clotheworker who of late bathe brought cc quarters of wheate oute of dansk to this cyty."[21] In November, 1562, Sir Thomas Smith, then in France, wrote to the Queen that as corn was likely to be very dear in England that year, there might be some trouble, especially if the Papists took advantage of the situation.   He advised as a preventive measure that she should take order with her merchants to bring from Dantzig to London a great store of wheat and rye.[22]   In April, 1574, we hear of the "Shipps of corne that cometh for this eytie out of Danske."[23]   Indeed we can have little doubt but that George Liesemann, a Steelyard merchant, spoke the truth in 1579 when he said that certain goods produced in the Eastland were indispensable to the English.   This was especially the case, he said, "of the precious grain, of which, it is true, they often have enough, but it also frequently happens that they have too little," just as shortly before there would have been a great riot in London on account of the scarcity of bread, had not ships soon procured a supply in Prussia.[24]

[19] A. P. C., III, p. 202.
[20] *Records at the Guildhall at London*, Repertory 13, Pt. II, f. 529.
[21] R. G. L., Repertory 13, Pt. II, f. 526 b.
[22] C. S. P., For., 1562, p. 435.
[23] R. G. L., Repertory 18, f. 191 b.
[24] Ehrenberg, *Hamburg und England im Zeitalter der Königin Elizabeth*, Jena, 1896, p. 150.

The last twenty years of Elizabeth's reign saw several
· failures of crops in England. In 1586 there must have
been a serious shortage of grain, especially in the
west of England, if we can rely upon an unsigned
document in which there is a discussion of the
price of grain for that year. This document sets forth
that "Duringe the moste parte of this somer corne continued at greate and highe prices, notwithstandinge all the
pollicie and consultacion taken against the same. This ex-
treamitie appeared and remayned more in the Countie of
Heref[ord] and the forest of Deane then in the cittie of
Glouc. and other partes in the Countie of Glouc. and more
in the Countie of Glouc. then in any other schiere adjoyn-
inge savinge in Bristoll, where for a space they were harde
and distressed." . . . The possible suffering was alle-
viated, however, by an importation of grain from the East.
The writer of this document continues, "the greate plentie
of corne that came to London from Dannske, Hamburge and
other places beyonde the seas kept downe the prices and
from thence good store came to Bristoll, parte wherof was
gotten hither from thence, and some provision was made
from London to Glouc." [25] In this year we hear of "William Gittens, Edward Longe and William Colston [who
were] retorning from Dansyke with corn." [26] The need
was apparently so pressing that the Privy Council gave
permission to certain merchants of Bristol to trade into
the East Parts with two or three ships and to return with
grain only, although this was breaking a monopoly of that
trade which they had granted some years before.[27] In
connection with this affair the Council spoke of the Baltic
countries as "those parts beyonde the Seas fromm hence

[25] Hist. MSS. Com. 12th Report, App. IX, p. 459. (The MSS. of
the Duke of Beaufort, the Earl of Donoughmore, and others.)
[26] A. P. C., XIV, p. 267.
[27] C. S. P., Dom., 1581-1590, p. 336.

plentye of grayne is vsuallie had.'' [28]   The municipal authorities of London also took steps to see that grain was brought from the East Parts to meet the demand that prevailed in the city.[29]

The suffering in 1586 furnished a lesson to the aldermen. The next year when a scarcity seemed imminent they ordered that a conference be held with certain Eastland merchants for ''a newe supplye of twentye or thrytye thowsand quarters of wheate and Rye for the Store and provysyon of thys cyttye.'' [30]   In 1589 Hugh Offley, one of these merchants, found in London a market for 2000 quarters of ''Eastland Rye good sweete and merchauntable.'' [31]

Although England did not send any great armies to the Continent in this period, even the small ones which she did send could not be provisioned from home. In 1590 and 1591 the English garrisons in the Low Countries were provisioned by corn purchased either there or at Dantzig.[32]

When Bacon wrote in 1592 that ''whereas England was wont to be fed by other countries from the East, it now sufficeth to feed other countries,'' [33] he was describing a condition that not only was of very recent origin but was also destined not to last many years. In 1594 and 1595 there was so great a dearth that in July of 1594 the aldermen of London ordered that 3000 quarters of rye and 1000 quarters of wheate be brought in [34] and in September of 1595 they called the Eastland merchants before them

[28] S. P., Dom., Eliz. 190, f. 60.
[29] R. G. L., Repertory 21, f. 288 b.
[30] R. G. L., Repertory 21, f. 363 b.
[31] R. G. L., Repertory 22, f. 128 b.
[32] C. S. P., Dom., 1591-1594, p. 115.
[33] Spedding, *Life and Letters of Francis Bacon*, London, 1861-1868, I, p. 158.
[34] R. G. L., Repertory 23, ff. 257 and 262.

and "treated with them to make provicion of som competent quantity of wheat and Rye to bee brought from hence.[35] The year 1596 saw large importations of grain into England from the Baltic countries. It is in that year that we hear of a "great arrival of Danske rye" at Newcastle,[36] and of the purchase, by the city of London of 500 quarters of "Danske wheat" from "John Wilkes, mᵣchaunttailor."[37] In the same season at least two committees of aldermen were instructed to "conferr wᵗʰ the mᵣchaunts trading the Easte contreyes for provision of corne to be brought to this cittie from the parts beyonde the Seas."[38] As a result of some of the contracts made at this time, we find that in the following spring thirty-two merchants brought into the port of London 740 quarters of wheat and 19,405 quarters of rye.[39] Wheeler in 1601 mentions corn as one of the imports from the Baltic countries[40] and we know that in the same year Roger Clark brought 200 quarters of rye from Dantzig to London.[41] This importation of grain was apparently of so much consequence that in 1606 the aldermen of London considered the question of applying to the Privy Council "That the English merchants trading into the Eastlands maye bring into this kingdome corne out of those countreys, and here to kepe a staple thereof."[42]

A trade which handled goods to meet a need so primary as this of grain in England, must have seemed then, as it does now, of great economic importance.

Besides naval stores and grain the East Country pro-

[35] R. G. L., Remembrancia [printed], II, p. 104.
[36] Hist. Mss. Com. Report on Hatfield House Mss., VI, p. 377.
[37] R. G. L., Repertory 24, f. 39.
[38] R. G. L., Repertory 23, ff. 571 b and 573.
[39] C. S. P., Dom., 1595-1597, p. 442.
[40] Wheeler, p. 23.
[41] R. G. L., Repertory 25, f. 262.
[42] R. G. L., Repertory 27, f. 305 b.

duced other things which England wanted. Among these
was nitre. Although the English made repeated efforts to
manufacture gunpowder at home and may in some cases
have succeeded, they never felt independent of the Continent for this important commodity. In 1561 Gresham was
engaged in bringing it from "Osterland" to England.[43]
In 1581 "Sault peter and gon-powlder" are mentioned
among the Baltic imports "whych her M^{atie} doth vse for
her higness shippes."[44] The importation continued and by
1591 it must have been considerable, for at that time Johan
Gerds, a servant of the Duke of Pomerania, informed
Burghley that "The said Duke lately granted free export
of a large quantity of nitre (the export of which, as well
as of munitions of war, from his dominion is . . . interdicted) because he was informed that it was purchased
for the use of the Queen's Majesty;"[45] . . .

The trade in nitre, however, was a matter of some uncertainty because of the widespread demand for that commodity and also because of its political importance. At
times the English could not be sure of getting it even from
the well-disposed Duke of Pomerania. For instance, in 1595
a " Mr. Furner, . . . a merchant of London . . .
being commanded to provide 100 lasts of saltpetre, which
he undertook to deliver within six months, to supply the
provisions that went out of the stores for the Cadiz voyage,
could not perform it, as the Duke of Pomerland would not
suffer his country to be weakened of a matter of such
strength . . ."[46] But in general the supply seems to
have been sufficient to warrant its being included in a list
of imports from Dantzig compiled by the customer, Plumpton, in the last years of Elizabeth's reign.[47]

[43] C. S. P., For., 1561-1562, pp. 1-2.
[44] S. P., Dom., Eliz. 150, No. 22.
[45] Hist. MSS. Com. Report on Hatfield House MSS., IV, p. 165.
[46] C. S. P., Dom., 1598-1601, pp. 470-1.
[47] Lansdowne 110, f. 157.

The East Country had been one of the main sources of
the supply of bowstaves for England. By 1574, however,
they seem not to have been especially valued there.
"These are not worth above 4 l. or 5 l. the hundred at
most, being hollow wood and full of sap by reason of
the coldness of the country."[48]

Furs are repeatedly mentioned among the imports from
the East Country, but by this time these must have been
only of minor importance.[49]

Wheeler also mentions soap-ashes as one of the imports
from the Baltic.[50] It is impossible to determine how great
was this import during the sixteenth century, but later it
assumed rather large proportions. On February 9, 1624,
the Eastland merchants declared potash to be a fourth part
of their trade. At that time they were importing £30,000
worth a year.[51]

Other articles brought into England by the Eastland
merchants were vitriol, copperas "better than could be
produced in England,"[52] stock-fish[52] and as Wheeler says
"almost whatsoever is made or groweth in the East
Countries."[53]

And now we must look upon the other side of the shield.
What had England to offer in exchange for these goods?
Or what did she produce for which she might be seeking
a foreign market? An investigation of this point shows
that woolen textiles were England's great export at this
time. Instead of exporting wool, as she had done in the
Middle Ages, she was now exporting cloth. In 1550 the
Steelyard merchants exported 43,000 pieces.[54] At the beginning of Elizabeth's reign the Merchant Adventurers

[48] Hist. MSS. Com. Report on Hatfield House MSS., II, pp. 82-3.
[49] Wheeler, p. 23; S. P., Dom., Eliz. 150, No. 22.
[50] Wheeler, p. 23.
[51] C. S. P., Dom., 1623-1625, pp. 128 and 154.
[52] Schanz, I, 233 n.; R. G. L., Remembrancia, II, p. 311.
[53] Wheeler, p. 23.   [54] Ehrenberg, p. 51.

were sending 100,000 pieces of cloth a year to the Continent.[55] In the years 1564 and 1565 England's total export amounted to about £1,000,000 of which wool and wool fells composed some £92,000, while woolen cloths and other woolen wares amounted to £896,000.[56] In 1601 Wheeler spoke of cloth as the "principallest commodity of the realm"[57] and the "Credite and Creame of the Land."[58]

That the English used cloth as an export to Eastland there is abundant proof. In September of 1551 Sir John Borthwick "the Kinges Majesties Agent in Danske" was required "to further the realease of iiij^{xx}xvj [96] clothes of Thomas Bannaster of London, stayed in the sayd towne."[59] In 1552 we hear of the "carseys" belonging to William Lane of London and John Baptist Cavalcant, Florentine, taken by the Marquis of Brandenburgh.[60] In 1553 Thomas Bannister had trouble getting cloths through the Sound.[61] In 1558 when Adolph, the Duke of Schleswig-Holstein was taking an interest in developing trade with England, cloth was considered the main article of export from England.[62] A document of the year 1561 on the sale of English cloths on the Continent sets forth that Suffolk cloths in colors, western reds and blues are wholly consumed in Eastland, Spain, Portugal and Barbary.[63] The next year Eric XIV of Sweden requested the Queen to grant to his factors the privilege of buying and exporting yearly sufficient cloth for clothing his retinue.[64] In

[55] Burgon, *The Life and Times of Sir Thomas Gresham*, London, 1839, I, p. 188.

[56] Ehrenberg, p. 80.

[57] Wheeler, p. 55.

[58] Wheeler, p. 62.

[59] A. P. C., III, p. 365.

[60] A. P. C., IV, pp. 74-75.

[61] C. S. P., For., 1553-1558, p. 168.

[62] C. S. P., For., 1558-1559, p. 13.

[63] C. S. P., For., 1560-1561, p. 524.

[64] C. S. P., For., 1562, p. 412.

1564 the Queen instructed the Marquis of Winchester to grant licence to certain persons to export colored cloths to Dantzig.[65] In the next year in a letter to the King of Denmark, the Queen remonstrated with that monarch for the excessive tolls he exacted at the Sound. In this remonstrance she mentions the four thalers levied on each piece of English cloth as the greatest hardship.[66] That same year (1565) the Merchant Adventurers sent in to the Privy Council a memorial on the condition of English trade at that time. In this they spoke of " suche of the said commodities as are to be spent in Media, Russia and Danswick, and by easte and northeeaste of the Sound, may be transported dyrectly to those places . . . Those commodities, beinge the greateste parte of the draperie of this realm, wich be to be spent in Denmarke, Swethyn, Pommerland, Mechelbroughe "[67] etc., etc. This kind of evidence exists for practically every year of Elizabeth's reign.

The Eastland trade in cloth was especially lucrative to the English merchants. In 1573 Dr. Valentine Dale had an interview with Katherine de Medici whose son, the Duke of Anjou, had just been elected to the throne of Poland, "whereupon he told her how ancient the amity had been between the Queen's [Elizabeth's] progenitors and the subjects of Poland and . . . how much her ships and mariners were in estimation with the Muscovite and the Kings of Denmark and Sweden, and what riches did come of the staple that was at Dantzig for cloth."[68] On March 30, 1603, Giovanni Carlo Scaramelli, Venetian Secretary in England, wrote to the Doge and Senate " . . . both the public and private revenues derive great profit

[65] C. S. P., Dom., 1547-1580, p. 237.
[66] 45th Rep. Dep. Keeper of Rec. App. II, p. 23.
[67] Kervyn de Lettenhove, *Relations Politiques de Pays-Bas et de l'Angleterre*, Brussels, 1882-1891, IV, p. 526.
[68] C. S. P., For., 1572-1574, p. 393.

rom the export of woollens, tin, lead, etc., from England
o Poland and Prussia;''[69] . . .

Although cloth was by far the greatest export from England to Eastland, it was not the only one. Cony skins were
taken thence, apparently in large numbers. In 1565
Thomas Allen took four ships laden with them and cloth
to Dantzig to obtain materials for the Queen's navy.[70] In
the latter part of Elizabeth's reign we hear of large quantities of them being sent through the Sound, as many as
500,000 in a single cargo.[71] Indeed, when, about this
time, Elizabeth gave a patent to two of her gentlemen pensioners for the sole licence to export conyskins, the
Eastland merchants protested vigorously, asserting that
the trade of transporting ''conyskynnes spetiallie grey
. . . hathe bene a great trade into the partes of Dansick and other Cuntreys beyond the Seas and diuerse merchants her Maiesties true and lovinge subiects brought vp
therein.''[72]

Other articles exported by the English to this region
were tin,[73] lead,[74] and coals from Newcastle.[74]

These then were the exports. It is noticeable that the
English found in Eastland a market for every kind of
goods which they had to offer.[75]

When the English traders in the early years of Elizabeth's reign set out to gain control of the Baltic trade they

[69] C. S. P., Venetian, 1592-1603, p. 556.

[70] 45th Rep. Dep. Keeper of Rec., App. II, p. 23.

[71] Rymer, *Foedera, Conventiones, Literae et cujuscunque generis
Acta Publica inter Reges Angliae*, Hagae Comitie edition, 1742, VII,
Pt. I, 203.

[72] S. P., Dom., Eliz., 265, f. 67.

[73] Rymer, *Foedera*, VII, Pt. I, p. 203; C. S. P., Dom., 1595-1597,
pp. 81-82; C. S. P., Venetian, 1592-1603, p. 556.

[74] C. S. P., For., 1579-1580, p. 263.

[75] A list of all of England's articles of export in the last decade
of Elizabeth's reign is found in the report of the customer, Plumpton. Lansdowne 110, f. 158.

were confronted with certain definite problems, certain obstacles to overcome. Some of these were purely physical,
others partook of an economic and political nature.

Of the purely physical dangers, the most important was
the actual peril of the voyage. To go from London to
Dantzig, Riga or Revel with a sailing vessel was no easy
feat. It meant crossing the stormy North Sea, following a
tortuous course through the Danish Sound or "Belt" [76]
and after that, if Riga were to be the destination "aboute
a thousande myles of daungerous saylynge." [77] Thomas
North, a mariner, writing to Walsingham in 1582 about
the specific dangers of passing through the Sound, relates
" . . . the road where the ships lie at anchor is an
open road with an easterly wind, and with a west or nor'
west wind, so that by storm from these two parts, many
ships are cast away, to the great loss and undoing of many
merchants, and also to the great charge of both merchants
and mariners . . ." [78] Concerning the voyage in general he declares, " . . . the voyage is as perilous into
the East parts as any that is traded of that distance. No,
there is none so perilous, but that it is traded in the summer time, in fair weather, yet there are more losses on that
voyage than on any other I know." [79]

Besides this purely physical danger, the Eastland merchants had to face a problem which at that time confronted all traders whose business required the transportation of goods over seas. This was the danger from pi-

[76] The voyage could be made in about a fortnight if all conditions
were favorable. In July of 1573 Dr. Valentine Dale, an English
representative in France, in reporting an audience which he had
with Katherine de Medici, relates that she mentioned to him that
"at Dieppe she did see a ship that had been coming from Dantzig
but 15 days" . . . C. S. P., For., 1572-1574, p. 393.

[77] Richard Eden, *The First Three English Books on America*,
Westminster, 1865, p. 314.

[78] C. S. P., For., 1581-1582, p. 648.

[79] C. S. P., For., 1581-1582, p. 651.

rates. The English pirates, with which the sea apparently abounded at this time, were no respecters of nationality, and apparently robbed their countrymen with no more compunction than they felt when preying upon foreigners. But they were not the only pirates on the sea. In 1565 the Queen wrote to Frederick II of Denmark in the interest of a certain William Peterson who had been despoiled by Danes.[80] In 1570 the "Danske Freebooters" came out with a fleet of six vessels to attack the English vessels bound for " the Narve."[81] In that same year a ship called the *Philip* of Sandwich belonging to Philip Lewes was captured by pirates[82] and two years later the ship of Thomas Boldnes, a London merchant, was also taken.[83] In 1575 the *Christopher* and the *Flying Hart,* two vessels freighted at Dantzig with the goods of English merchants were chased by pirates but were rescued by the Vice-Admiral of Norfolk.[84] In this they were more fortunate than the *Thornback,* a ship freighted by Alderman Thomas Pullison and other English merchants at the same port. This vessel was captured by pirates "under color of Commission from the Governour of the Lowe Countrey."[85] This was not an isolated case for "diverse other shippes laden with Englishe men's wares from Danske have been taken and spoiled under colour of soche Commissions either from the Governour or the Prince of Orenge."[85] In 1592 we hear of a Danish pirate, Hennison, who, by the capture of a ship and cargo five years before, had caused thirty-two Englishmen to suffer loss.[86]

Closely connected with the danger from pirates came

80 C. S. P., For., 1564-1565, p. 542.
81 Hakluyt, III, p. 167.
82 47th Rep. Dep. Keeper of Rec., App., p. 45.
83 47th Rep. Dep. Keeper of Rec., App., p. 46.
84 A. P. C., IX, pp. 29-30.
85 *Ibid.*
86 A. P. C., XXIII, p. 334; XXIV, p. 90.

the friction caused by the Danish-Swedish War, lasting from 1563 to 1570, though this should hardly be placed in the category of unmitigated calamities. In fact, it need not have been a calamity at all, had not the English yielded to the tempting offers of the Swedes to supply them with provisons for carrying on the war. Hardly had a state of hostilities been declared by Denmark before Eric XIV of Sweden wrote to the Queen desiring that she allow her subjects to furnish him with provisions and other necessaries "which they might bring to the ports of Halland or West Gothland."[87] To comply with such a request would have been a breach of the treaty relations which obtained between England and Denmark. However, the English must have either aided the Swedes or there were very strong rumors that they were about to do so, for Frederick II of Denmark asked her to prohibit her subjects from carrying provisions into Sweden. The Queen seemed not especially zealous in her efforts to prevent such a trade so that when she replied to Frederick, she promised to take care that the English should not take provisions to supply the King of Sweden's army but she declared that she could not prohibit them from carrying on the ordinary traffic with that country.[88]

The bolder spirits of the time seem to have been quite fascinated by the trade and adventures to be had by aiding Sweden. Under pretense of a legitimate trade to the East Country they carried supplies to that country and even occasionally acted as spies. In 1564 Thomas Valentine, while carrying letters for the Queen and some merchants into Sweden, used the opportunity to ascertain the plans of the King of Denmark and to carry them to the enemy.[89]

[87] C. S. P., For., 1563, p. 568.
[88] C. S. P., For., 1564-1565, p. 124.
[89] 45th Rep. Dep. Keeper of Rec., App. II, p. 23; C. S. P., For., 1564-1565, p. 282.

Denmark soon grew very impatient of these acts of hostility from the English and took definite steps to stop them. In January of 1565 Albert Knopper, the Danish ambassador, brought the matter to the Queen's notice. In a memorial addressed to her, he pointed out that according to the treaty made between King John of Denmark and Henry VII the subjects of neither prince should give assistance to the enemies of the other. He asserted that in the preceding summer several English merchants had taken warlike stores into Sweden. He then announced that the Danish King had chosen as a remedy for this, the closing of the Baltic navigation for a season "with which he hopes the Queen will not be offended, considering the exigencies of war." [90]

This threat aroused the English considerably. They maintained that if the Danes closed the Baltic it would be a clear violation of existing treaties. To placate the Dane, the Queen promised that she would charge her subjects to forbear from the carriage of any victuals or arms "whereby there might be any suspicion of their intention to aid either the King of Sweden or any other." [91] She suggested that instead of closing the Sound, he should exact pledges from the merchants that they would not carry provisions or warlike stores to the King of Sweden.[92] The Queen's promise and suggestion were unnecessary owing to the fact that Frederick had threatened more than he was either able or willing to carry out just at that time. Before the Queen's letter could possibly have reached him, he wrote that he would open "the navigation of his seas to all provided that they do not carry salt, arms or similar merchandise to his enemy." [93]

[90] C. S. P., For., 1564-1565, p. 279.
[91] *Ib*id.
[92] C. S. P., For., 1564-1565, p. 284.
[93] C. S. P., For., 1564-1565, p. 547.

In the spring of that same year (1565) Eric of Sweden
renewed his appeals to the Queen to enjoin her subjects
to bring provisions and munitions into those parts of Norway where his army was. He promised that they should
be well paid for their efforts.[94] There must have been at
least some response on the part of the English to this invitation for we find the Danes making a number of seiz-
ures of English vessels on the ground that they were aiding
the Swedes. In June, 1566, they captured the ship of
Gregory Parmort who was carrying corn to the King of
Sweden.[95] Later in the same year they took the *William
Joanna* of Plymouth, a vessel belonging to John and William Hawkins which they found in Norway.[96] At about
the same time they seized a ship called the *Julianna,* the
property of an Englishman by the name of Clynton.[97] In
1567 it was asserted by William Peterson, Thomas Bannister and "other the merchaunts of this . . . Realme"
that within the year preceding "Dyvers other of youre
Mat[es] subiects have bene spoyled of their shipps and goods
and their boddyes putt to Raunsone by the Servytures of
the sayd kinge of Denmarke."[98]

Notwithstanding the grave risks of seizure by Denmark
which they incurred, some Englishmen were still attracted
to this trade. In March of 1568 Frederick wrote to Elizabeth of one of her subjects, taken at Elsburg by the Danes
and afterward liberated on parole, who had then joined
the Swedes and who was at that very time in England preparing vessels for his enemies. He also mentions another
of her subjects who was engaged in the same kind of
enterprise.[99] In the following year we hear of the *Mathew*

[94] C. S. P., For., 1564-1565, p. 395.
[95] C. S. P., For., 1566-1568, p. 80.
[96] 47th Rep. Dep. Keeper of Rec., App., p. 44.
[97] *Ibid.*
[98] S. P., Dom., Eliz. 44, f. 59.
[99] C. S. P., For., 1566-1568, p. 430.

of Hull, an English ship seized by the Danish fleet at Revel.[100]

In 1570 the war came to a close and trade resumed its normal course.

It would appear, then, that the English did suffer losses and inconvenience and even came near being cut off entirely from the Baltic trade through the closing of the Sound, all because of the Danish-Swedish War. On the other hand, their hardships were, to a large degree, their own fault and it becomes a question as to whether, after all, their trade was not quickened and animated by the opportunities afforded by the war, more than it was checked and retarded by the punitive measures of Denmark.

But the serious trouble which confronted the English merchants in regard to the Baltic traffic was the competition of the Hanseatic League. For a long period the Hanse merchants had absolutely controlled the commerce of the "East Seas." With their staple at London they had been able to supply the English with Baltic products and in return export the English cloth. The entrance of the English into the Baltic trade created competition for these merchants and after they had once tasted the sweets of monopoly they were loath to give up their advantage. Consequently we find them opposing the English in the latter part of the fifteenth century and all during the sixteenth. Although the Treaty of Utrecht made with the towns by Edward IV provided for reciprocal privileges for the subjects of the two contracting powers, the competition, of the English seems not to have become really formidable until the time of Edward VI. As we have already seen, the English merchants at that time prepared to enter the lists in a way they had never attempted before. But when they tried to build up trade to Eastland, they encountered the determined opposition of the Hanse, led

[100] 47th Rep. Dep. Keeper of Rec., App., p. 45.

by Dantzig. The proclamation of Edward VI against the Steelyard sets forth that the treaty of reciprocity, made in the time of Edward IV whereby the English should have similar liberties in Prussia and other places of the Hanse, had been daily broken, especially in Dantzig, by the prohibition of Englishmen to buy and sell there and, though various requests for redress of such wrongs have been made, no reformation had ensued.[101]

After the English government had followed the advice of the merchants and had entered upon the policy of suppressing the Hanse privileges, Dantzig grew more drastic in her measures against the English merchants. By 1557 the situation was such that the English drew up "A Compendions declaration of such Iniuries, barbarous vsances, and vnfrendlie behauio[rs], as Hans Brandes Burrowm[r] and other naming them selves lordes of the Towne of Dansicke ministred, shewed, and vnnaturallie executed in, to and vpon the m[r]chauntes, Owners, masters, and marin[r]s of England beinge at Dansick in the monethes of Aprill, Maye, June, July and August A° 1557."[102] The English merchants declared that all of the English ships that had entered the port at Dantzig during the spring of 1557 were, upon their arrival and unloading, "comaunded to stay, not to departe at theire own will and libertie (as m[r]chauntes ought to do) w[th]out expresse and spiall licence craned and obteyned of the said Burrowmasters." There they were held until June 19, a delay which caused a loss of £20,000 [half a million dollars in modern values] to the English merchants and mariners. While they were being thus stayed, these Englishmen were mistreated in various ways.

[101] Contemporary translations of Edward's decree can be found in Lappenberg, *Urkundliche Geschichte des Hansischen Stahlhofes zu London*, Hamburg, 1851, p. 178 and in A. P. C., III, pp. 488-9.

[102] Lansdowne 170, f. 214. This declaration was delivered to the Privy Council by "Mr. Anthonyd Huse Gouerno[r] of the Marchauntes Aduenturers."

One of these was the refusal to allow them to purchase bread and beer within the town. This prohibition resulted in an exorbitant price being asked by persons just outside the town as well as a depreciation in the quality of the goods. The severity of the town was relaxed only when it was learned that the English were planning to go to another town where the Duke of Prussia and the municipal authorities had granted them permission to load what they pleased.[103]

When Elizabeth came to the throne the matter was in dispute. A few weeks after her accession, Thomas Gresham, the foremost financier of the period, pointed out to her certain measures necessary to a sound financial policy: she should reform the currency, grant as few licenses as she could, contract as few debts abroad as possible, keep up her credit at home and allow no special privileges to the Steelyard. On the question of the Hanse privileges he set forth, "the greatt ffreedome off the Stillyarde and grantinge of licence ffor the carringe off your woll and other comodytes ought off your reallme, which is nowe on off the cheffest pointes thatt your majestie hathe to forsee in this your comon well; thatt you neavir restore the steydes called the Stillyarde againe to ther privelydge, which hath bine the cheffest poyntte off the undoinge off this your reallme."[104] Gresham's final admonition to the new sovereign was to " kepp [up] your creditt, and specially with your owne merchants, for it is thaye must stand by youe att all eventes in your necessity."[105]

Keeping this advice in mind Elizabeth set out to settle the differences between her subjects and the Hanses and to do this she arranged a negotiation to be held in London in the spring and summer of 1560. A treaty was drawn

---

103 Lansdowne 170, ff. 201-203.
104 Burgon, I, p. 484.
105 Burgon, I, p. 486.

up which granted liberal concessions to the Hansards in England but all was made conditional upon the grant of equal privileges to the English in the Hanse Towns.[106] To this the Hanse refused to subscribe [107] and the oppression of the English in Dantzig continued. They were "driven to show openly their merchandise one day in the week, and then to sell to the burgesses of that town only." [108] Furthermore restrictions were placed upon them in such a way that one Englishman could not there bargain with another Englishman "without imprisonment or penalties." [109] The Merchant Adventurers maintained that the English were "used more ungratefully than any other nation that repairs thither for merchandise." [110]

Later in this decade the English were worsted in an attempt to force Dantzig to award justice to an English subject. In 1562 a certain William Marten sent his brother to Dantzig to collect a debt for which his father had received a judgment twenty-five years before.[111] The brother, armed with letters from Elizabeth to the magistrates of Dantzig and to the King of Poland, succeeded in having the case reopened. But he got no farther. From 1562 to 1568 the affair hung fire with many "shiftes and delayes." [112] Then William Marten, losing patience and fearing for the life of his brother who, it was later asserted "was stryken by his adersarye in place of Judgment in the p^rsence of the . . . maiestrats and no punyshment Done to thoffendo^r for the same," [113] ceased trying to obtain justice in Dantzig, recalled his brother

[106] C. S. P., For., 1560-1561, p. 214.
[107] Ehrenberg, p. 58.
[108] C. S. P., Dom., Add., 1547-1565, p. 520.
[109] Ibid.
[110] Ibid.
[111] The whole proceeding of William Marten's father is set forth in S. P., Dom., Eliz. 90, f. 21.
[112] S. P., Dom., Eliz. 90, f. 24.
[113] Ibid.

and laid his case before the English authorities. It was examined by Dr. Haddon, Judge of the Admiralty,[114] and soon the Alderman of the Steelyard was warned that unless justice were forthcoming to Marten within three months "her M^{atie} coulde not Denye the said Marten suche remedye as was Due to hym by lawe." [115] This warning being ignored by Dantzig, the queen granted Marten "aucthoritie to staye and arreste somoche of the goods of the maiestrats or inhabitaunces of ·Danske subiects of the kinge of Pole as myght aunswere the said Debte of 1938^{li} 15^s 5^d sterlinge wth all expences and Damages, wth a proviso nevertheles that no goods arrested should be soulde or Done awaye During the space of six monethes from the arrest. In wch tyme the maiestrats of Danske might compound wth the said Marten. And if they Dyd not then he might procead to the sayle of suche shippes as were vnder arreste for his satysfaccon." [116] Marten seems to have lost no time in putting into operation his letters patent.

If the English had really expected, by these measures, to force Dantzig to alter her course, they were doomed to disappointment. As soon as the magistrates heard of the steps taken in England, instead of "compounding" with Marten, they sent letters to protest to the Queen against her grant of arrest, and then to insure their fellow-citizens and themselves against possible losses, they seized and held all the English ships that came into their harbor. The ships proved to be "as well of London, Newcastell [from which place there were eight[117]] and hull as of other places." [118] These the Dantzigers held until an answer came from the Queen.

This seizure of the English ships caused such financial

114 S. P., Dom., Eliz. 90, f. 24.
115 *I*bid.
116 *I*bid.
117 S. P., Dom., Eliz. 47, f. 26.
118 S. P., Dom., Eliz. 47, f. 63.

distress among the Eastland merchants, especially those of Newcastle, that Dr. Lewes, to whom the matter was referred, advised the Privy Council to induce Marten to relent and set at liberty the ships and goods which he had staid and further to suspend his commission for a time "vntill sum other way may be devised . . . to vnderstand his matter rightlye and soe to fynishe the same." [119] But Dr. Lewes also considered it "verye harde for the po^r man" and recommended that the Council "take order that the m^rchants shall satisfye hym for his necessarye charges Defrayd about obteynynge and executing of the Comission wch may be sum relief to hym and no great burden to them beynge so many." [120] The Council followed Dr. Lewes' advice and "stayed execution" of their letters patent, while the merchants contributed sixty pounds to Marten's relief.[121] In this incident the "Danskers" certainly justified their reputation for high-handed conduct in dealing with the English.

But by the end of the sixties the scales commenced to tip on the side of the Queen's merchants. The Hanseatic League, once so powerful and so autocratic, had begun to show unmistakable signs of decay and disintegration. It was no longer able to hold its own members to a rigid adherence to its principles. And without such integrity these German cities could not possibly hope to dictate in commercial affairs to the vigorous young national organizations for trade which were appearing at this time. In 1567 occurred the defection of Hamburg from the principles and policy of the League. The Merchant Adventurers, energetic, wealthy and well-organized, were given a residence and extensive privileges there.[122] A little over

---

[119] S. P., Dom., Eliz. 47, f. 81.
[120] *Ibid.*
[121] S. P., Dom., Eliz. 90, ff. 24-25.
[122] Ehrenberg, p. 312.

a decade later the town of Elbing, a near neighbor of Dantzig, granted similar rights to the English in Prussia. These, with similar lapses on the part of other towns, left only time wanting for the complete triumph of the English and the rout of the Easterlings. By the end of the century the English merchants could speak of the Steelyard as the institution "vpon whose ruynes we were built."[123]

The question arises just how great or how important was this trade for which the English dared the perils of the sea and of pirates and for which the Easterlings waged such determined, though unavailing warfare against them. We have already seen that in so far as each region needed the products of the other, there was the basis for a very substantial trade between them. But the point of the actual bulk of the trade remains to be considered. Although it is impossible to obtain exact statistical evidence, a few figures have come down to us, which throw some light on this question. In the spring of 1557 during the quarrel between the Hanse Towns and the English, Dantzig, as has been seen, adopted the strenuous measure of stopping the English vessels as they came to the town. In the course of about eight weeks over fifty ships were thus held.[124] As has been already pointed out this delay meant the loss of £20,000 to the English merchants and mariners.[125] It would seem that there was a trade of no mean proportion at the very beginning of our period. As time went on and the Hanse lost its grip on the situation more and more, we find the English trade increasing. We have already seen how in 1573 Dantzig was considered a rich staple for English cloth.[126] In 1581 it was reported by John Rogers, the English agent in Poland,

[123] Sloane, 25, f. 13.
[124] Lansdowne 170, f. 203.
[125] Lansdowne 170, f. 214.
[126] C. S. P., For., 1572-1574, f. 393.

that the English merchants took from Elbing to the market at Thorn merchandise amounting in value to £82,380 [$2,059,500] and that the debts owed at that time by the Dantzigers to the English exceeded £65,900 [$1,647,-500].[127] In speaking of the friction between the English merchants and the King of Denmark, Thomas North, whom we have already quoted, estimated in 1582 that "if the King of Denmark pretended a quarrel towards our prince or nation, always about midsummer or Whitsuntide he might stay, that pass his Sounds, 50 or 60 sail of English ships, if he do 'deal upon the vantage'; for in the spring of the year, if he will suffer them to pass eastwards by 4 sail and 6 sail as they come, before those first ships return there may be 60, or 100 past and come within his 'danger,' which if he should stay, it would be a great foil to our merchants and owners of ships and also to a number of poor mariners."[128] In the same year the Queen wrote to the King of Denmark and mentioned "our people's trade into the sea of Öresund [the Sound] having much increased in quantity and value upon that of early times."[129]

As Elizabeth's reign drew to a close, the Eastland trade, although hampered in many ways, assumed such proportions as to enable the merchants engaged in it to compare themselves with the numerous and wealthy Merchant Adventurers both in the point of numbers and in the amount of their shipping.[130] Their ambitious assertion is, in a way, substantiated by a report made by the customer Plumpton for the month of May, 1596.[131] In this it is shown that, while there were 27 ships from the ports of Holland, 2 from Hamburg and 2 from Stade, there were

127 S. P., Poland, I, No. 9.
128 C. S. P., For., 1581-1582, p. 651.
129 C. S. P., For., 1581-1582, p. 632.
130 Sloane 25, f. 6 b.
131 Lansdowne 81, f. 123.

19 from Dantzig alone. And in 1603 the Venetian Se
retary, Giovanni Carlo Scaramelli, wrote to the Doge an
Senate that this trade was equal to the English trade c
the West Indies, Guiana and Brazil and greater than tha
of Venice, Ragusa, Lepanto, Constantinople and Syria.[1]
Just how much this was or how much this Venetian kne
about it, is impossible to determine, but this does sho
that in Scaramelli's eyes at least this was a very cousi
erable trade.

[132] C. S. P., Venetian, 1592-1603, p. 549.

CHAPTER II

THE EASTLAND COMPANY

It is usual to think of the sixteenth and seventeenth century commercial companies as organizations the aim of which was to open up or develop some new market for exports or to venture on some dangerous and distant voyage in search of certain highly prized goods. Such were the aims of the founders of the Muscovy Company, the Cathay Company, the Levant Company, the Barbary Company, the East India Company and a host of others. But with the Eastland Company the case was different. It is true, the voyage to Eastland was dangerous, but for a long time Englishmen had succeeded in trading there without the protection of an organization. The line of trade in that direction was one of the earliest to be followed by Englishmen. The home government had taken an interest in protectng and furthering it. The Baltic rulers had not at any time strenuously objected to it and in some cases had actually exerted themselves to encourage and favor it. Yet in 1579 we find the Eastland merchants organizing a company, modeled in some ways after that of the Merchant Adventurers. The query arises just why should these men, who were getting along fairly well as independent traders, form a company to carry on a regulated trade. The answer to this question seems to lie in the relation existing between these merchants and the problem of piracy, with the international complications arising therefrom.

The case that precipitated matters was that of John Peterson, a Dane. He had been despoiled of his ship and its cargo by certain English pirates, Hicks and Cal-

lice, about Easter time in 1577.[1] His grievance was taken
up by the Danish government and a restitution of the
spoil was vigorously demanded.[2] When Hicks and Callice
were captured, Peterson's ship was restored.[3] Since the
goods had been disposed of, the Privy Council decided
that for them he "shoulde be recompenced by certen fynes
to be put uppon suche as shoulde be founde to have ben
dealers withe pirattes, according to a Comission graunted
from her Majestic to that pourpose." . . . This resulted in the payment of £200 of the £1300 claimed by
Peterson. He was to receive the rest "as it was from
tyme to tyme to be leavied uppon the offendours." This,
apparently was too tardy a form of justice to suit Peterson and so, "on the sodane" he protested and departed
for Denmark.[4]

This course roused the English to take more effective
measures for indemnifying the irate Dane. The Council
feared that Denmark might adopt a policy of reprisals in
the Sound. Accordingly, "their Lordships foreseing
what inconvenience might follow thereby to suche her
Majesties subjectes as ether are there or hereafter shall
trade into the Est Partes," wrote to the Lord Mayor of
London on April 3, 1578.[5] In this letter they set forth
that they "have thought it good to require him to call
before him all suche of that Cittie as doe trade that way,
and to perswade them to leavie amongst them selfes, every
one according to his abillitie, soe muche money as re-
maynethe to be payed unto the said Peterson, which will
not be above mc[ll], which shall be payed unto them againe
as the fynes aforesaid shalbe leavied, which will not be
long; not doubting but they will the willinger yeild unto

[1] A. P. C., X, p. 57.
[2] Ibid; C. S. P., For., 1577-1578, p. 275.
[3] A. P. C., X, pp. 83 and 193.
[4] Ibid.
[5] A. P. C., X, p. 193.

[this] considering it is for their owne benefitte and they to be noe furder interested, but only the forbering of their money for a tyme, which maye be lesse burden unto them."[6] His Lordship was then instructed to inquire "what merchantes of Hull, Ipswich, Harwich and Newcastell doe trade that way, uppon the receipt of whose names from their Lordships the like order shalbe taken with them to assiste this contribucion."[7] The Lord Mayor must have followed this instruction, for such a list still exists. It gives, along with the names of the merchants trading to the East Countries, the rate of taxation for each. One hundred and forty-one names are included, among whom, judging by the tax rate, Thomas Pullison, Robert Hilson, William Cokayne, Hugh Offley, Richard Gurney, Edmund Boldero, and Roger Fludd were the wealthiest.[8]

By midsummer the idea of using the merchants for other purposes than merely to meet the demands of Peterson, had occurred to the Council. These merchants might be used to help send representatives to Denmark to negotiate upon the question of tolls collected at the Sound. On July 9, 1578, the Privy Council wrote again to the Lord Mayor "to confer with some of his brethern by calling before them soche marchantes of the Cittie as are interested in the trade towardes Danske, for the leavynge of 200[li] towardes the charges of soche persons as shall, apon motion made to the Quenes Majestic, be sent to the Kinge of Denmark, aswell for thexcessive customes demaunded by the saide King as also for the compounding of some controversies betwixt the subjectes of bothe realmes . . . their Lordships offeringe their assist-

[6] A. P. C., X, p. 193.
[7] Ibid.
[8] S. P., Dom., Eliz. 127, No. 73. It is impossible to determine whether this list contains only London merchants or whether those of the provincial towns are included.

inces to leavie and gather the same in equall and indiffer-
nt manner.'' [9]

In the following week "Mr. Alderman Pullison and
erteine other merchauntes tradinge Dantzig and the East
Partes" undertook and promised before the Lord Treasurer to pay over to Peterson the sum of £200, "towardes
the satisfaccion of the losses which he sustained by
Hickes.'' [10] The measures taken by the government had
so mollified Peterson that he had consented "in case he
maye presentlie have cc^{li}, to tarye some longer time
for the rest, for the levyinge wherof he is to understand
that it is ordered by their Lordships that iiij $^{xx^{li}}$ [80]
or therabout shalbe delivered out of the receipt of her
Majesties Exchequier by direction of the Lord Threasurer." [11] On July 16, 1578, the Council wrote to the Lord
Mayor to call Pullison and the other merchants before
him "and in their Lordships' name to enjoyne them to
make provision with speede convenient of the said cc^{li}
and xx^{li} more, or so much as shall suffise to meete
thother sum, iij$^{c\ li}$ and to cause the same [to be] brought
to the Lord Threasurer who will see it paid over to Peterson." [12]

Evidently Pullison and his companions were averse to
bearing the whole burden of this charge, for the next day
they appeared before the Council about the matter and
as a result, that body once more wrote to the Lord Mayor
requiring him to "sende for all such merchauntes as he
shall understande to trade into those partes, and in her
Majesties name to charge them to paie towardes the said
summe such severall porcions as everye of them is rated
at, and to commit suche as shall refuse to prison without

[9] A. P. C., X, p. 266.
[10] A. P. C., X, p. 277.
[11] A. P. C., X, p. 277.
[12] *Ibid.*

releasinge them by baile or otherwise without speciall warrant and order therin from their Lordships . . ."
His Lordship was particularly instructed, however, "to signifie unto them that it is meant the said severall porcions shalbe repaid unto them uppon such fines as shalbe gathered uppon pirates and their abbettours, wherin . . . their Lordships are minded substantiallie to proceede. . . ." [13]

Here was a peculiar situation. The inefficiency or indifference of the government in regard to piracy led to the endangering of English mercantile interests in the Baltic. The government, considering that it was the merchants who had most to lose in case Denmark undertook reprisals, thought it only fair that they should do most in preventing such a contingency. When the government sought to put its ideas into practice, a further problem arose. What would be an equitable distribution of the burden among the merchants, since all might share in the benefits? The solution that seems to have occurred to the merchants was the same as had been adopted for the solution of so many other difficulties of the merchants of the period, the formation of a chartered company; and so in the fall of 1578 we find them demanding joint privileges. [14]

Running parallel with this series of occurrences in England was another which may have had some influence in bringing about the formation of the company at this time. On the Continent events were so shaping themselves as to make it very necessary for the English merchants to effect some sort of organization. Since this subject comes up for full discussion later it need only be noted here that the old enemies of the English merchants, the Dantzigers, were doing all in their power to ruin the English trade in their city, while the people of a rival town, Elbing,

[13] A. P. C., X, p. 280.
[14] C. S. P. Dom., 1547-1580, p. 602.

vere just as anxious to attract and foster the trade of
Elizabeth's subjects. Only through organization could
he opposition of Dantzig be met and the overtures of
Elbing effectively turned to advantage.

What would be the attitude of the government toward
the new project of organization? Apparently the authorities felt that they had much to gain and nothing to lose.
In the future when such cases as that of Peterson arose
and menaced the Baltic trade, here would be an organization which could assume responsibilities. In fact the government might simply delegate powers to the Company
"to th'intent that suche disorders as happened heretofore in that trade might be avoyded and prevented." [15]
This organization might be given "libertie for that purpose to make actes and orders for their better government,
and authorite to sequester, committ and fine the transgressours therof." [16] Furthermore here was another instrument with which to work toward the attainment of
that most praiseworthy object, the expansion of English
commerce. Indeed here was an effective and impartial
"plat for all parties interested." [17]

Some time during the winter and spring of 1578-9 the
Eastland merchants presented a formal petition to the
Queen that "by her Highnes' Letters Patentes she would
vouchsafe to make them a Companie and Fellowshippe
Incorporate." [18] In this Alderman Thomas Pullison took
the lead. The Charter sets forth that "we [the Queen]
be credyblye informed by the reporte of our trustye sub-
jecte Thomas Pullyson Alderman of our Citie of London . . . That yowe our Subjectes Marchantes tradinge the Easte partes . . . by one assente and con-
sente are Wyllinge and desirous to gather congregate as-

15 A. P. C., XII, p. 207.
16 A. P. C., XII, p. 207.
17 C. S. P., Dom., 1547-1580, p. 602.
18 A. P. C., XI, p. 205.

semble and drawe your selves into one fellowshipp and coṁynaltye." [19]

A delay was now caused by the appearance of new complications. When the merchants presented their petition to the Queen, they enclosed an abstract of certain privileges which they desired.[20] This aroused the opposition of the Merchant Adventurers and the Spanish Merchants, for they considered "divers articles in the said abstracte as prejudiciall to their Chartres and Corporacions."[21] By August 5, 1579, however, the matter had been adjusted and on that day the Attorney General was instructed by the Privy Council "to acquainte the said Merchantes Adventurers and Spanishe Merchauntes with the said abstracte before he drawe upp the booke, that their consent be had to the articles which heretofore they misliked."[22]

In a few weeks after this (August 27) the charter was granted.[23]

It seems evident, then, that the formation of the Eastland Company was precipitated at least by the necessity on the part of the merchants of meeting this shifting by the English government of the burden of indemnification for piracy; other incentives to its formation are to be found in the efforts of the English to make the most of the situation in Prussia.

For the particular form of organization that the Eastland merchants were now about to assume, they had a

[19] The charter of the Eastland Company is found in the Patent Rolls, 21 Eliz., pt. 11 and also in S. P., Dom., Eliz. 131, No. 70. Extensive portions of it from the former source are printed in the appendix of the volume "*The Acts and Ordinances of the Eastland Company*," in the publications of the Camden Society, Third Series, XI. The quotation above comes from that volume, p. 142.

[20] A. P. C., XI, p. 205.

[21] *I*bid.

[22] A. P. C., XI, p. 205.

[23] C. S. P., Dom., 1547-1580, p. 630.

hoice between two models. The Company of Merchant dventurers had already shown that Englishmen as well as foreigners could unite and by a regulated trade both gain concessions abroad and protect themselves from dangerons competition among their own members. The Muscovy Company had demonstrated how co-operation by joint stock could be applied to overcome the obstacles of distant trading and the assumption of large risks. Of these two the Eastland merchants chose the former. This was only natural since the conditions with which they had to deal resembled the conditions of Germany far more than those of Russia. Reflecting the type of the company, the official name of "Governour, assistauntes and Fellowshipp of Marchaunte of Eastland "[24] was selected.

The charter is addressed to certain classes of administrative officials: admirals, castellans, customers, controllers, collectors of subsidies, keepers of havens on the seas, justices, escheators, coroners, mayors, sheriffs, "chiefe officers," bailiffs, constables, and "other our officers mynysters and subjectes."[25] This list probably includes all the officials of the government with whom the new company was at all likely to come in contact.

The purpose of the fellowship, as voiced by the charter, was the better regulation of the Eastland trade. The new Company was for the " honor and service of us and our lande inventynge [venting?] our comodytyes to the pffytte of us and our lande and cuntrye and sving [serving?]—our lande and cuntrye With the moste necessarye comodytyes of the said landes Nacyons countryes Cittyes and Townes Which thorough many unskylfull and disordered persons is sore altered to the greate hinderance of us and our lande and countrye."[26] The

[24] A. and O., p. 144.
[25] A. and O., p. 142.
[26] A. and O., p. 143.

relations of the English merchants to Denmark which we
have seen to be so important in bringing about the formation of the company, as well as the relations with the
Hanse Towns were only hinted at in the preamble of the
charter where it sets forth that by this instrument the
merchants were to be drawn into one body corporate and
politic "in dede and in name aswell for your better governemente Releiff and succours in those partes and re-
dressinge of suche wronges and injuryes as heretofore hathe
bene and hereafter myghte be layde unto and upon yowe
by dyvers and sundrye unlawfull and unreasonable taxes
exacyons and imposicions and other newe customes in
those partes contrarye to the entercourse betwene us and
our noble Progenitors and the princes States and comon-
altye and their Progenitors Auncestors and Predecessours
of the said Easte Countryes."[27]

A point much emphasized in the charter is that of de-
fining the geographical limits within which the Company
was to have the monopoly of trade. In certain regions
of the East Country no Englishmen except members of
this organization were hereafter to be privileged to buy
and sell. These places are beyond "the Sounde into the
. . . Realmes Kyngdomes Domynyons Dukedomes Cou-
tryes Cittyes and Townes of Norway Swethan Polland
and Terrytories of the same Kingdomes of Pole Norway
and Swethen lettow leefland and Prussen With the Terrytories of the same and also Pomerland from the Ryver of
Odera Eastward with Rye Revell Kynningburgh, Elbynge
Brounsburgh Dantzick Copenhawen and Elsenor Finland
Golland Ewland and Burntholme."[28] This included almost all the countries and islands touched by the Baltic.
Furthermore the few places not assigned exclusively to
the Eastland Merchants were taken care of. Narva, at

[27] A. and O., p. 144.
[28] A. and O., p. 144.

his time the one Russian port on the Baltic, already be-
onged to the Muscovy Company, so that now it was care-
ully excepted from the places assigned to the Eastland
Ierchants.[29] It would seem that the Eastland Merchants
at first had asked for a monopoly of all the lands bordering upon the Baltic; but to this the Merchant Adventurers
made objection. They resented the assignment to another
company of any portion of Germany since "all the Terry-
toris therof hathe ever benn insydente to their trade."[30]
This was probably one of the points in the dispute which
caused the delay in the granting of the Charter. A compromise was effected whereby the portions of northern
Germany west of the Oder, that is Pomerania west of the
Oder, Mechlenburg and Lübeck along with Denmark outside of Copenhagen and Elsinore, were to be held jointly
by the Eastland Company and the Merchant Adventurers. "We . . . doe by these psentes graunte to the
said Governour assistauntes and Fellowshipp̃ of Marchauntes adventurears of England . . . and to the
said Governour assistauntes and Fellowshipp̃ of Mar-
channtes of Eastelande . . . That the said severall Fel-
lowshipps and Companyes shall or maye . . . trade and
occupye into and with the kyngdomes Countryes Cytyes and
Townes hereafter expressed that is to saye into and
Withall Denmarke excepte Copen haven and Elseno Which
before is appoynted to the said Marchauntes of Eastelande
and their successours onely and into and With Mackelburgh
Jutland Selesia Moravia Lubeck Wysmore Rostock Sta-
tine Stralsound and the Whole Ryver of Odera any thinge
or matter in these psentes conteyned to the contrayre
notwithstandinge."[31]

Not only were there provisions as to the exclusive ter-

---

[29] A. and O., p. 144.
[30] S. P., Dom., Eliz. 126, f. 24.
[31] A. and O., pp. 149-150.

ritory of the Eastland Merchants but there were also
clauses prohibiting them from trading in other places.

"And We Wyll and comaunde and straightly inhibyte
our said Marchauntes of Eastelande and evye of them
that they nor their successours shall not occupy buy or
sell in any porte place or Towne of the Dukedome of
Holston the towne of Hamburg or the Ryver of Elve
or any of them or shall use the same otherwise then for
the Fre passage of their parsons and goodes Without
breakinge any Bulke to thende or intente to make sale of
any their Marchaundize Which places late recyted."[32]

When one finds a monopoly such as this one, the vital
questions for determining its real character are those concerning the membership. How many members were
there? What sort of people were they? How was the
membership recruited? Was the number limited in any
way?

In answer to the first of these questions it is found
that there were sixty-five charter members, sixty-four men
and one woman.[33]

When the merchants had first asked for privileges they
suggested that the membership be limited to persons who
had been engaged in the trade for a period of at least
ten years, that is, since January 1, 1568. But this was
considered a measure of doubtful propriety, "For that
there [are] many mere marchants that bathe benne Dealers in thos pties sence that tyme and nowe are [Wch] wolde
& myght think themselves hardly Deelte w[th]all, to be de-
barrid or phibetid the same."[34] Probably as a result of
this difference of opinion we find in the charter curiously
jumbled statements which were perhaps meant to evade

[32] A. and O., p. 150.

[33] In editing the Charter, Miss Sellers has seen fit to omit the
names of the charter members. This list will be found in the appendix to this volume.

[34] S. P., Dom., Eliz. 126, f. 24.

the issue. In the preamble the merchants are addressed as "yowe our Subjectes Marchauntes tradinge the Easte partes comonlye called the Dansicke Marchauntes or Marchanutes tradinge in or thorough the Sounde."[35]—Further on in the incorporating clause after the enumeration of their names they are spoken of as "mere marchaunts . .. which have had and lawfully did use or nowe have and doe lawfully use the trade of marchaundyze out of and from any of our Domynyons through the Sounde into [the various places set apart for the Eastland Company] . . . by transportinge out of the same or any of them any Marchaundyze or Comodytyes . . . into our Realme of England or into any other our Domynyons whatsoever or *which* have any traffique and did use any trade of marchaundyze in the said Realmes Kingdomes Domynyons Dukedomes Countryes Cyttyes and Townes aforesaid or any of them in and through the Sounde aforesaide before the firste daye of Januarye Which was in the yeare of our lord god 1568 & then in the saide yere of our lorde god 1568 aforesaid beinge lyvinge and their children and also their apprentyces which they then had or sythence that tyme have or had and hereafter shall have from henceforth, shalbe one fellowshipp and comynaltye . . . "[36]

In the list of charter members are the names of some of the most prominent merchants of the time. These men were distinguished not only in the Eastland trade but in the commerce with other places as well. They were among the people of influence in the municipal affairs of London. At the

[35] A. and O., p. 142.

[36] A. and O., pp. 143-144. In a comparison of the names contained in the Charter and those in the Lord Mayor's list, it is noticeable that eleven names appear in the Charter which are not contained in the other list. A possible explanation of this lies in the fact that one of these men, John Langton, was a resident of Poland and so very probably escaped the notice of his Lordship.

head of the list are four London Aldermen, Edward Osborne, Thomas Pullison, George Barnes and George Bond. Edward Osborne belonged to the oligarchy that controlled the city. He had married the daughter of Sir William Huet who had been Lord Mayor in 1559.[37] Thomas Pullison was one of the foremost merchants of his time. He traded to Spain, to the Netherlands and to the East Country.[38] Aldermen Barnes and Bond were among the substantial business men of London. In 1580 Barnes was one of the Governors of the Muscovy Company.[39] Bond belonged to a family prominent in business and city affairs. Another man of means in this company was William Bond, to whom the government owed at one time over £7000, a sum equal to $175,000 at the present time.[40] The one woman member, "Margarett Bond, wydowe" was very likely a relative of his; her name follows his in the list. Other well-to-do members were Christopher Hoddesdon, a Muscovy merchant and also one of the leading Merchant Adventurers; Thomas Wylford, the President of the Company trading Spain;[41] Thomas Allen, who had been the treasurer of the company which financed Frobisher in his voyages to the Northwest;[42] Hugh Offley, a merchant of wealth, who was often chosen to act as an arbitrator in mercantile cases and who later became an alderman;[43] Thomas Russell, at one time "one of the Queen's Majesties Purveyours";[44] Richard Staper, a man of broad interests who, with Alderman Osborne, had in 1575 sent at their own expense, John Wicht and Joseph Clements

[37] Stow, *Survey of London*, (Kingsford Edition, 1908) I, p. 223.

[38] C. S. P., Dom., 1547-1580, p. 489; C. S. P., Dom., Add., 1566-1579, p. 72; A. P. C., VIII, pp. 299-300; X, 107.

[39] C. S. P., Dom., Add., 1580-1625, p. 6.

[40] A. P. C., VIII, pp. 53-60.

[41] C. S. P., Dom., 1547-1580, p. 687.

[42] C. S. P., Dom., 1547-1580, p. 608.

[43] Stow, *Survey*, I, p. 151.

[44] A. P. C., VII, p. 241.

"by way of Poland to Constantinople, where the said
Joseph remained 18 months to procure a safe-conduct
from the grand Signior for M. William Harborne, then
factor for Sir Edward Osborne, to have free accesse into
his Highnes dominions, and obtained the same."[45] Osborne and Staper were also the patrons of Newberry and
Fitch in their journey to the Far East.[46] Besides these
men the membership included William Towerson, often
chosen by the Privy Council to help in the adjustment of
difficulties between merchants, both native and foreign;[47]
John Foxall, at this time a well-known trader to Spain,
Denmark and the East Country;[48] Robert Hilson and
Roger Fludd, both wealthy merchants, holding large interests in Dantzig;[49] and the Cokaynes who later became
so influential in and subscribed so heavily to the East
India Company.[50]

How was this number to be recruited? Of course, the
sons and apprentices of these men could get into the Company but what were the conditions put upon persons who
had no such claims for admission. The charter lays down
the rules for eligibility. Above all they must be
"mere" merchants.[51] Retailers, artificers, and handicraftsmen were absolutely excluded. Besides being "mere" merchants they had to be Englishmen, "subjects of us our
heires and successours."[52]

[45] Hakluyt, V, pp. 168-169.

[46] Arber, *English Garner*, Westminster, 1903-1904, III, p. 177;
Richard Staper was one of the leading merchants in the East
India Company. C. S. P. Col. East Indies, 1513-1616, pp. 99, 101,
109, and 116.

[47] A. P. C., VIII, pp. 167 and 287; X, p. 83.

[48] 45th Rep. Dep. Keeper of Rec., App. II, p. 48; C. S. P., For.,
1581-1582, p. 649.

[49] S. P., Poland, I, No. 11.

[50] C. S. P., Col., East Indies, 1513-1616, pp. 100, 101, 176, and
180.

[51] A. and O., pp. 143-144.

[52] A. and O., p. 143.

After this limitation as to the sort of persons to be admitted, comes a provision for the special favor of East-land Merchants in certain localities outside of London. The charter specifies that the company "shall take and shall not refuse to receyve into their fellowshipp all other Marchauntes . . . inhabytynge Within the townes of Brystowe, Excest Barstable Lyme Dertmouth Plymmouth Bridgewater Beaton and Tottnes Who synec the said firste day of Januarye in the yeare of our lorde god 1568 have in any one yeare transported any Wares or comodytyes of England into the said Easte partes through the sounde by Way of Marchaundyze or trade . . ."[53]

The question of entrance fee, or fine, as it was then called, was next taken up for discussion. There is no mention of any initial fee paid by the charter members other than the hint that certain persons are to be admitted hereafter "for such duetye as those nomynated in this charter are."[54] It seems fairly certain that the originators of this Company had to meet rather heavy expenses, since beside bearing the burden of indemnifying the Danes which Thomas North says was "made at the great suit of her [the Queen's] loving subjects,"[55] they had to secure the charter and perfect the organization. It is impossible to determine just how heavy these expenses were or how they were apportioned to the members. But in the case of the merchants to be taken in hereafter, the charter was quite explicit. The Eastland Merchants of the coast towns enumerated above were to be admitted upon the payment of £6 13s. 4d. "of good and lawfull money of England."[56] "All other Marchaunts Whatsoever," that is, merchants who had not traded to Eastland since 1568, whether they were of

[53] A. and O., p. 147.
[54] Ibid.
[55] C. S. P., For., 1581-1582, p. 650.
[56] A. and O., p. 147.

ondon or the coast towns, had to pay £20.[57] In both f these cases the children born since 1568 and the aprentices bound since that date were to be admitted on ayment of a sum equal to that paid by the charter memers.

There must have been considerable confusion in the inds of the framers of this charter as to the relation of this to other companies, if one can judge by the provisions found in the charter itself. We have already noted that before the granting of the charter there was some opposition on the part of the Merchant Adventurers and the Spanish merchants to the abstract of privileges presented by the Eastland Merchants and it is possible that this confusion in the charter is another result of an attempt to adjust difficulties. But whatever the cause of this obscurity, the charter first provided that this Company was to admit no merchants free of any other trading company. "And further we will and neverthelesse doe straightly comaunde the said Governour assistaunts and Fellowshipp of Marchauntes of Eastelande aforesaide and their successours That they and their successours doe not in any wyse admytt into their Fellowshipp any marchaunte free of any other companye or societie tradinge marchaundyze beyonde the Seas . . "[58] After this very definite prohibition came the exceptions which rob it of all significance. It was provided that "notwithstandinge any former excepcyon yet nevthelesse any other Marchauntes . . . beinge subjectes of us our heires or successours beinge of any other Fellowshipp or Marchauntes tradinge into any forreyne partes shall also be receyved and admytted into the said Fellowshipp of marchauntes of Easteland"[59] upon any one of three conditions: (1)

[57] A. and O., p. 147.
[58] A. and O., p. 146.
[59] A. and O., p. 147-8.

that they pay "in the name of a Fyne" such a sum of money to the use of the "said Fellowshipp of Marchauntes of Easteland as the Fellowshipp and companye Whereof they then be are used to take of any other psone or psons not beinge of their Fellowshipp for admyssion into their Company and Fellowshipp by redempcyon"; [60] (2) that they relinquish their membership in other companies; [61] since "Dyvers occacons may happen to Dryve [a] marchante From the vsuall trade wch he exersysethe in the fellowship wherof he is one; [62] (3) that they procure the free admission of a member of the Eastland Company into the other company. In this last case no fine was to be paid by the merchant for entrance into the Eastland Company. [63] The "mere" Merchant Adventurers and the "mere Marchauntes tradinge Spayne and Portingale" who had traded through the Sound into Eastland since 1568 were to be admitted on the payment of ten pounds. [64] This special concession was to be valid only one year after the granting of the charter. If there were any Merchant Adventurers and Spanish Merchants who had not traded to the East Parts but who were desirons of taking up that trade and entering the fellowship, they were to be received on the payment of forty marks. This concession was to be "Wythout lymytacyon of tyme." [65] In the first of these classes, the sons born after 1568 and the apprentices bound after 1568 were to be admitted on a fine equal to that paid by sons of charter members. [66] In the case of the second class only sons born or apprentices bound after their father's or master's en-

---

[60] A. and O., p. 148.
[61] Ibid.
[62] S. P., Dom., Eliz. 126, f. 24.
[63] A. and O., p. 148.
[64] Ibid.
[65] A. and O., p. 149.
[66] A. and O., p. 148.

'ance into the fellowship were to enjoy similar privi-
.ges.[67]

Beside providing for the territorial monopoly and the
1embership of this Company, the charter takes up the
uestion of internal organization. It provides for a body
f officials the most important of which were a governor,
. deputy governor and twenty-four assistants. In one
)lace the charter reads as if there was a possibility of more
:han one governor; it speaks of the "rule and governe-
nente of the said Governour or Governours his or their
eputye or deputyes and the said assistauntes or the greater
)arte of them then psente."[68] Since there is no men-
ion anywhere else of a dual or plural governorship, one
oncludes that this provision was worded in that way to
take care of a contingency that never arose. Alderman
Pullison was nominated the first governor[69] and Thomas
Russell his deputy. The first group of assistants were
also named in the charter.

The offices of governor and his deputy were to be filled
by annual elections. The charter goes into this matter
in great detail, describing both the manner of the regular
elections and the procedure in case of vacancies occurring
during the year of office. The twenty-four assistants
were to remain in office "for one whole yeare And further
soe longe as they shall behave themselves well in the said
office at the good discrecyon of the said Governor or his
Deputye and the most part of the said Assistants."[70]
Any member of the fellowship was eligible for the office
of assistant.[71]

The Company was given many powers. Among the

[67] A. and O., p. 149.
[68] A. and O., p. 146.
[69] This choice was perhaps the result of the prominent part which
Pullison took in raising the funds to pay Peterson, the Dane.
[70] S. P., Dom., Eliz. 131, No. 70.
[71] *Ibid.*

minor ones were the powers to purchase, possess and dispose of lands not exceeding one hundred pounds annually, to sue and be sued in the corporate name, and to
have a common seal.[72] The large power, however, was
that of governing absolutely the Eastland trade. For
this the provisions in the Charter are very general: "That
the said Governour or his deputye or deputyes and assistauntes aforesaid and their successours for the tyme beinge
or the greater parte of them then being psente and assembled together . . . for ever may and shall make
ordeyne and stablishe suche good statutes lawes and constitucyons and ordinaunces for the good government and
rule of the said fellowshipp as they shall thinke mete and
convenyente So as the said lawes ordynnces and con-
stytucyons be not repugnante or derogatorie to the lawes
and statutes of this Realme of Englande or contrarye to
any treatye league or covenntes betwene us our heires
and successours and eny other Prynce or Potentate."[73]
Further these "statutes lawes and constitucyons" could
be repealed whenever it should be deemed expedient to do
so by the authorities of the company.[74]

By way of machinery to put this in force the Company
was given the privilege of holding courts, that is, the privilege of having meetings for the above-mentioned legislation and the transaction of the common business. The
charter empowered them "to assemble assigne appoynte
and mete together and cause to be kepte courtes and con-
gregations of all the said Fellowshipp of Marchauntes of
Easteland."[75]

There can be little doubt but that the Eastland Merchants were anxious to follow the model of the Merchant
Adventurers more closely than has hitherto been suspected.

[72] S. P., Dom., Eliz. 131, No. 70.
[73] A. and O., p. 145.
[74] Ibid.
[75] A. and O., p. 144.

᠄ has been pointed out that the main difference in the
rganization of these two companies lies in the location
f the seat of government, the Merchant Adventurers hav-
ıg their governing body on the Continent, while the East-
ınd Merchants kept their base in London. But this de-
iation on the part of the latter was one forced upon them
ıy circumstances rather than as a policy consciously and
ndependently adopted. Apparently when the question of
ırganization was first broached, it was expected to have
,he governing body in the East Parts, but it was soon
ıeen that this would entail inconveniences upon the East-
and Merchants from which the more adjacent field of
ıctivity of the Merchant Adventurers delivered them.
Thus to "pvente that the said companye of theste
m'chants shall not inJoine such as wilbe free of their Sosyetye to Lose any tyme in travell abought the same over
the Seaes, yt may be pvyded for that all suche psonnes
as requyrithe the freedome of the sayd sosyetye may be
admitted into the same here in Inglande."[76] To meet
this situation the charter provided that there might be
assemblies and courts both in England and in the East
Parts,[77] provided that there were at least twenty members present, thirteen of whom had to be assistants.[78]
Both in England and in the East Parts courts could be
held as often as it seemed necessary to the "Governour or
his Deputye or Deputyes for the tyme beinge or any of
them for the proffytt or comodytye of the said Fellowshipp of Marchauntes of Eastelande aforesaid."[79]

There was also provision for a permanent local court
on the Continent, but since there could be but one real
head, this one was made subsidiary to the Court in England. The charter sets forth that the governing body

[76] S. P., Dom., Eliz. 126, f. 24.
[77] A. and O., p. 145.
[78] Ibid.
[79] Ibid.

"may and shall name chuse and appoint at theire will &
pleasure From tyme to tyme one or mo of the said Fellowshipp to be theire Governor or governors in the pts
beyond the See The wch Governor or Governors deputie or
deputies so named and chosen and euery of them shall
haue full power and auctoritie to elect and chuse to hym
or them Twelve of the discretest merchaunts there resident of the said Fellowshipp to associate the said Governor or Governors deputie or deputies in that place where
the said governor or governors deputie or deputies in the
said parts beyond the Sees shalbe resident. . . ." [80]
These officials so appointed were to rule and govern in the
East Parts within "such bounds and Lymitts as to them
by the said Governor and Assistants of the said Fellowshipp resident in England . . . shalbe proscribed and
assigned." [81] In practice it worked out that, instead of an
official called governor, there was a deputy in the East
Parts. The first person chosen to fill this position was a
resident of Elbing "and maryed in the Towne." [82] Later
a certain William Barker filled the post. [83]

Even after the granting of the Charter we find the tendency still present to give much power to the court on the
Continent. During the long negotiation between the Company and the town of Elbing and the King of Poland, the
deputy and his court at Elbing had great influence in
steering the course of those negotiations. [84] Later in the
century it showed great activity in the exercise of the judicial function. During a period of about sixty weeks
from October 31, 1600, to December, 1601, there were held
at Elbing thirty "seuerall courtes of Assistantes," an av-

[80] S. P., Dom., Eliz. 131, No. 70.
[81] *Ibid.*
[82] S. P., Poland, I, No. 11.
[83] Cottonian, Nero B. II, f. 202 b.
[84] S. P., Poland, I, document unnumbered, Herbert to Walsingham,
August 5-15, 1584; Cottonian, Vespasian F. XII, f. 145.

rage of one a fortnight, and during the same period there were twenty-five "seuerall Courtes and assemblies of Comtties" of the "most Auncient and discreet brethren of r Comp: there residinge." At these meetings important ases came up for settlement; allegations, proofs, accounts, lepositions, protests, and exceptions were produced and heard, evidence was weighed and decisions were reached by a majority vote of those present.[85]

It is obvious that if this organization was to be really effective in the government of the Eastland trade, its powers must go beyond its own membership and outside the realm of England. Accordingly we find the charter bestowing upon it the authority to execute its laws upon members and outsiders alike, both in England and the East countries. "Wherefore we for us our heires and successours doe straightlye charge and comaunde aswell all and singuler marchauntes of the said Fellowshipp and evye of them as also all other psons which be not nowe of the said Fellowshipp nor hereafter shalbe and usinge or tradinge the partes of Easteland aforesaid   . .

[85] Lansdowne 160, f. 179. In connection with the question of meetings comes the point of meeting places. In Elbing the Company owned buildings which were erected on land given them by the town. (Cottonian Galla D XIII, f. 42 b.) These are still standing. But in regard to the meeting place of the Society in London, the records have so far failed to yield information. A clue, perhaps, is given in R. G. L., Repertory 23, f. 573: "yt is ordred yt [a committee of aldermen] shall this afternoone treate wth the deputye and Assistants of the Companye of mrchaunts trading wth the Easte Contreyes at the founders hall for provisyon of corne and grayne to be brought to this citty from ye parts beyonde the Seas." It is possible that Founder's Hall was the regular meeting place of the Company. There would be nothing strange about it if they had met there since Stow tells us (I, p. 283) it was "a proper House" in Coleman street ward near Basinghall street, in the neighborhood of "fayre and large houses for marchauntes." This was within a stone's throw of the Guildhall. On the other hand it is quite as possible that this conference of the Company with the Aldermen may have been especially arranged to meet at Founder's Hall.

that they and evye of them be obediente unto all the said
statutes lawes and ordynnces and that they and evye
of them be and contynewe under the rule and governemente of the said Governour or Governours his or their
deputye or deputyes and the said assistauntes or the greater
parte of them then psente and to them shalbe obedyente
in the execucyon of the said statutes actes and ordynnces
and evye of them as is aforesaid to be made."[86]

A power bestowed exclusively upon the governing body
is that of taxation. It is provided that " the said Governour or his deputye . . . and assistauntes shall have
full and whole power and auctoritie to ympose and taxe all
reasonable imposycyons and somĉs of money Whatsoevere
aswell upon the parsons tradinge into the said Countryes
of Eastelande as also upon the marchaundyze to be transported and carryed into the said Countryes of Eastland
and Polland and other the domynyons afforesaid . . .
eyther by water or lande or to be broughte by any our
sujectes from thence suche taxe imposicions and somĉs of
money boothe on the goodes and vessells Wherein such
goodes are transported as to them shall seme necessarye
and convenyente for the supportacyon mayntenaunce and
good governemente of the said fellowshipp̃ and to be ym-
ployed onely for the benyfytt and comõdytye of the same
companye and not otherwyse"[87] . . .

To make this control of the Company over the Eastland
trade still more real, the organization was given not only
the right to pass acts and ordinances but the "authorite
to sequester, committ and fine the transgressours
thereof";[88] and in September of 1580 it was decided by
the Privy Council that there should be no appeal to the
higher English Courts from the decisions of the Court of

[86] A. and O., p. 146.
[87] *I*bid.
[88] A. P. C., XII, p. 207.

he Company.[89] As we have already seen the Court at Elbing was active in the judicial side of the Government of the Company.

Besides these large semi-political powers the government gave the Company certain smaller concessions. The members as a whole had the right to export yearly two hundred white cloths, though at this time it was lawful to export only colored cloths.[90] It was said later that this exception was to provide for the demand of white cloths as "weeds" for men of religious societies in the East Parts.[91] These cloths, however, had to be dressed according to the laws of the realm.[90] Furthermore the individual merchants were permitted "to carrye and take With theym in their purses the some of tenne poundes of curraunt money of Englande Without any forfeyture or penaltie whatsoev."[92]

Such, then, were the monopoly, organization and privileges of the Eastland Company. Its territory was extensive, its organization definite and its privileges large. But after all, the importance of these concessions to any one member depended upon the number of persons who should be allowed to enjoy them. As we have seen the charter provided that practically all merchants except artificers, handicraftsmen and retailers, who paid the appropriate entrance fee were eligible for membership and the company had to admit them.

During the first year of the Company's existence, it made a determined effort to exclude at least some persons through a peculiar interpretation of the Charter. It was held that a person who was both a Merchant Adventurer and a "merchant trading Spain" should not be considered a " mere Merchaunte of either of the said Societies, and

[89] A. P. C., XII, p. 207.
[90] A. and O., p. 149.
[91] Sloane 25, f. 5.
[92] A. and O., p. 151.

so by the wordes of theire corporacion not to be admitted, which onlie pretendeth for suche her Majesties subjectes as be mere Merchauntes Adventurers of Englande and mere marchauntes trading Spaigne and Portingall."[93] The question came up before the Privy Council, where, after consultation with the Master of the Rolls, the Attorney-General and the two Chief Justices,[94] it was decided that the narrow definition of a "mere marchaunt" put forward by the Company "was rather a cavell in effectt then of moment to debarre anie merchant of the said Companies of Marchauntes Adventurers and Merchauntes trading Spaigne and Portingall from being admitted into theire said Companie."[95] Naturally the Eastland Merchants had to withdraw their objections to the entrance of that class of candidates.[96] The Council further commanded the Company to extend the period three months for these persons to come in upon the special entrance fee of ten pounds, since the year allowed in the charter had almost elapsed.[97] Now the Eastland Merchants proved quite submissive and only meekly suggested to the Council that, since these persons were to be admitted to the benefits, it would be only fair if they were made to help bear the initial expenses of organizing the Company. The Council promised to look into the matter,[98] but whether it ever did so or not, we have no means of knowing.

In general, the Eastland Merchants considered that their Company was very easy of access. In 1602 they maintained that "any mchantt for a small some of money may be free wth vs (yf other of their trade decay) by a proviso in her ^maties charter."[99] And, indeed, there

93 A. P. C., XII, p. 146.
94 Ibid.
95 A. P. C., XII, p. 110.
96 A. P. C., XII, p. 111.
97 A. P. C., XII, p. 149.
98 Ibid.
99 Sloane 25, f. 6 b.

was probably much truth in their assertion. In spite of their trading place being somewhat distant and in spite of the fact that they labored under many disadvantages, by the end of the sixteenth century they could claim almost as many members as the Merchant Adventurers. Said they, "as the said advenn[r] be many in nomber so be we also,"[100] and as for the question of navigation "we think they will confesse that before this decay of our trade," by which the annual export of cloths had decreased 6000, "we haue mainteyned many more shipping then they euer did, and yett doe as many or rather more than thadven[r] now doe."[101]

It seems perfectly evident that an organization as powerful as this one and one that arose as it did out of an international problem, should bear a close relation to the English government. Some phases of this relationship come out in connection with piracy, others in connection with interlopers and still others in connection with the diplomatic activities of the time.

In view of the circumstances which led to the formation of the Company, it is interesting to find out how far the English government was able to put onto the shoulders of the merchants the solution of the problem of piracy and its complications in Denmark. In the first place the government lost no time in using the Company. Hardly had the charter been granted before the Council levied a collection upon them "for the answering of one of the King of Denmarkes subjectes."[102] The Company rose to the occasion and paid £505 7s. 10d. to the victims of Hicks and Callice.[103] By November 18, 1579, it was able to secure " A generall acquittance made by Thomas

---

[100] Sloane, f. 6 b. Wheeler estimates that at this time there were 3500 Merchant Adventurers. Wheeler, p. 57.

[101] Sloane 25, f. 6 b.

[102] A. Y. C., XI, p. 247.

[103] A. P. C., XI, p. 301.

Tynnacre, attorney for certen subjectes of the King of Denmarke in a cause of depredacion, and delivered unto the merchauntes of London trading to the Easte Partes, testifieng a full satisfaction and discharge of all suche losses as the subjectes of the said King in this case had sustayned." [104]

In 1586 occurred a peculiar case of piracy and indemnification. Martin Snering, a Dane, suffered the loss of his ship, " laden cheiflie with corne and other merchaundyzes," at the hands of the pirate, Diggory Piper. [105] The Privy Council ordered that the losses be appraised by John Foxall and William Watson, two members of the Eastland Company, and Herman Langerman and Yohanne Wonock, two " merchant strangers." This commission appraised the grain on the basis of the current price which at this time was very high in England, "and not as yt was worthe at the tyme of the spoile comytted." [106] This made the indemnification for the merchandise amount "to a double value over then they were worth to have byn sold where the same were taken." [107] The English must have refused or delayed paying this inflated indemnity and matters took their usual course. Goods of the English merchants were "stayed in Denmark to the value of the praysement." [108] This was a serious matter and the Council again intervened. January 2, 1587, a letter was sent to the Judge of the Admiralty instructing him to call the appraisers and the Governor of the Eastland Company before him, "dulie to consyder the qualities of those merchandize, and uppon their othe to value the same with all indyfferencie, that our merchantes maye not be charged to make restitucion of a greater somme then the

[104] A. P. C., XI, p. 300.
[105] A. P. C., XIV, p. 271.
[106] Ibid.
[107] Ibid.
[108] Ibid.

goodes spoiled did amount unto."[109] No evidence is available as to the outcome of this new investigation by the Judge of the Admiralty Court with the aid of the Governor of the Eastland Company. However, this fragment of the story shows how close were the relations between the government and the Company in regard to this matter of piracy. Besides taking it quite for granted that the merchants will pay the indemnity once it is properly adjusted as to the amount, the government used first the members of the Company and then the Governor of it as experts, as doubtless they were, in the settlement of the case.

So far we have seen only one side of the question. All we have seen so far has been the government forcing the merchants to meet the demand of the injured Danes. It remains to be shown how the government aided the merchants to recoup themselves for at least some of these losses. This can best be illustrated by another case arising out of the depredations of the above-mentioned Diggory Piper. In 1588, after a period of piratical activity on the part of that energetic corsair, the goods of the English merchants were again stopped in the Sound. The Eastland merchants paid the sums demanded for the redemption of their goods. Then they set out to procure some indemnification for their losses. They did not spare expense "as well . . . in the Admyraltie Court or in Denmarke." They found out that Piper had been "sett to the seas in warlyke sorte"[110] by a certain Josias Calmady, gentleman. They then petitioned the Privy Council to see to it that Calmady and "soche others as had bought the goodes taken by pyracie"[111] should be "compelled accordinge to equitie and reason to aunswer

[109] A. P. C., XIV, p. 271.
[110] A. P. C., XVI, p. 12.
[111] A. P. C., XVI, p. 12.

those sommes of monney for which their goodes were staied and arrested.''[112] The Council acted upon this petition and demanded a forfeiture of the bond which Calmady made for Piper's good behavior when he set out to sea. When confronted with this demand, Calmady ''dyd alleadge the smalnes of his livinge to be unhable to aunswer that somme which he stoode bound in for the good behavyour of the shipp wherein Piper went to seas.''[113] But the Eastland merchants were not to be balked in their efforts by such a pretext. They offered ''to receave all his livinge into their handes, as well landes as leases and all other proffyttes, to make that [what?] proffyt of the same they should be hable for the space of twelve yeres, and to yeeld him yerely towardes his maintenance in the meane season the somme of two hundredth poundes'' (equal in modern values to $5,000).[114] The Council evidently sympathized with the merchants, though they did not wish to be too severe with Calmady, so they gave him his choice between the plan suggested by the merchants ''or els that he shall give good assureaunce unto the said merchanntes to paie them yerely for the space of tenn yeres next ensuinge . . . towardes their repayment for soche sommes of money as they have dysboursed for the satysfyinge of the Daanes on whome the pyracie was commytted.'' Calmady decided that it would be to his interest to keep his business affairs in his own hands, so he accepted the second alternative. He seems to have failed to satisfy the merchants, however, for in June of 1592 he was summoned before the Council on this same charge. He was forthwith to ''answeare the objections made against him by Mr. Russell in the behalf of the merchantes trading within the Sound before the Judge of the Ad-

[112] A. P. C., XVI, p. 12.
[113] Ibid.
[114] Ibid,

miralty" and was "enjoyned not to depart hence untill he" had "put in good security to be forthcomming at all times to answeare the premisses there according to cours of law." [115]

Not only did the government try to get indemnity for money paid out by these merchants in this cause, as in the Calmady case, but it tried to avoid their having to pay it out in the first place. In cases where blame could be attached to well-to-do persons and they could be made to pay, the Council did not hesitate to make them do so. This is illustrated by the case of John Killegrew, "esquier, Captaine of the Castle of Pendenyce." [116] This gentleman seems to have become implicated in much the same way as Calmady. He was asked by the Council to answer to the amount of £440. He promised to pay it in February of 1588. When that time came he alleged that he had "taken order with a certaine merchaunt of Southampton to dyschardg the said somme." Now it was known that this merchant could not meet the obligation and therefore the Council concluded that the "said John Killygrewe dothe but seeke delaies." The situation was crucial with the Eastland Merchants. Spring was approaching, they would soon be ready to send out their ships but they dared not "use their accustomed trafficke for feare of arrestes" that were threatened "to be made of their goodes by the Kinge of Denmarke for the indemnytie of his subjectes." [117] This led the Council to take drastic measures. On April 10, 1588, a warrant was dispatched to the Sheriff of Cornwall "to apprehend the said Killygrewe, and to see him sent upp hether before their Lordships to answer his breache of promyse and contempt in not repairynge hether, beinge sent for by their

115 A. P. C. XXII, p. 538.
116 A. P. C., XVI, p. 13.
117 A. P. C., XVI, p. 14.

Lordships' commaundement, as also to take order to make present paiment of the said somme of monney."[118]

Sometimes the Council called upon the company merely to loan money to persons who were held to pay indemnity to the Danes but who were unable to meet their obligations at a certain time. Such was the Seymour case which arose in 1589. Edward Seymour was held to pay £350 to Gasper Primer, a subject of the King of Denmark. He paid £198 but seems to have been unable to raise the remaining £152 by the appointed time. This being the case, the Council wrote to the Eastland Company requiring them to advance that amount as a loan to Seymour. In the letter to the company, it was very carefully set forth that Seymour promised "to aunswer such reasonnable interest for the loane thereof as should be demaunded for the same";[119] and their Lordships promised that they "would at all times afford them their best furthraunce and fauvour in compelling him to observe such condicions as he offred to be bound unto." But however careful the government might be to see that justice was done in these matters, still the merchants were considerably burdened. In August, 1602, they complained that "many thousands of pounds haue bin taken from vs, without anie redresse" to make good the losses suffered by the Danes on account of the English pirates.[120]

In general it can be said that the Eastland Company did not relieve the government of responsibility in meeting the problem of indemnification for piracy. The Privy Council, the Admiralty Court, and the Court of Requests were the foremost agencies in adjusting the disputes that came up in consequence of the depredations of English pirates upon the Danes. In critical times, however, the

[118] A. P. C., XVI, p. 14.
[119] A. P. C., XVIII, p. 44.
[120] Cottonian, Nero B V, f. 53.

company was used to relieve the situation, through its furnishing money or advancing it temporarily to meet these demands.

Besides the drain on the Company to pay the Danes, it was occasionally taxed by the penurious government of Elizabeth for other things of consequence to its trade. For instance in 1601 we hear of its being assessed five marks to pay to the "Clarke of the Crowne in the Chauncerye the Purseuance and oth[r] offic[es] for sondry pclaymacōns and writts to be directed to the Maio[r] Sheriffs and Bayleffs of the severall counties & corporacons w[th]in the Countyes of Norff Suff and Essex towching the true and lawfull making of divers sorts of clothes."[121]

It will be remembered that the Eastland Company was given complete control over the Baltic trade in so far as Englishmen were concerned in it. But in the beginning it was necessary for the government to aid the Company in establishing its monopoly. After the organization had been in existence some months and had chosen Elbing in Poland as its "Mart-town," the Council sent letters to the customers and officers of the ports of London, Hull, Newcastle, Ipswich and Lynn instructing them to see to it "that no shipp doe passe owt of thoase portes under their offices towardes Eastland, unlesse they first take bandes of them in good sommes according to the valew of their merchandize, to her Majesties use, that they shall discharge their marchandizes only at Elbing."[122] This step seems at first not to have been completely effective in preventing "unorderly trading" and the company was forced to appeal to the crown. October 2, 1580, the Queen ordered that the clause in the charter denying appeal from the decisions of the Company to other courts, should be rigidly enforced and she forbade the Lord Chief Justice and the

[121] R. G. L., Repertory 25, f. 207 b.
[122] A. P. C., XI, p. 378.

rest of the Justices "of her Majesties Benche" to take cognizance of any such cases.[123]

The problem of the interloper seems to have confronted the Company more or less frequently. In 1591 it was reported to the Council that there were "divers froward persons in sondrie partes of this realme which doe refuse to conforme their selves to such governement and order as hath ben established by the said Governour, Assistantes and Fellowship bye vertue of her Majesty's charter." On December 29th of that year the Council instructed one of the messengers of her Majesty's Chamber "to repaier to all such places as the said Governour or Deputie and Assistance of the Companie shall from tyme to tyme by writing under their common seale signifie unto him, and that he shall will and comande all such persons so offending to make their undelaied repaires with him to London by such tyme as shalbe limitted by the Governour or Deputie and Assistantes and Fellowshipp, to answere to such matter as they shalbe charged withall."[124] In 1597 the Company made similar complaints and the Council took the same measures to guarantee the monopoly.[125]

It was not only at home that the Company needed the assistance of the government if it were to maintain a successful trade to the Baltic. There was another and more important element in the situation. This was the attitude of the government and municipalities in the East Countries. Should these decide to follow the policy of Spain in the Netherlands, the Eastland Company would fare no better than the Merchant Adventurers in Antwerp. In order to prevent such a misfortune, the Company did not depend merely upon the local desire for trade nor upon its own efforts to secure its position abroad. It sought to

[123] A. P. C., XII, p. 207.
[124] A. P. C., XXII, p. 132-133.
[125] A. P. C., XXVII, p. 331.

make its interests, national interests, as in a measure they were, and to use the prestige and power of the English government to aid it in gaining a foothold in the East Country, in trying to curb the Danes in their policy of exaction at the Sound and in securing redress for the wrongs committed against its merchants.

The government, on the other hand, seems to have been quite ready and willing to help the Company. In fact before the charter was granted the Queen wrote to Frederick of Denmark asking him for his sanction of the company about to be created.[126] A year later she wrote requesting free passage through the Sound for the Eastland Merchants.[127] In August of 1580 she sent Dr. John Rogers into Denmark and Poland for the express purpose of securing redress for grievances and of procuring "some satisfaction to the parties damnified,"[128] as well as "for causes of the Easte-land Merchauntes to the Kinge of Pollonia, his Magistrates of Elbing, etc."[129] In 1583 John Herbert was sent to Poland to look after the interests of the merchants there.

In 1586 the Company petitioned the government to urge the King of Denmark concerning their great losses and also for the better safety of their goods against the strict laws of that country.[130] That same year Daniel Rogers was sent to Denmark in behalf of the merchants.[131] In 1588 he was sent again at the death of Frederick II and again he made efforts to better conditions for the English traders.[132] In fact throughout the rest of Elizabeth's reign there were periodical negotiations with Denmark

126 Harleian 4943, f. 73.
127 45th Rep. Dep. Keeper of Rec., App. II, p. 25.
128 A. P. C., XII, p. 158.
129 A. P. C., XIII, p. 401.
130 C. S. P., Dom., 1581-1590, pp. 329 and 337.
131 Cat. Cottonian MSS., p. 213.
132 Cat. Landsdowne MSS., Pt. I, p. 107; Camden, History of Elizabeth, Queen of England, London, 1688, p. 421.

upon a group of differences which had arisen between the two countries; and in each negotiation the question of greater privileges for the merchants and indemnity for the losses they had sustained, was taken up by the English negotiators.

In 1594 the Company applied to Lord Burghley for the Queen's protection against the Dantzigers who were trying to get permission from the King of Poland to arrest English goods in reprisal for damages sustained by them at the hands of her Majesty's seamen.[133] In general it seems clear that the Company looked to the government to champion its cause abroad and it is also clear that the government willingly consented to enter the lists in its behalf.

But however much the government might like to see the merchants prosper, it was not willing to expend anything more than time and influence to aid them. The merchants had to meet the actual expenses of embassies and missions wherein their interests were involved. This is illustrated in the case of Dr. John Rogers, who was "with authoritye from her Majestie employed for causes of the Easte-land Merchauntes to the Kinge of Pollonia, his Magistrates of Elbing, etc., at the charges of the said marchauntes."[134] Once in a moment of extraordinary generosity the Queen agreed to pay half the expenses of an emissary to Dantzig, if the Company would pay the other half "by an imposition, with their consents to be laid on their cloths, to raise the same moiety; for the company is so poor as it will be hard for them to bear the whole charge or the one half by other means than some such course."[135] (December 23, 1594). In July of 1597 when an ambassador from the King of Poland was expected, the Council wrote to the

---

[133] Hist. MSS. Com. Report on Hatfield House MSS., V., pp. 16-17.
[134] A. P. C., XIII, p. 401.
[135] Hist. MSS. Com. Rep. on Hatfield House MSS., V, p. 46.

Lord Mayor concerning accommodations for him. The letter set forth, "her Majesty's pleasure is that your Lordship shall cause some convenient citizen's house that hathe good furniture in yt to be prepared and made ready in London where he maie be lodged and received for the tyme he shall make his aboad here, whereof we praie you to have care and to certefy us what house you shall thincke meet for that purpose. We thincke yt fitt yf there be any Dantzick merchante's house that shalbe convenient that he maie be there placed."[136]

Occasionally when the government prepared an embassage that was to take care of the interests of two or three companies, it levied upon all of them for a contribution toward paying the expenses. In 1600 when there was to be a formal negotiation with Denmark, the Council wrote to the Merchant Adventurers, the Muscovy Company and the Eastland Merchants. Each company was informed that " . . . her Majesty is at this presente to send Commissioners unto the cyttye of Embden to meete there with other that are sent from the King of Denmarke to treate of all matters that shall concerne the trafficque of your Companye and other her Majesty's merchauntes that trade into the East partes, and also the entercourse to Embden, and to establishe some good order for the good of you and other her Majesty's merchauntes. Forasmuch as this negotiacion doth concerne you in your trafficque and trade, and [it] is intended that three Commyssioners shalbe sent thither, being chosen of persons of honour, gravitye and learning, her Majesty's pleasure is you shall conferre amongst yourselves of some course to be taken by way of contribucion to leavye such a somme of money as may serve for the defraying of parte of the charges of those Commyssioners, wherein expedicion is to be used because the appointed time of the meeting wilbe shortly

[136] A. P. C., XXVII, pp. 302-3.

at hand . . . You must also have care to provide shipping to serve for theire transportacion." [137]

Although the government saw to it that the merchants helped bear the burden of expense in these affairs, it was no less active in preventing them from wasting their substance. On the day after the Council wrote to the Lord Mayor about accommodations for the Polish ambassador, mentioned above, an audience was accorded that functionary. On that occasion he behaved with such unprecedented discourtesy toward the Queen and made such threats against the English merchants in Poland that a letter was immediately despatched to the Governor of the Eastland Company "to make knowne to the merchantes that trade to Dantzick or to anie other partes in the East Contries that they forbeare all offices of ceremony towarde him, as of vysitacion, sending presentes or what soever else of like gratificacion untill you shall receive further direction from us in that behalf. Wherein we praie you to take speedy order." [138]

As for actual trading operations between the Company and the government, such were impossible since this was a regulated company and all the buying and selling was done by individuals. The government seems to have entrusted the purchasing of supplies for the navy to one individual who under Mary and Elizabeth is mentioned as the "Queen's merchant for Danske." In Mary's reign William Watson occupied the position. Upon his death in December of 1559 [139] Thomas Allen succeeded to the post, which he held until 1603. In the eighties he is enumerated among the officers of the navy and at that time he is credited with receiving the modest remunera-

---

[137] A. P. C., XXX, p. 195.
[138] A. P. C., XXVII, p. 307.
[139] Nicholas, *The Diary of Henry Machyn, Citizen and Merchant-Taylor of London*, Camden Society, XLII, 1847, p. 218.

tion of £30 per annum for his services.[140] Doubtless he did not rely upon that for his sole income. He was a charter member of the Eastland Company which would seem to indicate that he was a merchant of some means and influence.

Just how much was left to Allen's discretion in the exercise of his office is somewhat uncertain. In the sixties he seems to have been little more than an agent. In May of 1565 the Queen wrote to Frederick II of Denmark asking for free passage through the Sound for four ships laden with English cloth and rabbit skins which she was sending with Thomas Allen, to buy materials for the navy.[141] As time went on he seems to have assumed more responsibility. In 1572 he wrote to Burghley that he had spent £1800 of his own money in the Queen's service in rope-making.[142] This must have proved a not unprofitable investment for in 1590 he advanced the still greater sum of £3000 from his own funds.[143]

In May, 1603, he was succeeded by Simeon Furner [144] who in turn was succeeded by Francis Cherry in 1604.[145]

[140] 15th Rep. Hist. MSS. Com. V, p. 106.
[141] 45th Rep. Dep. Keeper of Rec., App. II, p. 23.
[142] Hist. MSS. Com. Report on Hatfield House MSS., II, p. 37.
[143] C. S. P., Dom., 1581-1590, p. 707.
[144] C. S. P., Dom., Add., 1580-1625, p. 423.
[145] C. S. P., Dom., 1603-1610, p. 119.

CHAPTER III

If the Eastland Merchants were to follow further the program adopted by the Merchant Adventurers to develop and increase the English trade with the Continent, then they had merely begun their labors when they obtained a charter from the queen. There now remained the equally essential and far more delicate business of securing concessions from the government of the country to which they purposed to trade. For, after all, the charter from the queen would be of little advantage to them, should the foreign government choose to withhold its favor.

And just here arises the question of what was the government to which the Eastland merchants must now sue for favor. Hitherto, for centuries, the English had regarded the Hanseatic League as the ruler of the commerce of the Baltic. For all practical purposes of trade, Dantzig was the real power in Prussia. The Treaty of Utrecht made by Edward IV with the Hanse in 1473 was always quoted as the document establishing the trading rights of the English in Prussia.[1] It is true, there were certain old treaties made between the English and the Grand Masters of the Teutonic Knights which remained theoretically in force.[2] It is also true that the English addressed occasional appeals in trade matters to Sigismund Augustus, the King of Poland and the overlord of Prussia. But the King, though very courteous to Elizabeth, showed

[1] All the English demands for rights were based upon this treaty. The sources for the subject of English-Hanse relations at this time abound with references to it.

[2] S. P., Dom., Eliz. 126, f. 25.

286

very little interest in commercial affairs, as well as very little inclination to antagonize the rich and haughty Dantzig.[3] Nevertheless there came a time when the kingship in Poland became the determining factor in Polish trade regulations, when this power was in active opposition to Dantzig and indifferent to the interests of the Hanse. With that change came new opportunities of which the English merchants, now organized, alert and ambitious, lost no time in taking advantage.

In 1572 Sigismund Augustus died and with him ended the line of the Jagiellos which had occupied the Polish throne for two centuries. The next four years saw in Poland many turbulent gatherings assembled to choose a new king. After the failure with Henry of Anjou and the subsequent incursions of the Tartars on the eastern border, the electors proceeded to a more serious consideration of the question of placing a suitable person upon the throne. But, in this, as in most other matters which came up for decision in Poland, there was little hope of a unanimous choice. The Senators of the Republic chose the Hapsburg Emperor, Maximilian II, while the gentry of the country declared for the Hungarian Prince of Transylvania, Stephan Bathory. Then ensued a race for the coronation in which Bathory, a man of strength and energy, as well as one of the ablest generals of his time, had little trouble in winning from his superannuated rival. He made his state entry into Cracow on March 23, 1576, and was crowned there on May 1 of that year.

Through his decisive and unfaltering policy in the first few months after his coronation, Bathory brought under his domination all of the heterogeneous elements of which Poland was composed at this time, except the free city of

[3] Perhaps the king was made more reluctant to intercede for the English because they so persistently afforded aid to the Czar, his enemy. He sets forth his position very well in his letters found in Cottonian, Nero B 11, ff. 91, 92 and 98.

Dantzig. The liberty-loving burghers, fearing that encroachments might be made upon the autonomy of their city, demanded of the new king the confirmation of its freedom and privileges and the abolition of certain abuses before they would acknowledge his authority.[4] Stephan, however, considered his coronation oath quite sufficient to cover the case.[5] Dantzig, secretly aided by the King of Denmark and the Emperor, held stoutly to its demands. Although negotiations went on for several months, they brought forth no solution of the problem. At last in March of 1577 the ban, proclaiming the Dantzigers as rebellious, was published, and means devised for putting down the city by force.[6] Then followed the famous siege which lasted until December of that year.

Although the King resorted to arms in this struggle, he realized that a more effective way to humble the proud and wealthy town lay in an attack upon its commerce. Situated at the western mouth of the Vistula it had, for a long time, served as the depot through which most of the products of the broad plains of eastern Europe had found their way to other lands.[7] And the Dantzigers made the most of their commercially strategic position. They enforced strictly the rule, adopted in most of the Hanse Towns, of compelling all foreign traders to have dealings only with a citizen and prohibiting all trade of "guest with guest." Even the Polish noblemen were not permitted to sell their grain to foreigners, a regulation under which they chafed considerably.[8] Now Stephan, in his

[4] Behring, *Beiträge zur Geschichte der Stadt Elbing*, Elbing, 1900, p. 2.

[5] Behring, p. 3.

[6] Behring, p. 3.

[7] Dantzig had not always enjoyed this advantage. It had been created in 1371 by a flood of the Vistula and the formation of a new mouth in the vicinity of the town. Petermann's *Geogr. Mitteilungen*, Vol. 5, (1905) pp. 41-42.

[8] Behring, p. 3.

"Universal" of March 17, 1577, moved the channel of Polish commerce from Dantzig to Elbing, a port on the Frische Haff near the mouth of the Nogat, the eastern arm of the Vistula.[9] This step was soon followed by another, more effective in attracting trade to the new route. Induced by the King's representative and by John Sprengel, a burgrave of the town who meditated upon the time when the geographical conditions had pointed to Elbing as the emporium of the Vistula system, Elbing granted free trade to foreigners and outsiders for a year.[10] Immediately trade responded to these inducements.[11]

On the other hand, it was to be expected that Dantzig would try to defend her trade as she tried to defend her walls. And for this she had two plans in mind; one to cut off the traffic by sea between Elbing and the rest of Europe by sending out privateers, the other to cut off the river traffic between Elbing and the interior by placing obstructions in the water ways in her vicinity.

To accomplish the first of these aims, early in May she set two ships to sea and a few weeks later she added four more.[12] A prize commission was also created to have oversight in these matters. Nor did this prove an unsuccessful plan. From the middle of July to the first of September seventeen vessels were captured at sea besides many grain barges on the Vistula. Occasionally a plundering expedition was carried through on the Vistula and into the Frische Haff.[13]

The second part of the program, that is, the obstruction of the Nogat River and the port at Elbing, was considered by the Dantzigers as a far more effective measure than the privateers. It was an exceedingly concrete and

[9] Behring, p. 3.
[10] Behring, p. 4.
[11] Ibid.
[12] Behring, p. 7.
[13] Ibid.

literal way not only to force trade away from Elbing but also to compel it to come back to Dantzig; but it was a method that appealed far more to the hot-headed masses than to the prudent councillors and aldermen who always kept in mind the time when peace would have to be made with the king.[14] Repeated demands for the execution of this plan came during the late spring and summer and each time they were evaded by the town authorities, until finally it was charged that the delays were caused by the machinations of certain selfish persons.[15] Coincident with this charge came the retreat of the besieging Polish army, whose frightful devastations in the surrounding country aroused the masses to a pitch wherewith the council could no longer cope.[16] Accordingly on September 20 the Dantzig fleet, aided by the Danish squadron, making in all an armada of some twenty vessels, on board of which were two hundred German soldiers, put to sea with the definite purpose of placing obstructions in the Nogat and the Elbing Rivers and of doing the enemies' places as much harm as possible.[17]

The next fortnight saw the execution of these plans. Although the Elbingers had, early in the summer, erected a block-house at the mouth of the Elbing River and in it had had quartered a company of a hundred men [18] and although the king responded to their appeals for aid by dispatching an able captain, Caspar Bekes, with five hundred Poles and five hundred Hungarians,[19] yet the Dantzigers were able to carry out their plans. Entering the Frische Haff they captured twenty-five merchant vessels,[20]

[14] Behring, p. 8.
[15] *Ibid.*
[16] Behring, p. 10.
[17] Behring, pp. 8 and 18.
[18] Behring, p. 7.
[19] Behring, p. 21.
[20] Behring, p. 19, note.

then coming on towards Elbing they stopped to levy tribute upon the coast towns of Braunsberg and Frauenberg,[21] and at last on September 26 they came to the mouth of the Elbing River. For two days they busied themselves plundering the neighborhood, burning granaries and doing whatever else of damage they could.[22] On the 28th they accomplished the main object of their expedition. First sinking three small vessels in the stream connecting Elbing with the Nogat, thus cutting off the town from communication with Marienberg where the king was, they effected a landing near the town.[23] While some of the Dantzigers were engaging the Elbing defense, others managed to start such fires in the granaries and lumber yards that the whole town was threatened with destruction. Whereupon the Elbing troops were forced to withdraw in order to help extinguish the flames.[24] The Dantzigers were then left free to complete their work. After destroying the bulwark at the mouth of the river, they proceeded to sink four large sea ships, loaded with brush, sand and stone, beside a couple of river barges at two places in the mouth of the Nogat.[25] Completing their work by setting fire to the block-house and several small villages near-by, they blew their trumpets, shot off their ordnance and departed.[26]

But the Dantzigers who had been so accustomed to carry things with a high hand, had at last overreached themselves. It is true they had carried through their program to the last detail, but they had also brought down upon their heads the enmity of those without whose cooperation they could not hold their position as absolute

21 *I*bid.
22 Behring, p. 21.
23 Behring, p. 23.
24 Behring, p. 24.
25 Behring, pp. 27 and 37.
26 Behring, p. 28.

rulers of the Polish trade. The distress of the Elbingers
was intense; the bulwark, upon which they depended to
keep the river within bounds, had been destroyed, obstructions had been placed in the rivers so that the water
rose and fell over the sunken ships "with a great noise," [27]
the block-house newly built that year, four villages and a
considerable portion of their own town reduced to ashes. [28]
It was scarcely to be expected that thereafter the Elbingers
should consider themselves bound to observe those principles of loyalty which contributed so largely to the commercial success of Dantzig. It would hardly be in accordance with human nature should the Elbingers not
seize the opportunity when it presented itself of seeking
a fitting revenge upon their enemy, especially since this
revenge was coupled with distinct profits to themselves.

Such an opportunity came when the English merchants
sought privileges in Poland. [29] It will be remembered that
just following these events in Poland, came the open
breach between England and the Hanse, brought about
by the expulsion of the Merchant Adventurers from Hamburg. In this affair Dantzig was a leader against the English. [30] Not only did she use all of her influence to bring
Hamburg back into the Hanseatic fold but she also made
conditions as unendurable as she could for the English.
The merchants maintained that they were "wourse vsed"
in Dantzig than were any other merchant strangers who
resorted there. [31] At last driven out "by meanes of most
grenons and intollerable Exactions, Impositions and ar-
rests," the English left the traditional trading place and

[27] Ibid.
[28] Ibid.
[29] Behring, p. 11, Ohne den Überfall auf Elbing und die gerechte
Erbitterung, welche er in der hart betroffenen Stadt hervorrief, wäre
die englische Residenz daselbst niemals möglich gewesen.
[30] Ehrenberg, pp. 131-158.
[31] S. P., Dom., Eliz. 126, f. 26; C. S. P., For., 1578-1579, pp. 494-
495.

went to Elbing.[32] Their reception there was all that they could expect. The Elbingers were now in a position to avenge the injuries they had received at the hands of the Dantzigers as they were also to have the more substantial gratification of seeing " themselues enriched, and ther towne beutifyed." [33]

From this time onward the question ceased to be one directly between England and the Hanse. The solidarity of the League had been irreparably broken. The English could now gain their ends quite independently of the League. With Elbing completely alienated from it, with the Polish King by no means well-disposed toward Dantzig, the English had at last found a situation in Prussia which made it possible to ignore the League. So quickly did they lose interest in the Hanse quarrel, as related to the Eastland trade, that John Herbert, the English ambassador sent to Poland (1583-1585) especially to establish the merchants there, wrote home in 1584, "I for my parte am lothe to enter into the action of the Hanses, for that I knowe they are intricate and require great lerning and deep judgment to enter into the depth of theim." [34]

The formal negotiations for privileges at Elbing were begun soon after the Eastland Company received its charter. A committee of five merchants [35] representing the Queen and the society went before the town authorities and offered to transfer all of the English trade to Elbing provided that the Queen was assured beforehand by letter from the magistrates that her merchants should have free navigation, immunity from new tolls and exactions and protection to depart in case any misfortune overtook them

[32] S. P., Poland, I, No. 11.
[33] S. P., Poland, I, No. 11.
[34] Cottonian, Galba D XIII, f. 10.
[35] S. P., Poland, I, No. 4. These merchants were George Ruchs [Rookes], Robert Walton, Matthew Gray, Thomas Gorney and John Briks.

there.[36] With this offer the Elbingers found no fault and on December 4, 1579, they replied in a letter to the Queen which set forth that they would willingly concede the "Libertie of traficque" to the English; that since there existed agreements and a covenant in regard to the tolls at the port, there was no reason to fear innovations; that so far as they were concerned none should be adopted without her consent; that since the King had granted liberty of commerce in the whole kingdom, they would do their part to see that it was enforced. Finally they promised to use their influence with his Majesty that he see to it that her merchants should remain free from difficulties placed in their way by the "malevolence and iniquity of others," the reference being, of course, to the Dantzigers.[37]

The English were quite satisfied with these assurances. An order was immediately sent out to the officers of the ports of London, Hull, Newcastle, Ipswich and Lynn that they should take bonds "in good sommes according to the valew of their merchandize" of all ships departing for the East Countries "that they shall discharge their marchandizes only at Elbing."[38] The Queen then very promptly replied to the Elbingers, stating her entire satisfaction with the preliminaries and asking for a formal treaty to concede certain definite privileges and immunities to the Eastland Company. She assured the magistrates of the good behavior of her subjects.[39] At the same time she wrote to Stephan about the affair.[40]

---

[36] S. P., Poland, I, No. 4.

[37] Ibid.

[38] A. P. C., XI, p. 378, February 6, 1580.

[39] Harleian, 4943, f. 16, February 9, 1580.

[40] Harleian, 4943, f. 18. In this letter the Queen writes as if this were not the first time she had approached him upon this subject and as if he had replied favorably to her advances. "Annus iam est ultimi Decembris mensis 21° die elapsus ex quo mercatorum nrorum causam que in libertate commerciorum exercendorum cum antiquorum priuilegiorum et si necesse sit nouorum etiam et auctiorum

The bearers of the Queen's letters, presumably merchants, were to act as her and the Company's representatives. Among them a certain John Langton who had been a resident in Poland for thirty years and bore an irreproachable reputation seems to have been the foremost.[41] Upon the delivery of the Queen's letter, the Elbingers immediately asked the Englishmen what privileges "they pretendid."[42] Whereupon the merchants very diplomatically responded only "suche as in old tyme to the whole Englishe nation and as of late tyme by the Hamburgers to the Merchant Adventurers were granted."[43] With this answer the magistrates were more than pleased.[44] Should they be accused hereafter of perfidy to the League they had only to point to the precedent established by Hamburg, one of its leading towns. They had only to repeat the arguments made by the Hamburgers but a decade before in order to justify their present course.

But however tactful the merchants might be, they were not equal to the occasion when formal negotiations were taken up with the town and the King of Poland. Possibly they realized "howe meanly, the Pollish Counsaile esteem a merchant, or any man not gentle borne."[45] Furthermore the news came that the Dantzigers had been using some "indirecte practises . . . to staye and w^{th}-draw" the Elbingers from their policy toward the English.[46] Very evidently there was needed a trained diplomat. However the merchants were not willing to entrust

donatione coniuncta concedenda SV comendauimus. In quo quidem negotio tam feliciter laborauimus ut eiusdem libertatis obtinende quatenus cum subditorum vrorum vniuersique Regni bono staret spem nobis faceret vra responsio."

[41] S. P., Poland, I, No. 11.
[42] Ibid.
[43] Ibid.
[44] S. P., Poland, I, No. 11.
[45] S. P., Poland, I, No. 28.
[46] Sloane, 2442, f. 41; S. P., Poland, I, No. 6.

their affairs entirely in the hands of a person not belonging to the Society. Accordingly they sent two commissioners, William Salkins, a merchant, and John Rogers, a "Doctor of the Civill Lawe" from Cambridge.[47] The latter had had some experience in diplomacy in Denmark in 1577 [48] and was considered an altogether competent person.[49]

Before starting for Elbing, Rogers made elaborate preparations. He searched the Tower, the Exchequer and the Rolls for documents which could aid him in his mission.[50] Old treaties made with the Grand Masters of the Teutonic Knights in the early part of the fifteenth century were resurrected, the Treaty of Utrecht brought out of the Exchequer, and the "bokes of the Anseas" copied.[51]

Being a representative of the Queen as well as of the Society, Rogers received instructions from both. The instructions from the Queen, issued in August, were of a general nature.[52] He was to conduct himself in such a way as to discourage the Elbingers from demanding anything which "may be thoughte by vs and o^r Counsaile not meete to be granted on o^r parte." He was to bind the English to no conclusions other than those to which they had already given their consent or which were included in "suche Charters as haue passed betweene o^r progenitors and the D. of Prussia and the townes vnder theire Jurisdiction." If a demand for such arose, he was to refer the matter to the Privy Council for further advice.

[47] S. P., Poland, I, No. 11; A. P. C., XII, p. 147.
[48] S. P., Poland, I, No. 11; C. S. P., For., 1577-1578, p. 18 [No. 28].
[49] Sloane, 2442, f. 41.
[50] S. P., Poland, I, No. 9 and 11.
[51] Ibid.
[52] The copy of the instructions in Sloane, 2442, ff. 41-43, bears only the date of August, 1580, but in A. P. C., XII, p. 158 there is a note for a special instruction to be sent to Rogers, August 25. A reference is made to this in S. P., Poland, I, No. 9 showing that this was sent the day following the issue of the first instructions.

Should a request be made for the revival of the old rate of custom which the Hanse Towns used to enjoy in England, he should demonstrate the impossibility of any such return owing to the recent changes in monetary values and to the great increase "in all matters of expences appertayninge to the state of kinges and prynces." He was to make "his repayre unto" the Duke of Prussia, who, she had been informed, had some interest in this matter; he was to acquaint the duke with her desire of fixing the trade of her merchants at Elbing and in her name to "request hys best furtherance thervnto." He was to deal with the King of Poland as with the Elbingers. For the particulars of his negotiation he was to receive his instructions from the merchants. Later he was furnished by them with fifty-two articles,[53] covering a great variety of subjects. He was to secure privileges for them in regard to all phases of life—legal protection, religious liberty, their demands extending even to such a concrete point as the right to use the common crane.

By the middle of September, 1580, Rogers was in Elbing[54] and ready to begin his work; but at the very outset he found his hands tied. As might be supposed, the most important document for him to have would be the Treaty of Hamburg and this he did not have. Before he left England he had realized its importance.[55] The merchants had obtained it, he had examined it and ordered that it be copied and the copy sealed and delivered to him.[56] When he was ready to embark he inquired for the treaty but was told that although it had been copied it had not yet been sealed, but that it would be sent to Elbing with Mr. Salkins who was to follow him in a few

[53] S. P., Poland, I, No. 9. He stopped only a few days with the King of Denmark. C. S. P., For., 1579-1580, p. 409.
[54] S. P., Poland, I, No. 11.
[55] Ibid.
[56] S. P., Poland, I, No. 11.

weeks.[57] Immediately upon Rogers' arrival the magistrates asked for the Treaty of Hamburg. He told them that Mr. Salkins was bringing it.[58] Consequently great was their disappointment when, upon Salkins' arrival, it was found not to be among the documents he had brought. The burgomaster in deep chagrin told Rogers that he "perceauyd now well, that it might be trewe, that the Danskers had reported" that the English would draw down upon the heads of the Elbingers not only the wrath of the Hanses but the displeasure of the King as well.[59] "And verely (quoth he) I haue bene founde alwayes to haue bene carefull for this Cittie and neuer reproched before my prince and rather than I wolde my old boarie bedde shulde be dishonored in this myn age I well take suche Corse, as I reckon to haue the Treatie of Hamburge in my possession."[60] Forthwith the town authorities refused absolutely to proceed with the negotiation unless the treaty were shown to them.[61] Rogers wrote, "Their Graunts so far forth to take place, as the Treatie of Hamburge were produced, and Negatiuely, conclude theye wolde not without thesame."[62] Rogers did everything he could to allay the wrath and suspicions of the burgomaster and to procure the treaty. He wrote letters home and he urged the deputy at Elbing to send for the treaty but their efforts brought forth no results. Rogers was much embarrassed over the affair. The burgomaster and magistrates never left the town but that, upon their return, they instantly inquired about "thesayd longe desyred Treatie."[63] The post or others had hardly arrived before they

[57] S. P., Poland, I, No. 11.
[58] Ibid.
[59] Ibid.
[60] Ibid.
[61] Ibid.; S. P., Poland, 1, No. 9 and 12.
[62] S. P., Poland, I, No. 11.
[63] Ibid.

clamored to know if it had come. "Notorious is it," wrote Rogers, "that at theyr owne charges this Cittie sent an expert and an expresse man to Hamburge ther meaninge by frindshippe or by Corruption of the secretarye or otherwyse to attayne thesaide Treatie; But so Secrett and firme wher they they cold not compasse thesame."[64]   At last early in March the burgomaster "withe suche vehement and ernest words . . . vtterid his mynde" that an express post was finally despatched.[65]

The question arises whether the merchants had any definite reason for so delaying the negotiation of Rogers or whether this was merely a case of negligence. In view of the fact that they were paying Rogers' expenses which were assuming rather large proportions, it seems hardly probable that they would ignore their own interests so persistently. It then remains to inquire what reason they might have had for retarding this negotiation. And this, according to Rogers, was to be found in the reluctance of some of the English merchants to leave Dantzig. He maintained, and the authorities of Elbing shared his views, that the whole cause was to be found in the machinations of certain Englishmen.[66] "To what perpose shall her Mat[ie] send letters to this Cittie, or Comissioners, when a fewe persons of wealthe shal by Sinister practise distorne her highnes intents to theyre factions. Wel it is knowen that Peter Kemerlinke a dansker and a Trader withe our nation hathe his first daughter marryed in Englande to Robert Hilson a rich merchaunt; his second daughter is marryed, to one Swister, a kinsman of Mr. Hilsones; his thirde daughter to John Barnel a riche merchaunte also; . . . Roger Fludde hathe marryed a danskers daughter, and is resident in danske, and vauntithe him so muche of his

[64] S. P., Poland, I, No. 11.
[65] Ibid.
[66] S. P., Poland, I, No. 11, 12, 23 and 24.

welthe, by his wyffe and trade, so he hathe spoken most
arrogant words against the authors of this trade, etc sayinge he wil be the destruction of this Elbinge trade etc.
Those mens capitalls be very great, and worke great ef-
fectes. Hughe Offeley (estemed here a very riche merchaunt) a great trader in fraunce (et quid non?) Mayntaynethe here a frenche factor namyd (Pattelier) who
hathe (as it were a licence) to destroye the trade at
Elbinge, and mayntaynethe wth defiance of the deputie,
his actions for danske, sayinge his M^r the worshippf M^r
Hughe Offeley, geuethe him meat and drincke besydes
wages, and he wil followe his aduises . . . Robert
Cooley, a factor sometimes of Mr. William Cockayne (but
vppon Cause now none) scheducethe thesaid Mr. Cockayne
his sonne and yonge prentise Thomas Stepney, and by all
meanes possible framithe the yonge lads for danske.
This Robert Cooley is an very factious person (the champion of Roger fludde) and is enamored cum venere
Gedanensi . . . Mr. Bodlighe hathe his sonne here
(frind withe Mr. Fludde) and fauore they (as I well
knowe) danske. Mr. Salkins (ioynt comissioner withe me)
bathe his seruant Jn. Parker continuallye . . . re-
mayninge always at danske. What he dothe there is not
unknowen to the magistrates of ye towne, to me and others
sincerely affected. Mr. deputie Russel hathe had (but)
2 factors or prentises a long tyme at danske. it is sayde
they be there to recouer debts but well know ye merchaunts here, what is ye cause (they obeyinge ordres *Sell
Not*)."[67]

Whether Rogers and the Elbingers were correct or not
in their assumption that these merchants prevented the

[67] S. P., Poland, I, No. 11. This condition of inter-marriage already existing between Englishmen and Dantzigers explains, perhaps, the absence of its prohibition in the charter. This may be
another case in which the conditions forced the Eastland Merchants
to modify their imitation of the Merchant Adventurers.

sending of the Treaty of Hamburg to Elbing, the fact remains that the treaty did not materialize for many months after Rogers went there, if indeed it ever did. And as has been pointed out the Elbingers refused to negotiate without it. In spite of that Rogers tried to have conferences with them, though with, little success. He also paid a visit to King Stephan at Warsaw in March, 1581. There he put forward the demands of the English for a residence at Elbing, for a definite legal status and for the jurisdiction of the governor of the Company over the Englishmen resident in Elbing.[68] Although the King was engrossed in the preparations for an invasion of Muscovy he seems to have listened quite willingly to Rogers and apparently approved the whole scheme in an informal way. For the Queen, Stephan had only the most gallant feelings. Rogers reports that throughout the interview "His highnes neuer made mention of her most gratious M^{atie} but euer raysed him (for honor) one foote from the place he sate on and toke of his Little polishe Cappe one halfe hand breadthe or rather more from his most honorable hedde."[69] After some discussion it was agreed, in view of the King's approaching absence, that he should appoint a commission of certain of his councillors who should repair to Elbing for the "more ample examjnation and disquisition" of the proposed agreement.[70] It was thought that this plan would cause little delay, seeing that so much unanimity of opinion and such amicable relations prevailed between the parties.[71] Before his departure into Muscovy, the King accordingly appointed a commission of several magnates, among whom Stanislaus Karnkouski, the primate of the kingdom, and John Kostka, Palatine of Sandomier and Captain of Marienburg, were

[68] S. P., Poland, I, No. 9.
[69] *I*bid.
[70] S. P., Poland, I, No. 9.
[71] *I*bid.

the principals.[72] Owing to the death of the latter, however, the commission was never able to act on the matter.[73]

Before Rogers could accomplish anything further with the Elbingers, he was recalled by the Privy Council. Apparently the merchants had succeeded in discrediting him with the home government. It is quite apparent why some of them whom he had accused of double-dealing, should be anxious for his removal. Others were dissatisfied with him because of his rather heavy and, as they considered, unnecessary expenses.[74] They maintained that his visit to the Polish court with all of its attendant outlay, was entirely unauthorized.[75] The Privy Council, reflecting this dissatisfaction, wrote in July, 1581, to Rogers and Salkins "touching their remisse dealinges in the negotiation with the Elbingers and to hasten the dispatche therof end their retorne homewardes."[76] Later came their definite recall. In the early autumn of 1581 Rogers obeyed and returned to England.[77]

In order that his year spent in Poland might not be entirely barren of tangible results, before he departed, Rogers drew up a model for a treaty which he left with the Elbingers for their ratification. This was then to be sent on to England after him.[78] It seems likely that Rogers was forced to depend upon his memory for the reproduction of the Treaty of Hamburg.[79] The document which he drew up contains much that is in that treaty, but it is cast in wholly dissimilar form.[80] The magistrates of Elbing, always anxious to retain the good-will of the

[72] S. P., Poland, I, No. 13.
[73] Ibid.
[74] Hatfield House MSS., 13, f. 78.
[75] Ibid.
[76] A. P. C., XIII, p. 133.
[77] S. P., Poland, I, No. 13.
[78] Cottonian, Nero B II, f. 155.
[79] This treaty is printed in Ehrenberg, pp. 312-326.
[80] Cottonian, Nero B II, ff. 155 b.-185.

Queen, followed Rogers' suggestion, though they did not ratify the convention entirely. Instead they placed their opinions beside each article in a parallel column. They agreed to the majority of the provisions; others, the most important ones, they referred to the King and a few they refused. And all were apparently left in suspense until it should be seen what the Queen purposed doing for the Elbingers.[81] This they drew up November 30, 1581. In general the document which Rogers drew up, with the apostils of the Elbingers, comprises a long and verbose document and one that quite justified Dr. John Hammond's opinion delivered a few months after this: "Most of the things concluded upon are such as needed no capitulation or articles, to my understanding, for they were to be looked for of common right in every country where there is any 'policy' and which is not barbarous; as license to sue and be sued by a proctor, justice against malefactors, recovery of stolen goods, and that one not to be punished or contended for any other's trespass or debt, and many other such like. Though these are specified in the 'intercourse' of Hamburg, I see no great reason in that precedent."[82]

Considering Rogers's mission as a whole, it had been a series of delays and fruitless endeavors. Nothing had been accomplished save an articulation of the privileges sought by the English. For these failures, Rogers was

---

[81] They had the advice of the King's councillors, who were at this time not entirely convinced of the sincerity of the English. John Herbert wrote August 16, 1583: "On monday being the fyft of this present I delyvered her Maty lre to the Bourgmasters, and having vsed som set speche, wherewth the [people] of this contrey is much delighted, among other I touched, by the way that her Maty was somewhat agreved wth the last Annotacons sent by the citysans of this towne. They replyed, that it was so prescribed vnto them by som of the k. Councell, that as then semed to dowbt of the yssue of this treaty, as a thing not ment by the Englishe nation." S. P., Poland, I, No. 27.

[82] C. S. P., For., 1581-1582, p. 657-658.

not wholly to blame. The absence of the King and the
death of his commissioner made it impossible to proceed
in the negotiation with the Polish government. The delays and double dealing of the English merchants made
it hard to get very far with the town. And lastly, it
becomes very apparent to anyone reading Dr. Rogers' letters, that his was hardly a personality to overcome all or
even a part of these difficulties. Throughout the whole
negotiation he displayed signal incapacity combined with
the most exaggerated estimate of his own powers and at-
tainments.[83]

After the recall of Rogers, the negotiation was carried
on by correspondence for nearly two years.[84] Upon the
arrival of his draft with its annotations by the Elbingers,
it was soon seen that this was too unwieldy a document
to be of much service, so it was revised and recast in a
form closely resembling that of the Treaty of Hamburg.
It now contained twenty-nine articles, most of which the
Elbingers had agreed to or had referred to the King. This
"formula" the Queen now sent to Elbing and to the King
for ratification.[85]

To secure the ratification of the King to this agreement
was no longer the simple matter it might once have been.
As the bitter feelings engendered by the clash between
Dantzig and the King, subsided, there appeared a very
marked tendency toward reconciliation on both sides.
Dantzig, in the realization of the powerlessness of the

[83] S. P., Poland, I, No. 7, 9 and 11. Perhaps his expenditure for
wine of £28 [$700 in modern values] accounts, in part, for his in-
capacity and "many disorders." Hatfield House MSS., 13, f. 78;
A. P. C., XIII, p. 401.

[84] In the autumn of 1582 the king sent Stanislaus Ossowinski,
chief gentlemen of the chamber [Cubicularium], with letters to
England. He had an audience with the queen but it does not appear that he contributed anything to the negotiation. S. P., Poland,
I, No. 18 and 20.

[85] S. P., Poland, I, No. 16, 17 and 19; Treaty Papers, LV.

Hanseatic League to prevent the English from making inroads into the Polish trade, now turned to the King and used every means in her power to induce him to withhold his consent from the proposed agreement. But one very substantial obstacle remained in the way. Soon after the King had moved the depot of Polish commerce from Dantzig to Elbing, he had placed a toll upon all goods going out of the latter port.[86] When peace was made with Dantzig, the town had promised to pay this toll also, but for four years it neglected to remit to the King. As long then as Elbing paid a toll which the Dantzigers evaded, the King would not be likely to do much to hinder the prosperity of the Elbingers. At last the Dantzigers saw this and hastened to remove the disadvantage under which they were laboring. Accordingly in the spring of 1582 they turned over to him a half of their port dues.[87] Since the Polish diets were notoriously penurious with the King, whose finances at this time were at a low ebb on account of his Muscovy campaign, it is scarcely a cause for wonder that the Dantzigers, through their grant, made a distinct impression upon Stephan. When, therefore, the Elbingers urged him to sanction their proceedings with the English, the answer came that his Majesty would decide nothing until the arrival of an envoy from Elizabeth and before he had summoned and heard the deputies of Elbing "and others, perhaps interested in the matter."[88]

This development much disturbed the Elbingers and they wrote urgently to the Queen to make haste and send a representation to counteract the influence of the Dantzigers.[89] However, their anxiety was premature, for Stephan was not a ruler who could grasp but a single

[86] Behring, p. 5.
[87] S. P., Poland, I, No. 23.
[88] Ibid.
[89] S. P., Poland, I, No. 15 and 23.

phase of a question nor one to be unduly influenced by money. He was still very well disposed toward the project of settling the English at Elbing. He inquiried in regard to the departure of Rogers [90] and later asked the Queen to send an envoy to his court. [91]

But the Queen did not immediately respond to this request. Her procrastination was no doubt due to the influence of the merchants who had to pay the expenses of these embassies and who were just now much disgruntled over Rogers' spending over five hundred pounds [\$12,500 in modern values] the year before. [92] She therefore waited to see what could be accomplished by the "formula" which the English had prepared. She answered the King's letter and stated that since there were so few things in connection with the matter that touched in any way the royal prerogative, she was sure there would be little difficulty in bringing the affair to a happy issue. [93]

Meanwhile the Dantzigers redoubled their efforts and, aided by certain of the English merchants who sympathized with them, they succeeded in keeping the whole negotiation at a standstill. [94]

In the spring of 1583 the Elbingers renewed their appeals to the Queen to send an envoy. [95] Finally it dawned upon the English that this was the only way by which the affair could ever be brought to a conclusion and so it was decided to send Mr. John Herbert, a Judge of the Admiralty, who just then was engaged in a mission to Denmark in regard to the Muscovy trade. [96] In this choice of Herbert the English were much more fortunate

90 S. P., Poland, I, No. 15.
91 S. P., Poland, I, No. 18.
92 Hatfield House, MSS., 13, f. 78.
93 S. P., Poland, I, No. 19.
94 S. P., Poland, I, No. 24.
95 Ibid.
96 S. P., Poland, I, No. 26 and a document unnumbered.

than they had been in that of Rogers. Herbert was a man of the highest type of intelligence and character.

In July, 1583, Walsingham wrote to Herbert in Denmark and instructed him that, upon the completion of his mission there he should proceed to Poland and bring matters to a conclusion for the Eastland Merchants. He was given full powers, and he was supplied with the draft of the treaty which Rogers had drawn up, with the apostils of the Elbingers added thereto and with the "formula" which had been drawn up on the basis of that draft. Like Rogers, his power was limited by the proviso that if any new matter came up, he was to refer it to the home government for further advice. Finally he was assured that the merchants would liberally contribute toward defraying the expenses incurred by him on their behalf, as well as toward compensating him for his labors.[97]

As soon as his mission was accomplished in Denmark he set out overland for Elbing and arrived there August 13, 1583.[98] There he found awaiting him his formal instructions and other necessary documents, the queen's letters to Stephan and to the town.[99]

The outlook now was fairly dubious. The Elbingers who had begun to despair of a successful issue, now took heart at Herbert's arrival.[100] But Herbert, himself, was not so sanguine in his hopes. On his way to Elbing he had stopped over in Dantzig for a few days and while there he had had a conference with the lords of the town and he perceived "by the sly speche of the chefe Burgomasters . . . that they make full accompt, that the king will graunt nothing to this Towne [Elbing] that may p'iudice the rest of his Ports in this quartre."[101]

97 S. P., Poland, I, No. 26.
98 S. P., Poland, I, No. 27.
99 Ibid.
100 Ibid.
101 Ibid.

In spite of his doubts, however, he set to work with a will.

The first matter at hand was to conclude with the town. This Herbert was able to accomplish in a few weeks.[102] In the main the "formula" prepared in England was satisfactory to the Elbingers so that now there was really nothing to provoke dissension. The final agreement contained thirty-three provisions which are as follows: [103] The first article established the "liberty of traffic." It declared the English merchants belonging to the Eastland Company free to come to Elbing and its port and territory, to remain there as long as they wished, to buy and sell goods, and to depart again, taking their goods with them, doing all these things at their own choice and convenience, precisely as if they were citizens of Elbing. Going along with this grant came the injunction that all goods imported by the English had to be brought to the city and exposed there in the market place for sale before they could be stored in ware-houses awaiting private sale or exported to other places. It was prohibited to ship directly to any other place in the East Countries or to transfer goods from one ship to another with that intention.

Next followed an article providing for the renting of an "ample and spacious" house which the English were to have for a definite sum paid annually. This they might occupy without any increase of price until a building could be erected by the Company upon land to be given them by the city for that purpose. In their "residence" the merchants were privileged to worship according to the dictates of the English Church. In case of death, the churches and churchyards were open to them for burial.

Turning now from that somewhat lugubrious provision came one of more practical importance for the develop-

[102] Cottonian, Galba, D XIII, ff. 42-45.
[103] Cottonian, Galba, D XIII, ff. 60-62.

ment of trade. The English were given the right of election of the officials of the Company, the elections to take place annually or at any other time that occasion might demand. It was required, however, that the governor take an oath to the Elbing magistrates that neither he nor his assistants would do anything to the "prejudice or damage" of the town. The governor was to have jurisdiction over all cases arising between two Englishmen, except those in which the public peace was disturbed. In those cases, as in all grave and serious affairs, the magistrates of the city were to take cognizance. There was a grant of privilege to the governor and assistants of formulating regulations to discipline the Englishmen to honesty of life as long as they remained in office. On the other hand before making rules or changing the existing ones on the subject of merchandise, these officials were compelled to obtain the consent of the Elbing authorities. The English were to be free to hold meetings and courts in their house at any time, providing they undertook nothing to the detriment of the town.

The legal rights of the English were very definitely fixed. As has been said before, over all civil cases arising among the English, the governor of the Society was to have jurisdiction; if an Englishman wished to bring suit against a citizen or a stranger, he might do this in the court of a magistrate of the city; if a citizen or stranger wished to bring suit against an Englishman, he could choose between the governor's court or that of a local magistrate. In this latter case, no appeal from the decision of the governor was allowed. In case of the insolvency of an Englishman, a report had first to be made to the deputy of the Company and opportunity given for an amicable agreement. If this failed the debtor was to be incarcerated in the prison used for detaining insolvent Elbingers, or otherwise proceeded against according to the common law regarding bankrupts. In all civil cases it was permitted to act through a proxy; the defendant in a criminal case, however, had to appear in court. It was permitted, also, to the English to produce witnesses and give testimony. All simple cases were to be terminated within forty days after the initial litigation. More serious matters were to be treated in the regular order of trials. Swift justice was to be meted out to any citizen or any stranger who in any way harmed an Englishman; likewise the governor was to see that any Englishman injuring citizens or strangers in Elbing, should be similarly punished. The English were to have the right of the recovery of stolen goods, provided the owner paid the expenses of the suit. The Company was to have the use of the town prison in which to place refractory members, though the magistrates were to be apprised each time before a person was committed.

Having established the legal status of the Society in Elbing, the privilege next provided for certain commonplace but none the less essential matters. Englishmen might lease buildings "as well public, as private," houses, shops, granaries and the like. In regard to the purchase of food and drink, they were to be subject only to such rules as applied to Elbingers. Next followed articles having to do with the buying and selling of merchandise. In general Englishmen were allowed to purchase any kind of goods in Elbing and export the same. If, however, a "pater familias" intervened in the bargain and wished to purchase the goods in question, especially if these were articles of domestic use, these were to be turned over to him without any increase in price. If for any reason Englishmen were not able to export the goods which they had purchased in Elbing, they were to be allowed to resell these goods at wholesale. In regard to cloth there was a special provision to the effect that it was to be sold only by the piece, an exception being made, though, of the very expensive kinds, which might be sold by the ell.

Leaving the question of merchandise, the privilege then took up the question of labor. The Society and the town jointly were to fix the price to be paid to laborers for loading and unloading vessels. If the Elbingers wished to undertake the work, they were to be given the first opportunity; if they refused, then the English might employ anybody they chose. The various petty officials of the town, weighers, measurers, masters of the crane, testors, etc., were to be chosen with the mutual consent of the Senate and the deputies of the Society. They were to take an oath of loyalty to both. In case they displayed negligence or want of good faith, they were to be held responsible for any damage that might occur through their negligence.

The last articles of the privilege treated a variety of subjects. Each Englishman was permitted to entertain as many visitors in his home as were permitted to citizens. He was allowed to dispose of his belongings by will according to the laws of England; with the reservation, however, that if he had come into possession of anything at Elbing either through a dowry or by inheritance, for these things he was to be governed by the local laws. The Society was to have the custody of the goods of a deceased member. Should an Englishman wish to leave the Society and become a citizen of Elbing, he would be accepted by the Elbingers upon his producing evidence of good character and of his dismissal from the Society. Thereafter he might hold real estate. Should an Englishman acquire property through the foreclosure of a mortgage, he was permitted to sell this in accordance with the prescriptions of the Civil Law on the subject. The English were to be free from all exactions put upon the citizens by the Senate.

At last came an article which had directly in view the interest of the Elbingers. By it they were granted privileges in England similar to those of the English in Elbing. Then followed an article providing for the denial by Elbingers of rights and privileges to dishonest Englishmen and the banishment of any such persons who might have acquired citizen rights; on the other hand any Elbingers who were "perfidious" or spoke ill of the city for this grant of privilege were to be cut off in England from participation in the benefits of the privilege. The final clause laid down the rule that should any case arise through the ambiguity of any clause in this agreement, its interpretation should be in accordance with the rule of equity set forth in the Civil Law; nor should the validity of the whole privilege be questioned on account of doubts which might arise in regard to particular stipulations.

After the town and the Company were brought to an agreement in the foregoing contract, there was still left to Herbert the increasingly difficult and delicate task of securing the King's sanction to it. Furthermore the King was to be sought to exempt the English merchants from the toll which he had established at Elbing and to which the Dantzigers had yielded. For almost a year the matter dragged. From the time of Herbert's arrival until Christmas of 1583 the King was inaccessible to him.[104] His Majesty was engaged in an extended trip.[105] Upon his return from that, the affair was brought to his attention and on February 9, 1584, he appointed a commission to look into the whole "cause."[106] Among the appointees to this body, was the Lord Treasurer whose preoccupation with other affairs prevented his attendance upon the com-

[104] S. P., Poland, I, No. 28.
[105] *Ibid.*
[106] Cottonian, Galba, D XIII, ff. 48b-49.

mission, and thereby obstructed the whole negotiation.[107]
So matters stood until May. Then the Dantzigers, ever
anxious to thwart the action of the Elbingers with the
English, served the city with a royal prohibitory mandate
"that no straungers should haue anie handlinge in village
Towne or Citie, Contrarie to the Constitutions privileges
and customes of this land of Pruse."[108] Immediately
Herbert had a conference with the Elbing Senators and
they decided to send to the King forthwith for his interpretation of the mandate and also to request him to em-
power the commission which he had appointed, to proceed without the presence of the Lord Treasurer.[109] Upon
the return of the messenger, for whose journey a month's
time was required, the Elbingers were reassured.[110] The
king had intended to stop only wandering peddlers who
tried to cheat the royal customs and the tolls of the nobility; he had not meant in any way to curtail the privileges
of the Elbingers.[111] In regard to the second request, he
was quite willing for the commission to begin its work
immediately.[112]

At last by the middle of the summer 1584 the serious
consideration of the treaty began. The commission, composed of Peter Costhca, Bishop of Culmen, Peter of Pol-
uticze, Palatine of Briesten, Stephan Grudzinski, Castellan
of Nakle, and Stanislaus Costhca, Vice-Chamberlain of
Culmen,[113] "Peeres of the Land of rare learninge, great
experience and Judgmᵗ"[114] came to Elbing in July to in-

[107] S. P., Poland, I, document unnumbered, Herbert to Walsingham, August 4/14 1584.

[108] Ibid.

[109] Ibid.

[110] Ibid.

[111] Ibid.

[112] Ibid.

[113] Cottonian, Galba, D XIII, f. 67b. John Dulski, originally appointed, did not come to Elbing.

[114] S. P., Poland, I, document unnumbered, Herbert to Walsingham,
August 4/14 1584.

vestigate the whole subject. On the 20th they received Herbert and the representatives of Elbing.[115] The next day they heard the deputies from Dantzig who presented every possible argument against permitting the English to gain permanent residence at Elbing.[116] To their attacks Herbert was permitted to make answer, though the more scurrilous ones he chose to ignore.[117] On the 25th the commission delivered to Herbert the opinion of the members concerning each article of the agreement and with that their work ended. They had been appointed only to investigate. When both sides of the question had been heard and a report made to send to the King, the work of the commission was over. Nevertheless at Herbert's urgent request he was permitted to speak and write further in refutation of the Dantzigers' arguments. On the 27th the conference was concluded.[118]

At this meeting were brought to light the possible points of objection which the King might have to the privileges accorded by the Elbingers. First it was contrary to the "perpetual pacts and privileges" of Prussia for the King to confine any nation that traded to his countries to any one town.[119] Then there was the much disputed point in regard to permitting trade of stranger with stranger. The Dantzigers maintained that such transactions were unlawful. Finally there was the point in regard to the King's tolls at the port, so lately conceded by Dantzig. The com-

[115] S. P., Poland, I, document unnumbered, Herbert to Walsingham, August 4/14, 1584.

[116] Ibid.; Cottonian, Galba D XIII, ff. 51-54. Herbert wrote of the Dantzigers, "They make themselues professed enymies to this cause and force (sic) not what charges they be at to hinder thesame, eyther, in expences or Rewardes, wherein they far surpasse this Towne and or Society."

[117] S. P., Poland, I, document unnumbered, Herbert to Walsingham, August 4/14, 1584; Cottonian, Galba D XIII, f. 65.

[118] S. P., Poland, I, document unnumbered, Herbert to Walsingham, August 4/14, 1584. [119] Ibid.

missioners thought the first point might be met by having the Queen "bynd her subiects to wᵗ towne or place she would." [120]   They apprehended little difficulty in securing royal sanction for free trade, seeing "that it was for the good of all the nobilitie, cytizens and Inhabitantes of Poland." [121]   Lastly they could express no opinion on the question of immunity from tolls, since that rested entirely with the King.[122]   But everybody realized that the action of the Dantzigers had made it "harde for them of Elbing to obteine Exemption." [123]   The King, always in need of funds, could hardly be expected to make a free gift to the English and place them in a position more advantageous than that of his own subjects.

This conference meant more to the English cause than the mere investigation and argument carried on at Elbing.   It also enabled Herbert to win over these commissioners to his side.   They seem to have been very much pleased with his personality and they treated him with the utmost of cordiality and friendliness.   Before leaving Elbing they promised him that should the matter come up before the Estates they would use their influence "to furder this action . . .   to the vttermost they may." [124] In view of their rank and prestige, this was no inconsiderable asset for the English.

Very shortly after this the King seems to have made up his mind to let the final decision of the matter rest with the Estates.   His chamberlain told Herbert that His Majesty "for the factions lately growen emong his nobilitie wolde not attempt any thing of importaunce to himself;

[120] S. P., Poland, I, document unnumbered, Herbert to Walsingham, August 4/14, 1584.

[121] *I*bid.

[122] *I*bid.

[123] *I*bid.

[124] *I*bid.   Herbert apparently knew how to win favor.   He wrote: "I gave them entretayment at my lodging and at Seabord, muche to their liking and contentment."

but wolde refer all to the generall assemblie.''[125] Accordingly the first step to be taken was to submit the question to a convocation of the nobility which had been called to meet at Lublin, August 20th. This assembly of the magnates was preliminary to the meeting of the larger body. Here it was decided what matters should come up for debate in the general assembly. When these points were determined upon they were then referred to the local assemblies for their consideration and in order that they might return members instructed how to vote in the Estates General.[126] It was now decided at Lublin that the English question should be one of four to be debated in the Estates, called to meet at Warsaw, January 15, 1585.[127]

Stephan, it seems, was by no means satisfied with the services of the commission which had visited Elbing. He was offended with the commissioners ''for that they yelded not up their opinions.''[128] In order, perhaps, to get first-hand information and also to give the English a fair hearing, he let it be known that he would grant Herbert and the deputies of Elbing an audience at Lublin.[129] They responded to the King's invitation with alacrity. On August 26th, ''being Sondaie, after Service and Sermon, at XI of the elok'' Herbert had an open audience.[130] There in the presence of the King and a large company of nobles he set forth the case in elaborate detail; and as he had been told beforehand by the Lord High Marshal that new commissioners ''might be chosen, oute of the bodie of the nobilitie there assembled'' he directed his

---

[125] Cottonian, Galba D XIII, f. 6, Herbert to Walsingham, November 6/16, 1584.
[126] S. P., Poland, I, document unnumbered, Herbert to Walsingham, November 8/18, 1584.
[127] *Ibid.*
[128] Cottonian, Galba D XIII, f. 6.
[129] *Ibid.*
[130] *Ibid.*

speech "to that end." [131]   He took up all these points in "such order," he wrote to Walsingham, "as the tyme and my small skill did give me leave." [132]   When he had finished the King called his chancellor to him, "and conferred long with him." [133]   Then the chancellor replied to Herbert's speech. The King, he said, was sorry for the long delays but "urgent affaires had bene cause thereof" and now owing to the many complications involved he had determined to appoint a new commission, "who should further debate of, and p'use the cause," and that thereupon Herbert should have "further answer and such as should be to hir Ma[ts] contentment." [134]

A few days later the King fulfilled his promise and appointed the commission which was to sit immediately at Levartow, a town in Lithuania, near Lublin. These commissioners, of whom Nicholas Firley was the most prominent, were "noblemen of birth, honored for their authoritie, and allotted to great estate by reason of their wisdome and experience." [135]   More important than their learning perhaps, from a practical point of view, was the fact that they were men "well affectioned to the cause." [136]

However, their instructions allowed them little latitude to aid the English. In the first place, they were not empowered to conclude anything, since that was to be left to the general assembly. They were apparently to discourage the English from asking for anything obviously impossible to grant. They were "to have due consideration of the late libertie, graunted by the king, to the Elbingers, touching the frer handling between straunger and straunger, with proviso and condition, that the reven[ue]

---

131 Cottonian, Galba D XIII, f. 6.
132 *I*bid.
133 *I*bid.
134 *I*bid.
135 *I*bid.
136 *I*bid.

of the Crowne might not therby any wies be deminished
and so carefullie that the English nation might be planted,
upon equal conditions, without any prejudice of the lawes
of the lande." [137]

The ten days (August 21 to September 1) [138] spent by
the commissioners at Levartow were crowded with activity.
Deputies from Dantzig and from Elbing were heard in
defense of their respective positions; petitions were received and considered; [139] letters passed back and forth to
and from the king; numerous consultations were held upon
the points in dispute. Herbert relates that one day he
was summoned to appear "by six of the clock in the morning" and that he remained with the commissioners until
night.[140]

Of the many points that came up for discussion and dispute, none apparently was so difficult of adjustment as
that in regard to the King's toll at the port. For some
reason the merchants seemed obsessed with the desire for
exemption from it.[141] The King, as has been seen, had
no reason to grant it and had instructed the commissioners
to refuse it. Herbert himself could see no grounds upon
which the English or the Elbingers could claim this exemption. However he held out for it until the last moment.
Finally the commissioners were on the point of leaving
Levartow, their carriages were in readiness for departure,
but they delayed long enough to come to Herbert's lodging
and there made one last appeal for the concession of this

---

[137] Cottonian, Galba D XIII, f. 6.

[138] Ibid.

[139] Ibid.; S. P., Poland, I, document unnumbered, copy of a petition of the Elbingers to the king.

[140] Cottonian, Galba D XIII, f. 6.

[141] An obsession with which Herbert had little patience. He considered it too small a matter, "not above on per cents," over which
to haggle. S. P., Poland, I, document unnumbered, Herbert to
Walsingham, August $\frac{5}{15}$, 1584.

point.[142]   Then with the advice of Mr. Salkins, the merchant, he yielded.[143]   At the same time he affixed the conditions that it should be levied upon *all* persons sailing from the port of Elbing and that there should be no increase of it either directly by raising it or indirectly through the high appraisement of goods.[144]   Several reasons, Herbert related to Walsingham, induced him to yield this point.[145]   He had been assured by the nobility at Lublin "that withoute yelding to that, nothing wolde be assented to";[146] an impression which seems to have prevailed with the Elbingers also, who urged him to compromise.   Should the negotiation fail, they would be "undone," not only because of the humiliation of having failed but also because of the large sums which they had expended.[147]   More than that, Herbert felt that if the English merchants "miss of their settling here now," they "are never like to obtein it hereafter."[148]   It would be very mortifying to the English "to be enforced by the sinister dealings of the Dansckers, to repaire to theim ageinst their willes."[149]

A second point upon which the commissioners insisted, came up in connection with the reciprocity clause in the privilege.   The Poles were not satisfied to have the reciprocal privileges limited to Elbingers, but asked that all the King's subjects be permitted to export cloths "upon English custome."[150]   With this notion Herbert had no sympathy.   To him this seemed a foible of the nobility who "regarde but the outeward shewe of the demaunde, and

[142] Cottonian, Galba D XIII, f. 6.
[143] *Ibid.;* Cottonian, Nero B II, f. 161.
[144] Cottonian, Galba D XIII, f. 6.
[145] *Ibid.*
[146] *Ibid.*
[147] *Ibid.*
[148] *Ibid.*
[149] *Ibid.*
[150] *Ibid.*

weigh not the just cause of the thing.''[151]   But should he
have been disposed to consider this, his instructions would
have forbade his conceding it.   Accordingly he labored
with the commissioners so earnestly that they promised
to use their influence to persuade the King to withdraw
the demand.[152]

On September 1 the commissioners left Levartow with
the understanding that, since they were only to investigate
the case and had no authority to conclude anything, they
would choose one of their number to report their findings
to the king ''wch could not well be done under the space
of five weekes.''[153]   For this office the commissioners selected the Castellan of Lublin.   Herbert was then to send
a messenger ''to attend on'' the spokesman.[154]

The next task that confronted Herbert was the campaign to bring over the nobility to favor the English
cause.   On their way back from Levartow to Elbing, he
and the burgomaster of Elbing paid a visit to the Archbishop of Guesne, the ''primus Poloniae Princeps,''[155]
with whom they conferred for three days.   Since the archbishop ''ever had bene an especiall favorer'' of the English, it was not a difficult matter to secure his active co-
operation.[156]   He immediately wrote letters to the King and
his chief officials in which he recommended the affair.[157]
Since he had ''great authoritie'' in the assembly as well
as at court, he was an ally of the first magnitude.[158]   But
Herbert did not cease his labors at this point.   Upon his

---

[151] Cottonian, Galba D XIII, f. 6.

[152] Ibid.

[153] Ibid.

[154] Ibid.; S. P., Poland, I, document unnumbered, Herbert to Veselinius, Stephan's Chamberlain, September 11, 1584.

[155] Cottonian, Galba D XIII, f. 6.; Nero B II, f. 161.

[156] Ibid.

[157] Ibid.; S. P., Poland, I, document unnumbered, copies of the
Archibishop's letters, dated, September 11, 1584.

[158] Cottonian, Galba D XIII, f. 6.

return to Elbing he wrote home to Walsingham and he urged that the cause be vigorously "pursued" by the home government. He advised that new letters be sent from Her Majesty "to the king particularlie and to the States in generall," from the Privy Council to the members of the two commissions which had considered the cause, from the Lord Chancellor of England to the Lord Chancellor of Poland, from the Archbishop of Canterbury to the Archbishop of Guesne "with a copie of Lindwood upon the constitutions provinciall of Canterbury; which he praied me to procure him," from the Lord Treasurer of England to the Lord Treasurer of "Littow," from the Earl of Leicester or the Lord Chamberlain to Stephan's Lord Chamberlain and finally from Walsingham to Baranowkie, the Polish chief secretary.[159] Herbert himself had written to or conferred with all of these persons.[160]

As further preparation for the obtaining of a favorable decision from the general assembly, Herbert wrote to Walsingham and requested him "to deale effectually with the Society, that ther be speedie order set, to haue monie taken vp to supplie the charges it standeth the Societies and oure nation much vpon to haue this vviage performed with much more credit and estimation then any of the former."[161]

Following Herbert's suggestion in regard to sending letters, Walsingham saw to it that letters were addressed in the Queen's name to the king, to the nobility, to the Elector of Brandenburg and others whose aid was re-

[159] Cottonian, Galba D XIII, f. 6.

[160] S. P., Poland, I, documents unnumbered, Herbert to Veselinius, Stephan's Chamberlain, September 11, 1584, with the reply of the Chamberlain, September 25, 1584, also Herbert to Baranowski, Stephan's chief secretary, September 11, 1584, with Baranowski's reply, September 25, 1584.

[161] S. P., Poland, I, document unnumbered, Herbert to Walsingham, November 8/18, 1584.

quested in the furtherance of the cause.[162] In regard to the sending of funds, it was thought in England that the Elbingers should aid in the expenses of the trip to Warsaw. The Queen's letter to that city definitely set forth such a request.[163] Owing, no doubt, to the difficulty of communication between Elbing and England, these letters did not reach their destination until after the general assembly had been in session for some weeks.

Herbert, who had also asked Walsingham for instructions in regard to his course at Warsaw, had foreseen the likelihood of their not reaching him before his departure. Accordingly, in order to have some guide for his policy there he had "p'suaded wth the Towne and Deputy and Assistants here to have certen colloquies what I might do, if further advice came not from yo H.^{r} Therein we spent two monethes and more, and wth much Difficultye have agreed of all points and articles"[164] . . . That his position as mediator was no enviable one, can be seen from his complaint: "I had much difficulty to agre the Towne deputies and the Assistants the Assistants being bent to have all liberties here that might any way further their Comodityes, the deputies of the Towne having regard to the Colloquie at Leuartow cold hardly be brought to assent to altre the same, as untill this veary mornyng the Articles were not signed. Therefore I am to crave pardon at y^r hands, for I fynd hit hard to please a multitude, that will not respect the dyversity betwene on naen and another."[165]

On January 7, 1585, Herbert set out for Warsaw[166] where he expected to meet the deputy and assistants of the Company who were to come there from a fair which

[162] Cottonian, Galba D XII, ff. 78-80; Nero B II, f. 164.
[163] Cottonian, Galba D XIII, f. 39.
[164] Cottonian, Vespasian F XII, f. 145.
[165] Ibid.
[166] Ibid.

they were visiting in the vicinity. There they waited for
nearly two months before they attained the object of their
quest. This delay was not caused by any uncertainty on
the part of the assembly as to the action it would take,
but merely through the press of businesss. All the local
assemblies of the nobility had favored the plan.[167] At
last on March 5, 1585, the Estates declared their approval
by endorsing the King's grant of free trade made at the
beginning of his reign.[168]

It is not difficult to see why the nobility displayed such
seeming generosity to the English. This was a measure
as much to their interest as to that of the subjects of
Elizabeth. When Herbert marveled at the extraordinary
courtesy extended to him and wrote that "Truly her
Mat[e] is much beholding to the nobility"[169] he innocently
ascribed to these gentlemen motives which probably played
little part in their actions. It is far more likely that they
were considering how opportune were these overtures of
the English who would deliver them from the commercial
tyranny of the Dantzigers. An open market where competition could have free play would mean as much to them
as it would mean to the English.

As soon as the general assembly had confirmed the grant
of free trade, Herbert requested the King to send to the
chancery and have a copy of the colloquies of Levartow [170]
made and sealed and presented to him.[171] These, with
the agreement made with the Elbingers, constituted the
basis upon which the English commercial rights were to
rest thereafter.

[167] Cottonian, Vespasian F XII, f. 145.

[168] S. P., Poland, I, document unnumbered, Herbert to Stephan,
March 6, 1585.

[169] S. P., Poland, I, document unnumbered, Herbert to Walsingham, November 8/18, 1584.

[170] Cottonian, Galba D XIII, f. 73.

[171] S. P., Poland, I, document unnumbered, Herbert to Stephan,
March 6, 1585.

There remained still one more duty to be performed before Herbert could return to England. This was a visit to the Duke of Prussia. It will be remembered that Dr. Rogers had been instructed to see him, though there was no specified request to be made other than for his good will. Neither Rogers nor Herbert up to this time had found opportunity to carry out that injunction. But now Herbert hastened to seek out the duke and solicit his favor for the merchants. This was of considerable practical importance since the duke controlled the Pillauer Tief and levied a tax there upon all ships passing through. The promise was now obtained of an unimpeded traffic upon the payment of the customary dues.[172]

After making on May 11, 1585, a more explicit, though no more extensive grant of privileges to the Elbingers in England, Herbert's work was at last accomplished.[173] He had spent almost two years of conscientious effort to that end and his success was complete. It is true he had not obtained for the merchants all for which they had asked, but he had obtained all that they could, in reason, have expected. And through it all, he preserved a dignified, modest demeanor worthy of the gentleman that he was. By the middle of the summer he had returned to the England for which he so longed during his protracted absence.[174]

[172] Cottonian, Nero B II, f. 166; Behring, p. 5.

[173] S. P., Poland, I, document unnumbered, endorsed "Sr Jh. Herberts Priuiledge to Elbinge."

[174] S. P., Poland, I, document unnumbered, Herbert to Walsingham, August ¦ 4/14, 1584: "To morow I must take my journey, god send me a spedy dispatch, and that I may once returne to England egaine. I here yo h: hath a determynacōn to send me to demark and so to prolong my repaire home. Truly yf it so happen I feare me I shall never se yo h: ageine. The extremyty of the wintre is suche, as I shall hardly be able to broke hit. Therefore let me intreat yo h: thowghe this acton take not place at Lublin, and p'haps may be referred to the generall states, that wilbe held at Christmas,

Once established at Elbing, the English remained there for almost half a century. During the later years of Elizabeth's reign, however, their stay there was repeatedly jeopardized by the inimical maneuvers of the Dantzigers and others, enemies of the English. But at each encounter the Elizabethan diplomats proved equal to the occasion and the mercantile interest was conserved. Not only the English but the Elbingers had reason to take pains to overcome the machinations against the trade, for, says Camden, "Elbing . . . oweth a great part of its Beauty and Splendour, and the great Resort of People to it, to the Commerce and Trade of the English."[175]

that I may have librety to repaire home afore the wintre. For over and besides that I distrust myne owne helth and know myne ability not to be able to beare the charges, I know it is not convenyent that so meane a p'sonage so meanely accompagned as I am like to be, shold represent the place I do, in so great an assembly."

[175] Camden, p. 539, annals for the years 1597-8.

CONCLUSION

In looking back over the field it appears that in the latter half of the sixteenth century English trade to Eastland developed such volume and importance as it had never attained before. Difficulties were met and overcome, or disregarded. The fact that the voyage was dangerous, that pirates infested the seas, that the Hanse offered stubborn opposition and keen competition—all of these combined could not undermine or destroy the trade. The goods of Eastland were too necessary to the English nation and Eastland was too good a market for English manufacturers for the merchants to allow these obstacles to hamper their activity. By persevering in their trade, even though conditions were often discouraging, by making the most of each opening and advantage, by using every means in their power, both at home and abroad, the Eastland merchants were at last rewarded with a good measure of success. By the end of the century they were carrying on a trade which was comparable in many respects to that of the Merchant Adventurers.

The rise of a new problem led to a new phase of development. In 1578 it fell to the lot of the Eastland merchants to aid in the indemnification of some Danes who had been the victims of the depredations of English pirates. With the advent of new difficulties came the effort to meet them the most effectively. To do this it seemed necessary and desirable to the men engaged in that traffic that they should organize a commercial company to carry on a regulated trade. The government was not averse to this idea and after some negotiation a charter was granted to the merchants. By this instrument the new Company was endowed with large powers and privileges which gave it the monopoly and control of the Baltic trade, so far as Englishmen were concerned in it.

In the exercise of these powers the organization came in contact with the government in various ways. The problem of piracy which had precipitated the formation of the Company continued to bring it constantly in touch with the government. Although the Company did not relieve the government of this embarrassment, as it was hoped that it would, at certain critical times it did help to tide over a breach with Denmark by the advancing of money to meet the claims of the Danes. The establishment and maintenance of the monopoly led the Company to enlist the aid of the government in its affairs. In addition to this the company looked to the government for aid in securing privileges abroad and for obtaining redress for injuries done them by foreign states. This aid, however, was confined to the use of prestige and influence, for the Company usually paid the actual expenses of the agents or embassies sent to negotiate on these questions.

Following close upon the heels of organization came the settling of the English merchants at Elbing. In this as in so many other things they showed their ability to turn what might seem to be a misfortune into an advantage. Scarcely had Dantzig turned them out before they grasped the drift of Polish politics and the significance for them of the enmity of the Elbingers for the Dantzigers. Making good use of this factor in the situation they were able to establish themselves at Elbing in a far more favorable position than they had ever enjoyed at Dantzig. Although the attainment of formal recognition, by the King and Estates of Poland, of their newly acquired privileges, involved a tedious and expensive process, they did not waver. In consequence, they continued to enjoy these privileges for half a century.

In general the development which took place in the Eastland trade is characteristic of that of all English trade under Elizabeth. In many cases the same merchants who were pushing out for trade into other portions of Germany, Russia and the Levant were engaged in it. The Eastland trade further illustrates how eager were the Elizabethan merchants for the advancement of their own and their country's economic well-being and how successful they were in overtaking and in some cases outstripping their competitors in the race for economic power.

APPENDIX

The merchants named in the charter of the Eastland Company. Patent Roll, 21 Elizabeth, part 11, membrane 21 [1] are ". . . . Edwarde Osborne Thomas Pullyson [2] George Barne George Bonde [3] Aldermen of our said Cittye of London Cristofer Hoddesdon Thomas Wylford Roberte Hilson Wylliam Cokayne Hughe Offley Thomas Allen Rychard Gourney [4] Edmonde Boldro John and Henrye Isham of our said Cittye of London mercers Richard Staper John Burnell Roger Watson thelder Wyllyam Salkyns [5] John Bodleigh [6] thelder Wyllyam Bonde Margarette Bonde wydowe Nicholas Pierson Thomas Russell Roger Floide [7] Willyam Watson draper John Langton John Collett Peter Collett Stephen Collett Blase Freman John Howgh [8] Robert Maiott Richard Wyllys [9] Edmonde Burlace Wyllyam Towerson John Foxall Hugh Gold Wyllyam Barker Jerome Bele Godfry Wylson [10] Thomas Bramley George Holmes Thomas Cambell Augustyne Fulkes Richard Lewis armerer Hugh More [11] Jervys Symondes Robert Coley [12] Anthonye Stanlack James Newman Frauncys Clerke [13] Thomas Tenycar [14] Wyllyam Helman Robert Walton Roberte Strete Humfrey Lee George Rookes Henrye Walton John Taylor [15] Thomas Cokayne [16] John Bodligh the yonger Nicholas Sympson Thomas Gurney [17] Bryan Carmarden and Thomas Slatter . . . ."

[1] A copy of the charter is in S. P., Dom., Eliz. 131, No. 70. Some of the names are there spelled differently. Such differences are noted below.
[2] S. P., Pullison.
[3] S. P., Bond.
[4] S. P., Gorney.
[5] S. P., Salkins.
[6] S. P., Bodligh.
[7] S. P., Fludd.
[8] S. P., Howghe.
[9] S. P., Willis.
[10] S. P., Wilson.
[11] S. P., Moore.
[12] S. P., Coly.
[13] S. P., Clarke.
[14] S. P., Tynaker.
[15] S. P., Tailor.
[16] S. P., Cokayn.
[17] S. P., Gorney.

BIBLIOGRAPHICAL NOTES

Primary Sources.

    The MSS. sources consulted in the preparation of this monograph are those found in the Record Office, the British Museum, the Guildhall at London, and the collection of the Marquis of Salisbury at Hatfield House. The materials at the Record Office that proved of most value were those classified in the State Papers, Poland. The first paper in Bundle I bears the date 1578. Although the Calendar of State Papers, Foreign, now extends through the year 1582, so far the Polish papers have not been included. In making references to these documents it has been necessary to refer to them by number since they have not as yet been bound nor the folios marked. The State Papers, Domestic, yielded much material that is only suggested by the brief entries in the calendar. At the British Museum the Lansdowne, the Cottonian, the Harleian, the Sloane, and the Royal Collections all yielded something of value. The Cottonian proved the richest field for research. The records at the Guildhall contained many suggestive entries. This was particularly true of the Repertories. The generous excerpts given by the Historical MSS. Commission of the MSS. at Hatfield House were adequate in most instances, though in one or two cases an examination of the originals brought to light further material of importance for this study.

    Of the sources that have found their way into print the Acts of the Privy Council, New Series, London, 1890—, furnished information of the greatest value.

    The Calendars of State Papers, Domestic, for the period furnish many suggestive entries but the fact that in many cases important documents are dismissed in a sentence renders them much less useful than they might otherwise have been.

    The Calendars of State Papers, Foreign, were very good for the period they cover. Liberal paraphrases of the documents and numerous direct quotations make them of special value. However as has been said the series at present ends with the year 1582.

    The Calendars of State Papers, Spanish, Venetian, and Colonial, East Indies, afford a little material.

    The Forty-fifth and Forty-seventh Reports of the Deputy Keeper of the Public Records in the appendices contain reports on the archives of Denmark and on the libraries of Sweden by Rev. William Dunn Macray. The documents calendared there were often very illuminating.

The Reports of the Historical MSS. Commission, particularly the reports of the Hatfield House MSS., proved of some value.

Rymer, Foedera, Conventiones, Literae et cujuscunque generis Acta Publica inter Reges Angliae. Hagae Comitie Edition, 1742.

The Acts and Ordinances of the Eastland Company, London, 1906. Edited by Maud Sellers and published by the Camden Society, 3d Series, XI.

Hakluyt, Principal Navigations, Voyages, Traffiques, and Discoveries of the English Nation. 12 vols. Glasgow, 1903-1905.

Wheeler, A Treatise of Commerce, London, 1601.

Camden, History of Elizabeth, Queen of England. London, 1688.

Stow, Survey of London. Kingsford Edition, Oxford, 1908.

Behring, Beiträge zur Geschichte der Stadt Elbing, Elbing, 1900. In this book are printed the sources for the account of the relations between Dantzig and Elbing during the summer of 1577.

Secondary Works.

Allen, Histoire de Danemark depuis les temps le plus recules a nos jours—traduit d'apres la septieme edition danoise par E. Beauvois, 2 vol. Copenhagen 1878. This is the best general history of Denmark. It contains a bibliography of a hundred pages.

Bain, Slavonic Europe, a Political History of Poland and Russia 1447 to 1796. Cambridge, 1908.

Lingelbach, The Internal Organization of the Merchant Adventurers of England. Philadelphia, 1903.

Burgon, Life and Letters of Sir Thomas Gresham. 2 vol. London, 1839.

Schanz, Englische Handelspolitik gegen Ende des Mittelalters, 2 vol. Leipzig, 1881.

Ehrenberg, England und Hamburg im Zeitalter der Königin Elizabeth. Jena, 1896.

Other books used for but a single reference in the thesis, are mentioned in the footnotes.

INDEX

Abdullah Khan, favorable to Muscovy Company, 148, 151, 154, 156; privileges granted by, 151, 153; death of, 156.

Adams, Clement, 8.

Admiralty Court, verdict against interlopers, 52.

Agents of Muscovy Company, 16, 35; duties and powers of, 35, 201; authority of, in Russia, 75; instructions to, 93, 129; difficulties of, 133, 151, 159, 171, 202; quarrels among, 155, 159, 176; independent, for Persia, 200; achievement of, 210.

Alcock, Thomas, in service of Muscovy Company, 56; factor for Persia, 154; murder of, *i*bid.

Allen, Thomas, sent to Dantzig to purchase ship-stores, 222-223; charter member of Eastland Company, 260; commissioned to supply English navy with ship-stores, 284-285.

Ambassadors, Venetian, in England, 12, 20, 24, 55; Swedish, in England, 55; Danish, in England, 58; from the East to Russia, 140; English, at the Porte, 223; Polish, in England, 282, 284; English, in Russia, *see* Bowes, Fletcher, Horsey, Jenkinson, Randolph, and Sylvester; English, in Poland, *see* Rogers and Herbert; Russian, in England, *see* Mikouleve, Napea, Pissemsky, and Saviena.

Apprentices, 261, 263, 264.

Ardebil, 149, 168, 176.

Armada, Spanish, 91.

Armenia, trading rights granted to Muscovy Company, 50.

Armenians, rivalry of, 168, 205.

Arrash, 149, 151, 168, 179.

Artificers, English, sent to Russia, 55, 59, 60.

Assistants, of Eastland Company, 265; of Muscovy Company, *see* Consuls and Assistants.

Astrakhan, 84; Russian outpost, 132; a mart town, 132, 203; besieged, 175, 188; proposed center of Persian trade, 184, 185; English preparations at, 206.

Attorney General, the, 254, 272.

Bacon, Francis, 227.

Baku, factors at, 189, 190.

Bannister, Thomas, 40, 43, 64, 84, 222, 231, 238; factor for Persia, 175; granted trading privileges, 177; activities of, 177, 178, 179; death of, 179.

Barbarini, Raphael, overthrown by Muscovy Company, 164.

Barnel, John, 299.

Barnes, George, 26, 28, 30, 260.

Bassendine, James, 104, 105, 106.

Bathory, Stephan, chosen king of Poland, 287; quarrel with Dantzig, 288-289; Rogers sent to, 297; visited by Rogers, 301; conciliated by Dantzig, 305; appoints commission to deal with Herbert, 312; limitation of powers, 314; refers English question to the Estates, 315; displeased with Elbing com-

Lightning Source UK Ltd.
Milton Keynes UK
UKHW032017280119
336360UK00013B/1434/P